China's Grandmothers

Over the past century and a half, China has experienced foreign invasion, warfare, political turmoil and revolution, along with massive economic and technological change. Through all this change there is one stable element: grandmothers, as child-carers, household managers, religious devotees, transmitters of culture and, above all, sources of love, warmth and affection. In this interdisciplinary and longitudinal study, *China's Grandmothers* sheds light on the status and lives of grandmothers in China over the years from the late Qing Dynasty to the twenty-first century. Combining a wide range of historical and biographical materials, Diana Lary explores the changes and continuities in the lives of grandmothers through revolution, wars and radical upheaval to the present phase of economic growth. Informed by her own experience as a grandchild and grandmother, Lary offers a fresh and compelling way of looking at gender, family and ageing in modern Chinese society.

DIANA LARY is Professor Emeritus of Modern Chinese History at University of British Columbia.

China's Grandmothers

Gender, Family and Ageing from Late Qing to Twenty-First Century

Diana Lary

The University of British Columbia

CAMBRIDGE
UNIVERSITY PRESS

CAMBRIDGE
UNIVERSITY PRESS

University Printing House, Cambridge CB2 8BS, United Kingdom

One Liberty Plaza, 20th Floor, New York, NY 10006, USA

477 Williamstown Road, Port Melbourne, VIC 3207, Australia

314–321, 3rd Floor, Plot 3, Splendor Forum, Jasola District Centre,
New Delhi – 110025, India

103 Penang Road, #05–06/07, Visioncrest Commercial, Singapore 238467

Cambridge University Press is part of the University of Cambridge.

It furthers the University's mission by disseminating knowledge in the pursuit of
education, learning, and research at the highest international levels of excellence.

www.cambridge.org
Information on this title: www.cambridge.org/9781316513354
DOI: 10.1017/9781009064781

First published 2022

A catalogue record for this publication is available from the British Library.

ISBN 978-1-316-51335-4 Hardback
ISBN 978-1-009-07362-2 Paperback

This book is dedicated with love and gratitude to

My Three Treasures
三寶
Mabel Milsted
美寶
Jack Carney
英寶
Misha Carney
加寶

Contents

Illustrations

Tables

Boxes

Acknowledgements

This will be my last book. Over many decades I have benefited enormously from the help and insights of many people.

My first debt, as a historian working on Republican China, is to the great generation of Chinese social scientists of the 1930s and 1940s, brought up in the traditional culture and educated in Western academic disciplines. They started the scientific study of Chinese society. Their work was interrupted by war and revolution, and much of their talent wasted. They were Chen Da (Ch'en Ta) 陳達, Chen Hansheng (Ch'en Han-seng) 陳翰笙, Fang Xianting (H.D. Fong) 方顯廷, Fei Xiaotong (Fei Hsiao-tung) 費孝通, Fu Sinian 傅斯年, Lin Yaohua 林耀華 (Lin Yueh-hwa), Ma Yinchu 馬寅初, Ji Chaoding (Chi Ch'ao-ting) 冀朝鼎, Sun Benwen 孫本文, Tao Menghe (L.K. Tao) 陶孟和, Xu Liangguang (Francis Hsu) 徐粮光 and Yang Maochun (Martin Yang) 楊懋春.

My teacher Chen Zhirang (Jerome Ch'en) 陳志讓 studied with some of them at the Southwest United University during the Anti-Japanese War, shortly before he left China for England on a Boxer Indemnity scholarship. Jerome and my other two teachers and mentors, D.C. Lau 劉殿爵 and Dennis Twitchett, gave me an unparalleled education.

Two people have given me the understanding and love of Chinese proverbs and sayings, 成語語言 (*chengyu yuyan*), the form of language that carries much of Chinese culture. They are Wang Bingsheng 王冰生 and Jan Walls 王健.

My deep thanks go to colleagues and friends who have helped me in many different ways: Alison Bailey, Timothy Brook, Jenni Calder, Phil Calvert, Denise Chong, Ezra Vogel, Gu Xiong, Hai Chi-yuet 溪治月, Judith Hall, Charlotte Ikels, David Jones, Kenzie Kwong 劉兢秀, Colleen Leung, Chantal Meagher, Penny Milsom, Isobel Nanton, Kenneth Pai 白先勇, Joanne Poon, Fay Sims, Norman Smith, Sarah Tsang, Endymion Wilkinson, Beryl Williams, Alexander Woodside, Yu Chun-fang 于春方, Eleanor Yuen 袁家瑜 and Victor Zatsepine. I remember two much-missed friends, Delia Davin and Janet Salaff, pioneers in the study of Chinese women.

Over the years I have spent oceans of time talking with my grandmother friends, sharing our love of our grandchildren, our pride in their achievements, our hopes for them and our anxieties about them. They are Marianne Bruguière, Jenni Calder, Pauline Carney, Jean Chaplin, Cristina Delano, Joan Dublanko, Helen Duff, Deborah Hobson, Betsy Johnson, Felicity Pope, Qi Wenxin, Vanessa Stone, Marjorie Weir, Natasha Wilson, Yu Chun-fang and Eleanor Yuen.

My immediate family has been my inspiration and my constant support. The departed members are: my grandmothers Margaret Lainson and Mabel Symmes, my parents Arthur and M.M.E. Lainson. The living are: my sisters Polly Clompus and Victoria Woodward; my daughters Tanya and Anna Lary; my grandchildren Mabel Milsted, Jack and Misha Carney; my nephews and niece Mark, Daniel and Harriet Clompus and William Daniels.

I have had a long and happy connection with Cambridge University Press, and am deeply grateful to the press, especially for the constant support and help from four wonderful editors: Marigold Acland, Lucy Rhymer, Rachel Blaifeder and Emily Plater. Many thanks for invaluable help in editing to John Gaunt. I thank Aaron Throness for his invaluable help with the images for the book, and James Duff for his impressive ability to solve my technology problems.

Finally my thanks go to three people who have greatly improved my work: the two anonymous readers who read the manuscript for CUP with great care and gave me many helpful suggestions, and my dear friend Mary Boyd, who understands contemporary China better than anyone else I know. In the induced isolation of the pandemic she read the last draft with meticulous care.

Preface

In Praise of Grandmothers

Chinese grandmothers are integral parts of their grandchildren's lives, a major source of care, love and security. They love their grandchildren and are loved in return. They give unstintingly of their time and energy to their 'treasures'. They have done this for a long time.

The practice of grandmothers raising small children is embedded. Some parents have always gone away, to work or study, and been separated from their children, for weeks, months or years. The anguish for parents at leaving beloved children is immense, made easier by implicit trust that they will be well cared for. Today the separations are concentrated in the children of rural migrants. Grandmothers are in charge of the children for fifty weeks of the year, the parents home for only two weeks' annual holiday. Without the legion of grandmothers China's sustained economic boom would have been impossible.

In the past, grandmothers dominated their family. They were simultaneously loving grandmothers and harsh mothers-in-law, i.e. they mistreated their grand-children's mother. The old system, so hard on young women, had to change, and it did. Old women have lost much of their power, but while the family remains the cornerstone of society, parts of the old internal dynamics survive. China is now a wealthy nation, but one that provides only limited social welfare benefits – healthcare, pensions, unemployment insurance, education. In the name of Confucian values, China makes younger generations of families responsible for the care of their seniors. In return the elders take a major role in the care of their grandchildren.

The book covers a long time span. Change has been constant. There are major variations by period, region, class, good luck, bad luck and personality in all these issues, but one constant: grandmothers are hugely important to their families.

This book covers the period from the mid-Qing Dynasty to the present. The way Chinese is written on the Mainland has changed; characters have been simplified since 1956. Here is an example: dragon (*long*) is now written 龙, replacing 龍. Simplified characters are easier to learn and to read but they lack the beauty and the historical connection of traditional ones. They cannot be used for one of the greatest art forms in Chinese culture, calligraphy. Outside the Mainland (Taiwan, Hong Kong, Overseas Chinese communities) traditional characters are still used. I found it hard to abandon the traditional characters for traditional sayings and for poetry; for them and for names and terms used before 1956 I use traditional characters.

    This is a personal book. As a granddaughter and a grandmother I could not help inserting myself into it. There are many shared experiences of old women, whether in China or elsewhere. The universal joy of being the grandmother of the most delightful of human beings, babies and small children, makes us members of an elderly sisterhood.

Introduction

The writer Chiang Yee was in England in the 1930s when he painted in ILLUSTRATION 0.1 of himself with his grandparents. It was painted from memory, by a man who called himself 'the silent traveller', isolated and alien. The picture took him back to a place of perfect happiness, with two lovely old people who adored him.

The picture of the grandmother of the celebrated Wong family of Vancouver shows a poised, clear-eyed woman. She is wearing a sombre silk gown. Her hair is pulled back, her face unadorned. She has jade hoops in her ears. She is confident, she has a natural dignity, she is a woman fulfilled. She was born in the late Qing Dynasty. She had three sons and seventeen grandchildren, ten of them born in Vancouver.

In traditional China getting older was not threatening. Old women came into their own, in control of their households, basking in the love of their sons, living with their grandchildren. Their husbands were less important in the family. Old men moved into quiescence, engaging in gentle activities – calligraphy, *taiqi*, hanging out with other old men. The grandchildren were a joy. Each new grandchild added to the happiness, 'piling up happiness':

累積快樂
leiji kuaile

The number, especially of grandsons, mattered: the more there were, the greater proof an old person had of success in life. Pearl Buck, the interpreter of China for generations of Western readers, gave a lyrical description of the happiness of Wang Lung, the main character in *The Good Earth*: 'In the space of five years he had four grandsons and three granddaughters and the courts were filled with their laughter and their weeping.'[1] The only greater happiness was to see great-grandchildren, to have 四世同堂 *sishi tongtang*, 'four generations under one roof'. The ideal image was of a respected patriarch, surrounded by grandchildren, his days passing in quiet pleasure.

Old women were busy and self-confident. They did not fit saccharine Western images of plump, smiling grannies, knitting and sewing in a corner, undemanding and passive. And there are no Chinese versions of dotty old

ILLUSTRATION 0.1 Grandparents with their favourite

women, as played by Maggie Smith: the working-class, combative Muriel Donnelly in *The Best Exotic Marigold Hotel* or the crazy Miss Shepherd in *The Lady in the Van*. Her Dowager Lady Grantham in *Downton Abbey* is a matriarch who might be recognisable in China, though she had no formal power in her family beyond her autocratic personality.

Comparisons between China and the West that seem unavoidable may also be problematic. They may be facile assumptions about differences and similarities between cultures, assumptions that lead to blind alleys of complacent

ILLUSTRATION 0.2 The Wongs' grandmother

ignorance. That is one possibility. Another is that there *is* a history of comparisons; the China–West binary has been used since the nineteenth century (late
Qing Dynasty), a pattern of analysis known as the *tiyong* dichotomy, 'Chinese
knowledge as the essence, Western knowledge for practical use':

中學為骵 西學為用
zhongxue weiti xixue weiyong

The core of the dichotomy is that there is a Chinese essence that cannot
be touched by material and technological change. The essence is made up
of values and beliefs, evolved over millennia of history. Originally developed in the government sphere, it came to encompass society, closely
associated with Confucian values. In social terms it means that Chinese
families are expected to respect and care for their elders, Western families
much less so. *Tiyong* has survived the arrival of a Western ideology,
Marxism, and it continues to survive in the age of *Socialism with Chinese*

Characteristics. It is used explicitly to congratulate China on conquering COVID, counterposed to the lack of success in the undisciplined liberal West (the origin of the virus is not mentioned). In looking at the lives of old women ILLUSTRATION, comparisons may help, to point up the advantages and the restrictions of the Chinese way, as seen from the point of view of old women/grandmothers.

ILLUSTRATION 0.3 The kiss

Love and Affection

Grandparents were/are tremendously important to their grandchildren; they were the source of love. The cartoonist Feng Zikai 豐子愷 captured this love. The role of parents was/is to be strict with their children, to prepare them for the harshness of a competitive world. The dearth of overt parental affection created a space for grandparents to give grandchildren warmth and expressions of love.

Chinese adults often remember their grandparents' giving of love, the gift of the old to the young. The love is reciprocated. The grandchildren think of their grandparents with love and gratitude – and with respect for their fortitude and resilience. Li Jie dedicates her beautiful book about her childhood in Shanghai to her grandparents, who 'first illuminated for me the human vitality and personal meaning of a baffling and tumultuous century'.[2]

Generations

There is no such thing as a typical Chinese family, but there has been a common feature: power within the family resided in the senior generation. There was a twist to the tradition of male dominance: as men grew older they withdrew; women became more powerful, as matriarchs. The matriarch was in charge of everything within her household, leaving her husband (later her sons) to manage affairs outside the family. Literate or illiterate, she was supposed to be shrewd, devoted to the welfare of the family. She kept track of income and expenditures – at whatever level of wealth or poverty – she managed relations between family members and she led the observance of rituals and ceremonies.

Her role was as true of peasant (the term 农民 nongmin is now often translated as 'farmer') families, the vast majority of the population, as of rich families. In the family economy grandmothers were essential. They were household managers, they looked after the children and they helped out in the fields at the busy times, planting and harvest. This is a prosperous village in Yunnan in the 1940s; the old women were at work at harvest time:[3]

We often found old women, even those above sixty, busily working in the fields. It will not be too far from the truth to say that the female population of the community turns out en masse during the busy season. They may be at work in the fields or busy in the kitchen preparing food for the workers. On the other hand men could be found at all times in the shops, gambling houses and opium dens enjoying their idle bliss.

Class

I have just mentioned that older women were dominant in families, whether rich or poor. This brings up the issue of class. Defining social class has been an enormous issue in modern China. In the Mao Era (1950 on), often called the

Red Era (红色时代 *hongse shidai*), political upheaval and class struggle demanded class classification (阶级分别 *jieji fenbie*). The process used many metrics (land ownership, income, family background) which varied by place and time. The process was tumultuous and antagonistic. This system has gone out of usage. I have borrowed a simpler approach, from the pioneer sociologist Chen Da 陳達 in the 1930s, which fits today's society better than the Mao Era classification: rich, middle class and lower class.

Child Care

Until very recently paternal grandmothers were accepted as repositories of wisdom in the care of infants and small children. They took over much of the baby care from their inexperienced daughters-in-law, holding the infant in their arms, rocking, soothing, kissing, crooning, singing lullabies to get a baby to sleep, doing everything except feed the baby – that was left to the mother. They dressed babies in elaborate clothes and hats. They were baby-worshippers. Their skills and attention helped to produce the most charming of creatures, a placid, smiling infant.

I have come across very few references to a new mother's lack of trust in a grandmother's competence to care for her children, even though the grandmother was her mother-in-law. This has always intrigued me; it is quite contradictory to Western concepts, where baby and child care has gone through cycles of belief and practice that have one thing in common: mothers doubt the knowledge and competence of grandmothers. In China, the expertise of grandmothers seems to go unquestioned. The pattern of trust has shown cracks recently. The state worries about the quality of care of the tens of millions of 'left-behind children' (留守儿童 *liushou ertong*), whose parents, migrant workers, are away for a year or longer at a time. The lack of trust is not the parents', however, but the state's.

The role of the grandmother as child carer has increased over time, and has extended from infants and small children to older ones. Grandmothers have come to care for grandchildren for long periods – weeks, months or even years. This extension of care started with the beginnings of industrialisation at the end of the Qing Dynasty and the employment of more and more young women outside the home. After 1949 and the establishment of the Communist government, the Party demanded that young women (i.e. mothers) participate in the revolution. Maternal grandmothers as well as paternal grandmothers were drawn in. Now that millions upon millions of people work away from home, separated from their children, the separations are accepted as part of the new economy.

Contributions to the Family Economy

Grandmothers contributed to the family economy. Their unpaid work within the household was a substitute for money. They preserved vegetables, eggs, meat, fish and fruit; they made noodles, pickles, bean curd. They made household items, bedding, clothing, shoes. And they made handcrafts for sale. Every locality had its tradition of handcraft products, made by women working in convivial groups in the courtyard or at the house gate. Baskets and mats were woven from reeds and osiers; toys were moulded from paste, thread was spun and woven into cloth. Older women taught the local crafts to younger women in their family.

Elders

Old women, as old people, have benefited from the Confucian tradition of respect for age. They are assumed to have accumulated experiences, good and bad, to have absorbed them, and acquired wisdom. The ancient text 韓非子 *Han Feizi* says, 'the old horse knows the road': 老馬識途 *laoma shi tu*. On a more cynical level is 'an old reprobate knows all the tricks': 老奸巨猾 *laojian juhua*. Wisdom was not gendered, though a rule of thumb was that from men came rather lofty advice, from women practical help and understanding.

The respect for age has held fairly steady in China, with major exceptions. The young radicals in the 1920s and 1930s revolted against the old patriarchal order. Revolt included sympathy for their mothers and grandmothers as victims of patriarchy. In the Mao Era respect for age was turned on its head; youth was in control and old people were repositories of feudal backwardness. The present government has reversed this. Confucian respect for age is mobilised to make up for limited provision of pensions and health care; there are legal and moral provisions that require children to look after their parents and their grandparents. The celebrations to honour the elderly, banned in the Mao Era, have returned. From sixty on the decade birthdays (大壽 *dashou*) are occasions for major gifts and lavish celebrations.

Grandmothers inculcated traditional culture into their grandchildren, through stories, songs, picture books, proverbs. They taught them religion, praying to household deities, taking them to shrines and temples. They told them stories. Chiang Yee remembered sitting at his grandmother's knee with his siblings and cousins on hot summer evenings:[4]

It was her habit to tell us legends and stories about immortals and spirits, or about her life as a girl and a young wife, or about the city and its history. Some of the stories interested me and others did not, but we were all impressed by Grandmother's knowledge. After a cup or two of *kaoliang* (a Chinese strong white wine made of barley [actually a spirit made of sorghum]) she was always in good humour and ready to entertain us.

Grandfathers had different responsibilities in cultural transmission. Literate grandfathers were responsible for passing on the higher culture to their grandchildren. The first stage, when the child was very small, was to teach the rudiments of calligraphy, from single strokes to simple characters. They might be written in sand, or with water on a stone floor, or, as the child improved, on paper. The beautiful 2015 film about the great calligrapher Qi Gong 启功, *The Calligraphy Master*, shows his grandfather teaching him the first stages of calligraphy.

Grandfathers took ancestral succession seriously. They taught their grandchildren about their forebears, and in the telling created continuity between the ancestors and the children. Whether the family had a written genealogy or not, all families had a sense of where they came from, who their relatives were. The genealogies and the oral histories might or might not be factual, but they existed, and the older generation had a duty to pass them on.

Grandparents played a key role in a child's language development. They spoke to their grandchildren in their native dialect. Standard Chinese (國語 *guoyu*/普通话 *putonghua*) was not introduced until the Republic (1912 on) and took a long time to be universally spoken; until recently most people spoke a dialect. Younger people became bilingual, in dialect and standard Chinese, but the grandparents seldom did. They were their grandchildren's instructors in dialect. This turned out to have long-term value; certain dialects (Beijing, Shanghai, Minnan, Cantonese) have brought their speakers advantage in the economic boom that started in the 1980s.

The Power of Older Women

Older women wielded powerful social control. They were in close touch with their neighbours, with other grandmothers, exchanging the latest local news, gossiping. In the Mao Era the Communist Party called on them to run street committees and watch their neighbours for signs of opposition to the Party. That role has declined, replaced by social media and electronic surveillance.

Old women were/are devotees of the female deities who play an enormous role, in Buddhism, Daoism, popular religion and Christianity. The various deities have their own cults and temples, but their roles are similar. All are loving and caring, protecting mortals in distress. They were immensely popular, which is perhaps why they were attacked so ferociously during the Mao Era, their shrines destroyed and their images smashed. They are now back, stronger than ever, worshipped in countless temples and shrines, some of them of extravagant size and lavishness.

Grandmothers in Literature

China's most famous grandmother, the Lady Dowager of the Jia Family 賈母, is a central character in the eighteenth-century novel *A Dream of Red Mansions*, and in cartoons, films, radio and television series, and on playing cards and cigarette cards. The Jia mansion and its garden, the 大觀園 *Daguanyuan*, have been re-created in Beijing. She feels familiar to all Chinese, a commanding and respected figure (see Chapter 2).

Grandmothers are downplayed in academic and official literature on women in Chinese society; they hardly exist. The focus in feminist history is on girls and young women, on the miseries that women in those age groups have suffered: foot binding, arranged marriage. The push towards raising the status of women since the late Qing has focussed on young women and their contributions to revolution and social change. Older women are absent, unless as domineering mothers-in-law or as carers for the children of their own absent children. I have scoured the literature on Chinese women for discussion of old women, with very slim pickings.[5]

Other genres of literature value grandmothers, notably biography and autobiography. Traditional biographies were detailed, year-by-year accounts that left out women. In the 1930s a more introspective form of biography emerged. Three autobiographies in English describe childhood in late imperial and early Republican China. Sheng Cheng wrote about his family in Yichang 宜昌 (Hubei), Tan Shihua about his in Sichuan and Ling Shuhua 凌叔華 about hers in Beijing.[6] All were from rich families and had foreign connections. Vita Sackville-West, a member of the Bloomsbury Group, wrote the introduction to Ling's work.

The poor were illiterate, they could not write about themselves, so biographies of the poor are rare. One that does stand out is the oral biography of Ning Lao Taitai told to Ida Pruitt in the 1930s, *Daughter of Han*.[7] Gail Hershatter's *Gender of Memory* is a fascinating compilation based on more than seventy interviews that she did in the 1990s with her colleague Gao Xiaoxian, in villages in Shaanxi. They interviewed old women about their lives as young women in the early years of the Mao Era.[8]

After 1949 biography took on a sinister aspect; people were required to write autobiographies to establish their past in class terms, often with the consequence of a bad 'label'. In published literature hagiographies of major revolutionary figures were published in great numbers. In the Mao Era demonologies of enemies such as the Four Great Families (四大家族 *sida jiazu*), the leading families of the Republic, balanced the hagiographies, lurid tales of hideous tyrants and poisonous weeds.

Since the early 1980s there has been an explosion of memoir (回忆录 *huiyilu*) writing. These may be written by or about a subject. They are often thinly veiled efforts to 'revise history', to give people who had previously been vilified back their rightful place in history. Others are efforts at reflected glory, written about famous figures with whom the author has a connection. Memoirs are positive; awkward periods are omitted, as are salacious details of private lives. To offset the probity of memoirs there are 'outside histories' (外史 *waishi*), books packed with lurid and sometimes improbable details of the lives of the famous. Printed books have now given way to online material.

Autobiography disguised as fiction is a major genre for understanding the family and its transformation in modern China. Ba Jin's 巴金 novels, published in serial form in the early 1930s, gave detailed descriptions of his family in Sichuan. François Cheng's (Cheng Baoyi 程抱一) novel *The River Below*, first published in 1998, closely follows Cheng's childhood in Jiangxi, and his wartime youth in Sichuan.[9]

Sentiment

Western sophisticates often feel queasy about liberal expression of sentiment. It is dismissed as 'sentimentality' or 'schmaltz', too sugary, cloying or syrupy to be taken seriously. Overt sentiment seems false, hypocritical, squirm-making, mawkish. It arouses 'feelings of embarrassment and anxiety'.[10] It is class-based: the less educated are more likely to indulge in sentiment than the more educated. And it is overtly commercial – greeting cards, floral tributes. It may go beyond sensible bounds. When my children were small it was common to have a baby's first boot bronzed; there must be millions of bronze boots around.

There is a countertradition in China. Expressions of overweening sentiment are quite acceptable, not the least embarrassing. Nowhere does lush sentiment appear more vividly than in portrayals of infants. Babies are shown as laughing, rosy creatures, plump to the point of obesity.

Periodisation and Chronology

Many of the topics I look at in this book recur over time; others mutate, change dramatically or disappear. There is no absolute linear chronology. There are surprises in what comes back, what does not. The best example is Confucian values. They were the foundation of government and society in the Qing, attacked by the Taiping Heavenly Kingdom (太平天國 *taiping tianguo*) (1850–64), by Republican iconoclasts and by the Communist Party – and are now back again, sponsored by the state. One topic is relatively recent: the growth of population, which stressed the old social system.

In the late Qing Dynasty and the early Republic, social change was slight in most parts of China. The family was the centre of life, traditional values and customs were still dominant, migration was limited to a few regions. Major social changes got under way slowly after the 1911 Revolution. The new political system had limited impact, but industrialisation, new transport systems and constant low-level warfare all combined to accelerate changes in society, concentrated in the cities and coastal regions. In 1937 Japan invaded China. There followed twelve years of warfare, the War of Resistance (1937–1945),

---

Box 0.1 Population

China's population is the largest of any state in the world, and has been since time immemorial. For much of that time it was fairly stable, around two hundred million; since the eighteenth century it has more than quadrupled; it passed a billion in the 1980s and is now around 1.4 billion. The population is no longer growing, and concern now is about shrinkage and the imbalance between young and old. I use vague numbers because until the Census of 1981 there was no rigorous census. Historically the bulk of the population was rural; now more than half are permanent or temporary urban residents. In infancy and childhood males have outnumbered females; in old age women outnumber men. Life expectancy has risen dramatically since 1949, from around forty to over seventy, though one generation, born in the early 1960s famine, is significantly smaller. As many as 50 million people of Chinese descent live outside Mainland China; 24 million are in Taiwan, more than 7 million in Hong Kong.[1]

[1] For greater detail on historical demographics see Ge Jianxiong 葛剑雄, 中国人口史 *Zhongguo renkou shi* (*A History of China's Population*) (Shanghai: Fudan, 2002); Endymion Wilkinson, *Chinese History: A New Manual,* 3rd edition (Cambridge, MA: Harvard University Asia Center, 2013), pp. 289–292, 308–311.

---

then the civil war between the Nationalists and the Communists (1946–1949). The wars brought refugee flights, economic collapse, social upheaval and chaos. The old social order, already compromised, was effectively destroyed.

During the Mao Era the Communist government made radical efforts to remake China along socialist lines. Old values were trashed as 'feudal'. The Party took precedence over the family. Mass migrations redistributed people across China. China was isolated from the world and from Overseas communities. Tumultuous political movements caused huge disruption, economic hardship and famine; the greatest turmoil was the Cultural Revolution (1966–1976). The Communist Party survived the excesses of the Mao Era. A new leadership ushered in an era of 'change and opening up' (改革开放 *gaige kaifang*). The last four decades of the Reform Era have seen the rebirth of many traditional norms, grafted onto the wreckage left by the Mao Era. There has been unprecedented economic growth and fundamental social change. Restrictions on family size have changed family dynamics. From rural China hundreds of millions of peasants have moved to work in new industries; they do not move permanently, but remain attached to their villages, where their children live with their grandparents.

Over the past century of political turmoil, economic growth and techno-logical innovation, much of Chinese society has changed beyond recognition. In the lifetime of the old women interviewed by Hershatter and Gao a mind-numbing succession of political movements blurred into each other; they identified clearly two big turning points: 'Life got better twice, once in the 1950s and again in the 1980s.'[11]

Beyond political periodisation is personal periodisation, the key dates in a person's life: birth, marriage, birth of first child. Today's grandmothers see their lives in personal terms – and they see that through all the societal change the role of grandmothers has changed, but not fundamentally. They have continued to be child-carers, household managers, religious devotees – and above all sources of love, warmth and affection.

1   Precious Treasures

寶貝

baobei

The happiest aspect of getting older, the compensation for infirmity and fragility, is having 'golden boys and jade girls' (金童玉女 *jintong yunü*). Grandchildren are 'precious treasures' (寶貝 *baobei*), the rewards for life.

Being a grandmother is a long stage of life. It can start as early as a woman's mid-thirties – but it usually starts around the time of menopause. The grandmother hypothesis suggests that the active role of grandmothers in child care differentiates humans from other animals. The grandmother foregoes her reproduction at menopause; her long post-menopausal life is devoted to the care of the offspring of her own children. Her support guarantees that more infants will survive. In the wild, primate mothers can no longer care for an older infant once another is born; this greatly limits the first one's chances of survival. With humans the survival of children until they can fend for themselves is made possible by the grandmother's help to the mother.

In traditional China grandmothers were respected. A woman's life was lived on an upward trajectory. A short childhood led to a hard time as a young wife and mother, under the thumb of her mother-in-law, to a later stage when her household tasks were onerous, to older age when she was respected and dominant. The happiness and status of older women depended on being a grandmother – and it was assumed that all women would be grandmothers. In the past this meant being a paternal grandmother; there was an absolute distinction between paternal and maternal grandmothers, one in which the maternal grandmother barely counted.

Secure in the love and material support of her sons, the paternal grandmother had reached an honoured stage of life. She expected to live in a family headed by her husband or, if he was dead or incapable, her eldest son. (For polygamous families see Chapter 7.) The idea that she might live elsewhere was almost inconceivable; the only alternative was a nunnery. She loved her grandchildren and was loved by them. Physically this was a relatively easy stage of life. The horrors of pregnancy and childbirth were past. Her household duties were not

---

Box 1.1 Terms for grandmother

Until the Communist revolution, 'grandmother' effectively meant a child's father's mother. She alone had access to her grandchildren. The stark difference between paternal and maternal grandmothers appears in the language: the paternal grandmother is 祖母 *zumu*, the maternal grandmother is 外祖母 *waizumu*, 'outside grandmother'. Table 1.1 provides some informal terms, distinguished by paternal/maternal, and by region.

Table 1.1 *Chinese terms for grandmother*

Paternal grandmother, north China	*nainai* 奶奶
Maternal grandmother, north China	*laolao* 姥姥
Paternal grandmother, south China	*ama* 阿媽
Maternal grandmother, south China	*popo* 婆婆
Paternal grandmother, Taiwan	*ama* 阿媽
Maternal grandmother, Taiwan	*apo* 阿婆

physically tiring but they required alertness and constant supervision of her daughters-in-law, her unmarried daughters and (if she was wealthy) her servants.

This trajectory lasted into the Republic (1912 on). Then the world of grandmothers started to change. Few of the new ways enhanced their status or compensated for the sufferings of their younger lives. The biggest changes were after 1949: later age of marriage, smaller family size, more education, better health. These changes are what make the lives of women in contemporary society almost unrecognisable in comparison to the traditional one. There is one major continuum: their critical role as grandmothers.

Stages of Life

Being a grandmother (even better, a great grandmother) was the last stage in the life of Chinese women. For those who survived the early stages, life got better. The birth of a girl was the arrival of a temporary member of a family, someone who would be gone in less than two decades. Her name would not be entered in the family genealogy (家谱 *jiapu*). A girl would be betrothed early in life, an arrangement made by her family. This is a description of the process in rural China by the anthropologist Fei Xiaotong:[1]

When a girl is six or seven her parents approach a matchmaker. The matchmaker takes a red paper with the hour, day, month, and year of the girl's birth written on it. She visits a series of eligible boys, from different villages. The boy's mother takes the papers to a fortune teller. The fortune teller examines the relative merits of the proposals. Once a girl has been selected the matchmaker goes back to her family and serious negotiations start, focussing on how much the boy's family will send to the bride's family in gifts. These will be returned to the groom's family as her dowry, along with major contributions from the bride's own family. Eventually, when the girl and boy are in their mid-teens, the groom will be sent to fetch his bride to his home, where a large feast is prepared. The bride bows to her husband's ancestors – and then meets him, for the first time.

Girls were brought up to embody feminine virtues of modesty, obedience, chastity and submissiveness. If a family's income allowed it they lived cloistered lives, kept away in separate quarters from the larger society. Girls were expected to obey their father, as they would later obey their husbands. They might be loved by their families, but affection was an option, not a requirement. Girls got little education; the hard-headed thinking was that educating a girl was an investment without return. Family resources had to go to sons. They were unlikely to be taught to read; this at least saved her from having to read the turgid *Biographies of Exemplary Women* (列女傳 *Lienüzhuan*), the severe Confucian code of female behaviour.

Childhood and brief adolescence were periods of training for married life. From their mothers and grandmothers girls learned domestic skills. These skills depended on the wealth or poverty of the family. A girl from a family that kept its own cook did not learn how to cook; she learned how to supervise a cook, tasting the food as it was prepared. In the film *Crazy Rich Asians*, the matriarch Eleanor Young (Michelle Yeoh) supervises a legion of cooks before a large party; in Western kitchens no cook would tolerate such interference. All girls learned needlework. Poorer girls learned to sew clothing and bedding, and embroidery. More affluent girls learned only embroidery. All girls were taught to grow flowers, and to make and serve tea.

This training was different in detail but not in concept from the training given to Western girls. What *was* different was that in the West girls had some hand in finding a husband. Lev Tolstoi (*Anna Karenina*) and Jane Austen (*Pride and Prejudice*) describe in exquisite and excruciating detail the suspense and anxiety of girls on the brink of marriage.

The space for Western girls to find a good match was very small. By the time she was in her early twenties, she was 'on the shelf', a spinster, an old maid. Chinese girls had no role in finding a husband but every girl got one; there were no spinsters in China. The only unmarried women were nuns and prostitutes. In the West girls hoped for love as a prelude to marriage. In China love might follow marriage, but it could not come before it. The bride and groom did not meet until the wedding ceremony, when the bride was brought into her husband's house; the word for 'to marry' is a house with a woman radical (嫁 *jia*). The newly-weds were just as likely to hate each other as to fall in love. An irony: she kept her surname in her new family, Madam Wang 王氏 or Madam Li 李氏, without a given name. This is the opposite of the Western tradition, where a bride lost her maiden name. Within the household a woman would be known by her status and relationship. If she was married to the second son of the family she would be called Second Daughter-in-Law (二媳婦 *erxifu*); as mother of the eldest son she would be Mother of Oldest Son (老大他媽 *laoda tama*).

Her children had no formal relationship with their maternal grandmother (姥姥 *laolao*). Her natal family (娘家 *niangjia*) could do little to help her if her marriage was unhappy. Four of the five daughters of the Confucian mandarin Zeng Guofan 曾國藩 had unhappy marriages; three died young. Despite his prominence, Zeng could not make their situations better. Part of the daughters' unhappiness was his fault. They were married with small dowries; the upright Confucian was opposed to excessive spending. Their relative poverty made them vulnerable in their husbands' families.[2] The family of a mistreated wife might feel responsibility for arranging a bad match. Ning Lao Taitai, a poor woman from Shandong, told her life story to Ida Pruitt. Her mother helped her survive a disastrous marriage:[3]

Because my husband smoked opium and did not bring home food, I stayed longer with my mother than was the custom (half the time). While she [her mother] was alive I had a place of refuge. She sent food and grain to me, and flour. I was my family's baby. They always loved me and fought for me.

A maternal grandmother might step in to care for an orphaned grand-daughter. Lin Daiyu 林黛玉, the heroine of *A Dream of Red Mansions*, was taken in by her mother's mother, the Lady Dowager, after her parents' deaths. This was a rare example, as was the case of the writer Peng Hui 彭慧. Her widowed mother transferred what she could of her husband's estate to her own family when she knew she was dying. She distrusted her husband's feckless brother. The money paid for the care and education of her four daughters.[4]

Where married daughters lived close to their natal family, contact was more likely, but help was discretionary. General Li Zongren 李宗仁 was born to a peasant family in Guangxi in 1890. One of his most searing childhood memories was of going with his mother to borrow rice from his wealthy maternal grandmother. His family was going hungry, and needed rice to tide them over until the harvest. His grandmother, who made her money through lending grain at interest, was hard-hearted:[5]

My mother explained that our shortage was due to the size of our family [eight children] not to laziness. As mother and daughter they spoke frankly and with little restraint. They quarreled bitterly, neither willing to give in. Mother grew so angry, tears flowed from her eyes, and she decided not to borrow.

The steely grandmother stuck to the requirement that help went only to sons, not to daughters. Li adored his mother, and admired her hard work and determination. The memory of her humiliation by her own mother stayed with him until old age.

For a woman to flourish in her married family it was critical to have sons. They secured her husband's family line and assured her of care in later life. Son-preference was absolute and unquestioned.

This preference has not gone away. I had two daughters. Chinese friends were horrified that I did not try for a son. Without a son, how could I guarantee a happy old age? If my attitude was hard to grasp, the choice of some Western women not to have children at all was incomprehensible.

As a woman lived longer, and produced sons, her status in the family improved. By the time she became a grandmother, she was secure. Most of the miseries of life were behind her.

Obligations and Rewards

Grandparents were the direct link between past and future generations. There was an obligation on the young to produce grandchildren for their parents. The elders had their own obligation, to teach the younger members of the family about their forebears; otherwise the younger generations might grow up in ignorance of the family line:

老人不講話後生會失譜

laoren bu jianghua housheng hui shipu

This prescription was less a threat than a statement of the key role of the old in a family. They were the bedrock of the family; the family was the bedrock of society.

The Chinese family expected much of grandmothers. A contemporary North American grandmother has some choice about how much she will do for her grandchildren. She may be intimately involved with them, or she may see them only occasionally. She is unlikely to live with them. Advertisements show older people, always handsome couples, enjoying life in retirement (with the slogan 'Freedom 55'), playing golf in warm climes, cruising the world on luxury liners. Adventurous grannies are off sailing solo round the world, or climbing Everest. Some are looking for new love, on websites such as Age Match, Our Time or Love Again. Some are in public office, or running major corporations. The choice is theirs.

Not for Chinese grandmothers. They have always understood that their first duty is to their family. This was not a burden. A traditional grandmother basked in the love of her grandchildren and took credit for their survival, proof of the

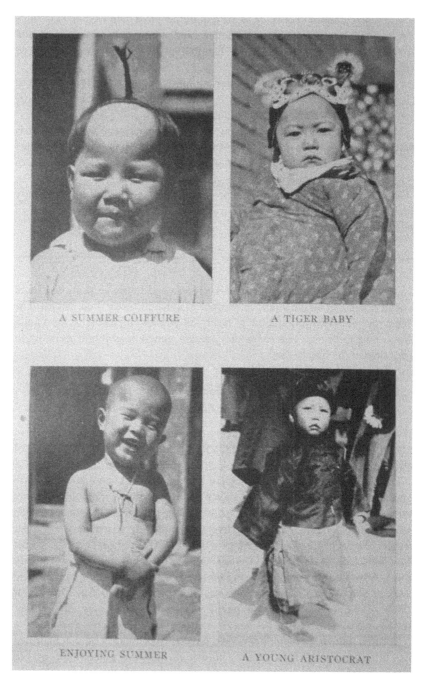

ILLUSTRATION 1.1 Baby boys

efforts she had made for them, the food she had fed them, the prayers she had said over them. Their success was her success. In the delicate business of competitive grandmothering, she congratulated herself on having more and cleverer 'precious treasures' than other grandmothers.

The recitation of the achievements, beauty and competence of the treasures had a practical application: matchmaking. The task of matchmaking was formally ascribed to the parents of the prospective bride or groom, but grandmothers were often heavily involved. They had more time; they had more connections. Old women visited each other or met at temples and shrines. They relished the task of making a good match for the young ones they loved. They scanned their natal families for potential brides or grooms, i.e. cousin marriage. The concept of 'cousin' in Chinese society is complex; there are distinct terms for different kinds of cousin. Paternal cousins (堂 tang), with the same surname, the children of brothers, a boy and girl who shared a surname, could not marry. Maternal cousins (表 biao) could marry. The genetic dangers of cousin marriage, which made it unacceptable in most Western countries, were not recognised. In the most famous love triangle in *The Dream of Red Mansions*, Jia Baoyu 賈寶玉 loved his beautiful cousin Lin Daiyu, daughter of his father's sister. But his loving grandmother could see that the fragile, hypersensitive girl was not a suitable wife for the heir to a great family. The matriarch choose instead to marry him to another cousin, Xue Baochai 薛寶釵, equally beautiful but sensible and competent. She was a maternal relative, the daughter of his mother's sister, a less close relative than Lin Daiyu.[6]

The pinnacle of a grandmother's success was to have a grandson pass one level of the imperial examinations. Success in the highly competitive examinations, with minuscule pass rates, brought prestige to the whole family. The mother and grandmother of the successful candidate experienced intense gratification. An almost unheard of success was that of Lady Wang 王夫人, Jia Baoyu's mother. He passed the second level of the examinations in the same session as her grandson Jia Lan 賈蘭, the son of her dead first son. This extraordinary success was blasted by the disappearance of Baoyu before the results were announced.

After the examination system was abolished in 1905, clear proof of success was more complicated. Respect for financial success, in the port cities and overseas, was diminished by the Confucian contempt for money and profit. Military success, the new route to power, was tainted by traditional contempt for soldiers.

好鐵不打釘 好人不當兵

Haotie bu da ding haoren by dang bing

Good iron does not make nails, good men do not become soldiers

Intellectual achievement came to be associated not with Confucian scholars but with the young iconoclasts who were breaking away from the tradition. All three types of 'modern' success dismayed the older generation. Eight decades later, examinations are back as the first step on the way to a brilliant career. The Gaokao 高考, the examinations for entrance to university, take place every year, on the same two days across China. Ten million young people sit them. Like the traditional examinations, they bring success to a few, disappointment to many, many more.

Love and Warmth

One of grandmothers' greatest contributions to their families is the love and affection essential for young children to thrive. The love of grandmothers for their grandchildren is universal. This is from an early nineteenth-century German text:[7] 'The grandmother's tenderness towards the grandchildren and that of the child towards the grandmother must be regarded not as a product of civilisation but a general trait of the human soul.'

In China the love was intense, felt both by the child and by the grandmother. It flowed freely. Grandmothers had been denied romantic love in their youth. As mothers their duty had been to mould their children for success; mother love was expressed in discipline and attention, not in hugs and kisses, gentleness and kindness. Amy Chua is the protagonist of the tough Chinese mother. Her book *Battle Hymn of the Tiger Mother* attributes the academic success of children of Chinese origin to rigorous discipline; bans on play dates, sleepovers or television; and acceptance of no grade below an A.[8]

Box 1.2 The concept of a 'Chinese mother'

Amy Chua popularised the concept of the 'Chinese tiger mother', with her prescription for how to raise high-achieving children.[1] She counterpoised the 'Chinese mother', tough and determined, with the 'Western' mother who raises the 'soft, entitled child' (pp. 13, 22). 'Chinese mothers' do not have to be Chinese – they may be Korean, Iranian, Pakistani, Korean. And not all Chinese mothers are 'Chinese mothers' (p. 4). Achievement is defined as getting into a top US university.

Chua is disarmingly open about the perils of tough parenting. She describes what she did as 'extreme parenting', and herself as an 'overbearing, fanatic mother' (p. 48). Her tactics worked with her elder daughter, but at times her relationship with her younger daughter was 'all-out nuclear warfare'. And she could not persuade her daughters that they were Chinese (pp. 56, 205). 'When Chinese parenting succeeds, there's

Box 1.2 (Cont.)

nothing like it. But it doesn't always succeed' (p. 212). She has paid a cost; she seems to have experienced few of the joys of having children: 'the truth is I'm not good at enjoying life' (p. 97).

[1] Amy Chua, *Battle Hymn of the Tiger Mother* (New York: Penguin, 2011), page references in parentheses.

Grandmothers gave grandchildren what their parents could not: expressions of unconditional love. Chua was astounded by the behaviour of her ultra-strict parents towards their granddaughters: 'ridiculously unstrict in a way completely inconsistent with the way they'd raised me'. Her mother warned Amy that she was too strict in disciplining her younger daughter: 'You're going to regret it.'[9]

As primary child-carers for their grandchildren, grandmothers found their task easier than caring for their own children had been. These are Taiwanese grandmothers in the 1960s: 'Child care, instead of being a burden among other burdens, is a pleasure, since grandchildren need only to be loved, not trained.'[10]

Grandchildren were the daily companions of their grandmothers; their loving care gave the child a sense of self-worth and self-confidence. In return the grandchildren gave their grandmothers cuddles and comfort. Grandchildren slept with their grandmothers. A warm little body was a living hot-water bottle.

Child care had no set limits; the grandmother did what was necessary, extending to full-time care if the parents were absent, working hard for the revolution. Jian Ping, daughter of two Communist Party cadres, feared her stern and often absent mother, but adored her 奶奶 *nainai* (father's mother), as did her five siblings:[11]

Nainai was soft-spoken and patient. No matter what my siblings and I did, she never raised her voice or lost her temper. I was always afraid of Mother. She had high expectations of us and was very strict. But Nainai set no rules and passed no judgements.

Her *nainai* slept with her, and gave her frequent treats and, above all, her total attention.

Care and love come together in food. For many grandchildren, the fondest memories of their grandmothers have to do with the food they cooked. Leslie Li's affectionate memoir of her grandmother, Li Xiuwen 李秀文, the first wife of Li Zongren, focusses on food: 'Food was at the heart of Nai-nai's existence. Not so much the eating of it as the cooking of it. She relished good food. She revered its two basic premises, the freshest ingredients (homegrown if possible) and diligent preparation.'[12] This loving grandmother, who did not have a common spoken language with her daughter-in-law or her four granddaughters, took over their suburban New York kitchen. She grew vegetables in the backyard. Out went fish fingers and spaghetti, in came simple but delicious Chinese home cooking (家常菜 *jiachangcai*). The language of her love was food.

The love from grandmothers to their grandchildren was natural and extravagant. This is the Communist heroine Liu Hulan 刘胡兰, with her grandmother:[13]

One day at twilight little Hu-lan sat in her Granny's lap clasping her neck with her two small hands while Granny rocked gently with half-closed eyes listening to the sweet childish voice, singing her local ballads.

When the song came to an end Granny became even quieter. She hugged Hu-lan tighter and smothered this favourite granddaughter of hers with kisses.

There were dark sides of such intimacy. Children born as late as the 1970s understood something of the cruelty of the past, from their grandmother's feet (see Chapter 3). Her bare feet when she washed them showed the pain that she lived with. Zhu Xiaodi saw his grandmother's feet as a child in the early 1960s:[14]

It was amazing to me that a grown-up could have such small and pointed feet. Under her socks she wrapped her feet with a long cloth band. Late every afternoon, after unwrapping the long cloth, she washed her feet. I was amazed by the length of the band. Once her foot emerged it was really terrifying. All her toes were bent over to one side and the shape of her foot looked awful.

Today's Grandmothers

The Reform Era, starting in the early 1980s, has given grandmothers renewed importance. Hundreds of millions of peasants have left their homes and their children to work in the factories that produce vast quantities of goods for export. Legions of rural grandmothers have taken over child care to allow parents to leave home. In the cities, working parents depend on grandparents for child care. Urban women retire at fifty, young enough to be child carers. Grandmothers do this work without recognition from the state, though they provide social services that in many countries are provided by the state. They save the state enormous amounts of money, in wages no longer paid, and in the absence of subsidies for child care.

The material situation of many of today's elderly is light years away from what they knew in their youth. There have been huge improvements in sanitation in the cities. Running water, indoor toilets and bathrooms are standard. The old 'honey' carts that once collected human waste every morning have disappeared, as have noisome public toilets and bath houses. Rural areas are less developed, but access to electricity and to cell phone networks is standard. Cell phones have

Table 1.2 *Death tolls in modern China*

Resistance War	1937–1945	20–30,000,000
Civil War	1945–1949	7–8,000,00
Land reform	1948–1951	Several million
Great Famine	1960–1962	30,000,000
Cultural Revolution	1965–1975	20,000,000

become the major means of contact with family, of shopping and of social intercourse. The revolution in communications has been a boon for the elderly. By phone, Skype, WeChat and social media they keep in constant touch with their children and grandchildren – often more than the young ones would like.

Life expectancy in China has risen dramatically; it is now over seventy-five, slightly higher for women than for men. A half-century ago life expectancy was thirty years less. The rise has happened despite the massive casualties of recent history. Table 1.2 gives estimated death tolls for 1937 to 1975.

These figures are so huge that they seem incomprehensible, but not to elderly Chinese; they have been touched by one or more of these disasters. In the almost four decades of stability in the Reform Era, premature deaths have plummeted.

With increased life expectancy, women will be grandmothers for up to a third of their lives. They are healthier, less threatened by the epidemic diseases that once swept through China – cholera, malaria, plague, typhoid, smallpox – though more threatened by the diseases that affect people who live longer – cancer, heart disease and stroke.

Through all this change, expectations of grandmothers have changed but not diminished. The old assumption that the paternal grandmother would be the one that counted in bringing up the grandchildren has gone – now availability and closeness are key, in which case the maternal grandmother may be more important than the paternal. In the past a *nainai* ruled alone over a brood of grandchildren living in the same household. Now she shares equal status with the *laolao*. Today's grandmothers have fewer grandchildren, a result of the One Child per Family policy, introduced in 1979 and abandoned in 2015. In an extreme case there are four grandparents for one grandchild, four old people to hover over a single precious treasure. The deluge of attention is almost enough to 'drown the child in love' (溺爱 *niai*).

Competitive grandparenting has emerged; paternal and maternal grandparents try to outdo each other. They have been blamed for contributing to a generation of spoiled singletons, children so indulged and petted that they turn into monsters. The little ones may be overweight, their mouths constantly filled with snacks. Their obesity may be why psychoanalyst Wu Zhihong 武志红 has

---

Box 1.3 Putuoshan 普陀山

Putuo Mountain is one of the most important pilgrimage sites in China. It
dominates Putuo Island, in the Zhoushan archipelago south-east of Shanghai.
The whole island is dedicated to the worship of Guanyin, the Goddess of Mercy
and the bringer of sons. Every year millions of pilgrims visit the island, many to
pray for a son or grandson. The mountain is topped by a thirty-metre-tall statue of
the goddess, erected in 1998, clad in gold so that her light streams out across the
sea for miles around. It is one of many huge statues built recently. The tallest
Buddhist image may be the Big Buddha in Lushan 鲁山大佛 (Henan); it is 208
metres high.

---

referred to today's China as 'a nation of giant infants (巨婴国 *juyingguo*), in
which adults have the mentality of a small child: demanding, noisy and
undisciplined.[15]

Today's grandchildren are called 'emperors and empresses', most often
'little emperor'. Son-preference is alive and well. Grandparents are often
blamed for its perpetuation. The desire for a grandson can bring the paternal
grandparents to pressure their daughter-in-law to have a son. The young wife
and her mother-in-law may visit a maternal deity to pray for her help (see
Chapter 8). The most desirable trip is to Putuoshan 普陀山, to ask for the help
of Guanyin in 'sending a son'.

It is often claimed that son-preference leads to early-stage abortions. An
ultrasound test to determine the sex of a foetus is followed by abortion of
a female foetus. Another outcome is the abandonment of girl infants to
orphanages. There are no reliable statistics on either of these practices.

As the children grow the demand for financial help from grandparents
increases. Both sets of grandparents give close attention to the grandchildren's
education, and pay application fees for good schools, school fees and coaching
fees. Daily supervision in preparation for the Gaokao is expected. This is the
main character of Chen Ran's book *A Private Life*:[16]

I lived through and witnessed the closing years of the 1970s and the restoration of the
university entrance examinations in the early 1980s, which pitted middle school graduates ruthlessly against one another as they converged like swarms of wasps on the
universities.

Grandmothers come into their own in preparing their grandchildren for the
Gaokao, a 24/7 job. They live with them, and supervise what they eat, how long
they sleep, what exercise they take. Xu Shangfa's 徐上发 wife moved from their
village in Gaoan 高安 (Jiangxi) into the county town to supervise the day-to-day

---

Box 1.4 Western models of grandmothers

The online self-help phenomenon is strong in China. WikiHow tells Chinese grandmothers how they should make themselves 'fit for purpose as (paternal) grannies' (如何做一个称职的奶奶 *ruhe zuo yige chengshi de nainai*). It offers them a Western-style blueprint for happy relations between the generations. A grandmother must be heavily involved in the grandchildren's lives, but she must leave discipline to the parents; she must not interfere with their parenting. A big part of her job is to show love for the children, with much hugging and kissing (多报报亲亲 *duo baobao qinqin*), but not spoiling them with it. She gives them a sense of security (给他们安全感 *gei tamen anquan gan*). She must also tell the grandchildren about the family's history (讲家史 *jiang jiashi*).

---

life of their brilliant grandson. The old man longed for his wife to return so that they could 'pass their later years in peace' (安度晚年 *andu wannian*).[17] Intensive care is not the only means of seeking success; grandmothers pray for the grandchild's success, consult fortune tellers, burn incense. There are echoes here of the imperial examinations, with one great change – girls can compete as well as boys.

Pride in the achievements of grandchildren is counterpoised with horror at the behaviour of teenage grandchildren. For the first time in Chinese history adolescence is a recognised stage of life. Only in Shanghai, for a brief period before 1949, could young people be teenagers. Zhou Caiqin 周采芹 (the actress Tsai Chin) went out on dates, dressed as a bobby-soxer.[18] In the Mao Era young people devoted themselves to the Great Leader; they shunned self-indulgence, stylish clothes, dates or parties. Half a century later young people are adolescents. Their coloured hair, their dating, their music, their clothes appall their grannies who grew up in Maoist puritanism. Western grandmothers have been through these experiences. In the 1960s, already married, I wore (quite decorous) miniskirts, three inches above my knees. My husband's grandmother prayed for my safety and my immortal soul. Fortunately she never saw my sister Vicky's hot pants.

Chinese grandmothers today have to deal with two particular issues. One is that they are out of step with modern ideas on child care, often based on foreign models circulating on the Internet with the message that grandparents should defer to parents.

The second issue is their radical youth; they have to keep the memory of their youth in the vault. Six decades ago, their hearts full of revolutionary fervour, they attacked their elders as 'bourgeois' or 'feudal'. The Red Guard rampages lasted a few years; then they were sent off to live in rural China (下乡 *xiaxiang*), often for years. Their revolutionary fervour damaged the people they attacked but it also damaged them. They lost their youth.

2 Archetypes and Images of Grandmothers

盡善盡美

Jinshan jinmei

Confucius extolled the possibility of being 'most perfect, most beautiful'. Old women sometimes came close, as grandmothers. Two celebrated grandmothers appear in *The Dream of Red Mansions*. The most famous sat at the pinnacle of society; the other was a poor peasant woman. Both were indomitable, self-confident, nurturing, wise. The Lady Dowager Jia (賈母 Jia Mu) presided over a huge household – a thousand strong – of family members and servants. She was benevolent, generous and very much in control. Granny Liu 劉姥姥 was a rustic woman. The two old women are known to every Chinese.

The Lady Dowager loved her many grandchildren, but adored only one, Jia Baoyu, the boy born with a piece of jade in his mouth. Much as his grandmother adored him, his father, her own son, did not. The scholar official Jia Zheng 賈政 was disappointed with the boy from early in his life:[1]

on his first birthday Jia Zheng tested his disposition by setting all sorts of different objects before him to see which he would select. Believe it or not, ignoring everything else he reached out for the rouge, powder boxes, hair ornaments and bangles! His father was furious and swore that he'd grow up to be a dissolute rake.

Baoyu spent much of his young life with his grandmother, his sisters and his female cousins. His grandmother's indulgence told him that he could ignore rules, and behave as he liked. He was the epitome of a wilful, spoiled boy – and a figure of great charm. When the teenage boy played truant, his father flew into rage, had him tied up and beat him: 'With clenched teeth he rained down dozens of vicious blows. . .he belabored his son mercilessly.'[2] Servants rushed to get the old lady. She stormed into her son's study, swore at him, grabbed the bleeding boy and took him into her own chambers. She refused to see her son for days. He was shamed and humiliated before the whole household.

Granny Liu lacked the Lady Dowager's authority. She made no pretence to be anything but a simple old woman. She had no position, no money. She was teased, even mocked, by the superior young people who lived in the Daguanyuan.

劉姥姥進大觀園

Liu Laolao jin Daguanyuan

Granny Liu visits the Daguanyuan

The expression is still used to show up people who are deceived by first impressions. But she was the person who got things done, who sorted out awkward situation without seeking money or gratitude. She was discreet and unpretentious. She was the fixer for the Jia family. She sorted out the problems that the family elders could not deal with themselves, given the restrictions of their position. She saved a young granddaughter of the house, Jia Qiaojie 賈巧姐, from being sold as a concubine to a prince from the frontiers (read Bluebeard or Dracula) by her unscrupulous uncles. Granny Liu dressed the girl up as her own granddaughter and smuggled her out to her village, where the girl married and settled down happily.[3] This was a classic example of the superiority of common sense over weeping and wailing, all that the young ladies of the house had been capable of.

However great their difference in social standing, the two old women were proof of the traditional assumption that women's experience of life produced shrewdness mixed with kindness, firmness mitigated by love. These qualities were needed to care for a family. The Lady Dowager's dominance is obvious, Granny Liu's less so, but equally real. Both were matriarchs.

Matriarchs

Box 2.1 Matriarch/matron

The word 'matriarch' belongs to another era, in China and in the West, when women of the elite dominated and controlled large households, filled with family members and a legion of servants. Queen Victoria was one, so was her contemporary the Empress Dowager. Queen Elizabeth is not. Despite her God-given status, her huge household and wealth, her descendants are not under her thumb. Some of the activities of her unruly sons and grandsons have caused her great grief.

There was once a lesser matriarch, the matron, a sensible, competent woman who managed her domestic world. That word lost its domestic meaning as it came to be used for women who managed institutions such as hospitals or schools. The adjective 'matronly' continues to refer to women in an unflattering way: middle-aged, stout, staid, boring.

There were real matriarchs as well as fictional ones in traditional society, great numbers of them. The embedded custom that created them was the mother–son bond; the matriarchs' position depended less on their husbands than on their sons. If they were widowed, their dominance in the household actually increased; a son was more likely to be obedient than a husband. In Europe and North America widows fared less well, from top to bottom of society. In an aristocratic household a widow was put out of the mansion, dispatched to the much smaller dower house. Her daughter-in-law became the chatelaine of the mansion, the title, the possessions and the great household. At the bottom of the social scale widowhood might mean an alms house or the poor house. There was no legal obligation on their children to care for them. Chinese matriarchs, on the other hand, kept control of their households as long as they lived. By custom and by law sons were under obligation to respect their mother as head of the household. Her sons were expected to show her love and open affection.

The devotion of sons to their mothers grew as the mother got older. There is a genre of biography written by sons about their mother; the title starts with the phrase 我的母亲 *wode muqin* ('my mother'). They ascribe their achievements – and the men who write them are successful – to the love and guidance of their mothers. Their mothers were loving and gentle, strict but patient, devoted to their son. The devotion was reciprocated; a son would always love his mother, even a bad one.

狗不嫌家貧 兒不嫌母丑

Gou buxian jiapin, er buxian muchou

A dog does not abandon a family because it is poor,
a son does not abandon his mother because she is ugly

The devotion of mothers to sons was potent. This is the perceptive sociologist Delia Davin:[4]

A mother's affection for her son might be the strongest emotion of her life. Her marriage was unlikely to be an important emotional outlet and she compensated for this in her devotion to her children and above all to her sons who were her insurance for old age and who brought her an improvement in her status in her married home.

The love was reciprocated, in the lasting devotion of the son. The contrast to Freudian anxieties over a too-intense relationship between a domineering mother and her sons is enormous. What Freud saw as pernicious, Chinese sons celebrated, without ever imagining the connotations that Freud put on excessive love between mothers and sons.

The position of the matriarch/grandmother had nothing to do with feminism. It was matriarchy within patriarchy, a system that kept *young* women subservient to older women, and older women dominant in the family. The anthropologist Margery Wolf saw this in Taiwan in the 1950s. Elderly men withdrew; their wives were at the heart of their families. Until they were 'completely senile or physically handicapped' they did all kinds of 'minor but time-consuming' tasks, nursing sick children, getting babies to sleep, sewing and knitting.[5] They were household managers. They assigned the tasks within the household, made the arrangements for the celebration of festivals and birthdays, supervised store rooms and planned supplies for the family. They abhorred waste; they made sure that all cooked food was eaten, and that anything that might be reused was stored away; no piece of string or rubber band was ever thrown away.

Some matriarchs lived long enough to dominate households of five generations, fulfilling the super-ideal of 'five generations under one roof' (五世同堂 *wushi tongtang*). Zeng Jifen, the daughter of Zeng Guofan, achieved it. She had thirteen children. When she died at the age of ninety her descendants (some no longer alive) numbered 123: children, grandchildren, great-grandchildren and great-great-grandchildren.[6] Queen Victoria, the 'Grandmother of Europe', had nine children, forty-two grandchildren and eighty-seven great grandchildren, for a total of 138. I have come across a six-generation family. Zhu Zhengshi celebrated her 119th birthday in August 2019, in Chengdu (Sichuan). Five generations of her descendants were at her birthday, sharing a lavish two-tier birthday cake.[7]

The matriarch was in charge of a host of women: umarried daughters, daughters-in-law, granddaughters, and, in rich families, concubines, servants and slave girls. Everything within the walls of the family compound was under her control; she reigned supreme. Zeng Jifen's widowed sister-in-law, Guo Yan, presided with love and strictness over her huge family, children, grandchildren, nieces, nephews, all living in Prosperity Hall (*Fuyu tang* 富裕堂), the Zeng mansion in Xiangxiang 湘鄉 (Hunan).[8]

Although she didn't get about much she knew everything great and small that went on in her home and served as the arbiter of right and wrong. She was very reasonable in administering discipline and instruction, never reprimanding a wrongdoer in front of others. Instead she would call whoever was at fault into her room and quietly explain what they had done wrong, comparing it to incidents in the past. Her aim was to show them the error of their ways, to urge them to repent and to change their ways.

The rich matriarch controlled her husband's concubines and the concubine's children. Wang Lanfeng, matriarch of the Lee family in Hong Kong, took the first son of her husband's first concubine into her own quarters in the huge Lee family home in Happy Valley. All the children, including those born to concubines, called her 'mother', and were beholden to her. Senator Vivienne Poy 利德蕙 is the daughter of that son.

She lived until 1956, a widow for much of the time; her position was never imperiled, by war, Japanese occupation or revolution.[9] She dominated her family through love and through constant, meticulous attention.

The ideal type of matriarch must be counterposed against the tyrant matriarch. The archetype of the tyrant matriarch was the Empress Dowager Cixi 慈禧太后, the terrifying dominatrice of the late Qing Dynasty. She presided over palaces and government, but not over direct descendants; her only child, the Tongzhi Emperor 同治皇帝, died young, without issue. Cixi made up for his loss by dominating her nephew, the hapless Guangxu Emperor 光绪皇帝, and all other males, Manchu and Chinese, in the Qing administration. Cixi has been the butt of unending, vicious, misogynist criticism, but she did save the faltering Qing Dynasty from an earlier demise than its actual end in 1911.

China was/is a patriarchal society. In the leadership of government and society men dominated. In families, this was less so; as age came on men tended to decline, dying earlier than women. Women moved into dominance within their families. So long as multi-generational households were the norm the dominance was guaranteed. Martin Yang's description of his village in Shandong in the early Republic describes the process of an older woman achieving power within her family, as her husband retired from fieldwork and sank into lethargy:[10]

When a couple reaches the age of fifty or sixty the wife generally becomes the dominant person in the household. She is now the mother-in-law of one, two or even four daughters-in-law. She is the grandmother of a long line of children and also the overseer of a large household. The middle-aged sons have almost invariably developed strong attachment to their mother but not to their father.

Grandmothers were expected to go on caring for their grandchildren and great-grandchildren for as long as they were still able to drag their old bones about. That has not changed. This is the anthropologist Ellen Judd writing in the 1990s:[11]

Women in China very often continue to perform child care and domestic labour as long as they are able to do so, which may extend into their eighties. There is much less evidence of older people in the countryside 'retiring' from work than the culture's explicit value of age would seem to indicate.

The figure of the matriarch came under threat from the early Republic on. The withering of the large multi-generational family, migration, urbanisation, the gradual rise in the age of marriage for women and the disruptions of war and revolution all worked against the status of the traditional matriarch, as did the growing desire of young people for love, to choose their own life's partner, and to build their own households.

There were efforts to create modern versions of the large household that allowed a little more autonomy to the young. Some families were rich enough to maintain establishments that accommodated the young while continuing to live in large families. The Zhu family of Shanghai built, in the 1920s, a huge compound, a mansion for the parents and smaller houses for each of their many sons. The matriarch was in constant touch with her daughters-in-law and her grandchildren, and kept a close eye on them. The plan was not without its shortcomings. It took little account of the wishes of the young people. In 1924, the marriage of Zhao Chengjun and Zhu Jisheng (Ignace) was arranged by their parents. Chengjun was an accomplished girl; she spoke French and English, and had a strong sense of herself. The wedding was in church; both families were Roman Catholic. Before the altar, when the priest asked her if she would take Jisheng to be her wedded husband, she said firmly, 'No'. Chaos ensued. The priest, the French consul and her father all tried to get her to change her mind. She was firm. She fled to a Catholic convent, where she spent the rest of her life. The jilted fiancé went to bed. The wedding breakfast was ready and, as many of the guests arrived not knowing that the marriage had not taken place, the banquet was served. The lurid Shanghai press had a field day with the scandal.[12] One of the Zhu sons was as recalcitrant as his brother's fiancée. He became a priest, and never married. In the Resistance War (1937–1945) the family scattered, never to be reunited. The carefully conceived plan was negated in less than two decades.

The figure of the matriarch seems now to belong to another age. There are no large families any more; three-generation households are still common, ones of four or more generations rare. There are no matriarchs at the top of Chinese society. The two most important women in modern history, Song Qingling 宋慶齡, the wife of Sun Yat-sen 孫中山, and her sister Song Meiling 宋美齡, the wife of Chiang Kai-shek 蔣介石 (Jiang Jieshi), were neither mothers nor grandmothers. Jiang Qing 江青, the last wife of Mao Zedong 毛澤東, was a tyrant, not a matriarch. Anson Chan 陳方安生, the former chief secretary of Hong Kong, has the characteristics of a matriarch, kindness and authority, but she has lived a modern, middle-class life with her husband and two children. Tsai Ing-wen 蔡英文, the president of the Republic of China (Taiwan), is not married. If the matriarch is gone for good, the ideal of wise, caring old women is still very much around.

Physical Images

The faces of traditional grandmothers, photographed from the late Qing on, had authority and patience written on them, along with wrinkles, the sign of long life, as the face of a Shandong peasant woman in Image 2.1 shows.

ILLUSTRATION 2.1 The beauty of old age

The images of the Communist Era poster art were Soviet-influenced; dimpled, smiling creatures. One of the most popular was the grandmother in *Pulling up the Giant Turnip*, a Russian folk tale repurposed with Chinese characteristics (Image 2.2).

Old women's faces were unadorned. The old-woman role in opera, the 老旦 *laodan*, is played with almost no make-up, in an art form where other characters are heavily made up. They dressed in sombre colours, dark blue, grey or black. Their grey or white hair was pulled back in a decorous bun, and covered with a black velvet cap. Some decoration was permissible, in the form of embroidery on jackets and shoes.

The colour palette is close to that worn by older Western women, though the constraints are different. In China dark colours are signs of propriety; white is the colour of mourning. In the West black was the colour of full mourning, grey, lilac or mauve the colours of half mourning. It was almost impossible for a Western woman to live to old age without being in permanent or partial mourning, for

ILLUSTRATION 2.2 Giant turnip

a dead husband, child or close relative. Western mourning jewellery was made of black jet; lockets or rings had the hair of the dear departed plaited into them. Elderly Chinese women wore vivid green jade pins or rings, the gifts of their devoted sons on their decade birthdays. The quality and colour of the jade was crucial. I once spent an afternoon in the deserted antique shop at Tanzhesi 谭柘寺 outside Beijing, helping my dear friend Hai Chi-yuet find the perfect stone for her mother's sixtieth birthday. In those days, just before the revival of Confucianism (the mid-1980s), the antique seller was so impressed with her filial devotion that, declaring that he did not have a fine enough piece in stock, he sought out an exquisite piece and brought it to her in the city.

The grandmothers of the present may look back with some envy on their predecessors, who (as paternal grandmothers) might have large numbers of devoted descendants. Present and future Chinese grandmothers will have far fewer, and they will never be matriarchs; the traditional multi-generational family is moribund.

3   Baby Seekers/Baby Lovers

In traditional China all women married. Not all men did; the combination of higher rates of survival of infant boys, polygamy amongst wealthy men and sheer poverty meant that up to 20 per cent of men never married. They were 'bare sticks' (光棍 *guanggun*) (see Chapter 10).[1] Marriage was early, usually under twenty. Early marriage led to compressed generations. The Lady Dowager remarked that over the fifty-four years that she had been in the Jia family, there had been seven generations: 'I came to this house as the bride of a great-grandson, and now I have great grand-daughters-in law myself.'[2] Compressed generations made a major contribution to population growth, which was offset by a short life expectancy; few people lived beyond four decades. Even so, China's population more than doubled during the Qing Dynasty.

Mothers-in-Law

Grandmothers-to-be were mothers-in-law first. The Chinese mother-in-law is one of the most reviled figures in fiction and in fact. Her relationship with her daughter-in-law was the ultimate bad relationship. This is Fei Xiaotong: 'It comes to be taken more or less for granted that the mother-in-law is a potential enemy of the daughter-in-law. Friction between them is taken as usual and harmony as worth special praise.'[3] Chinese mothers-in-law appear in a much harsher light than the figures of fun they are in the West. The inner history of the bad relationship between mother-in-law and daughter-in-law in China was that the mother-in-law had once been a defenceless daughter-in-law herself: 'the daughter-in-law of many years becomes a mother-in-law'.

多年的媳婦熬成婆

duoniande xifu ao cheng po

A mother-in-law took out years of built-up resentment on her daughters-in-law. This was her revenge for what she had suffered as a daughter-in-law. The teenage bride had to make a double adjustment: marriage, to a stranger; servant to her mother-in-law. Daughters-in-laws were required to produce grandchildren for their husbands' mothers and to cater to the old women's daily needs. The women who would be loving grandmothers could be tyrants to the grandchildren's mothers.

The writer Lu Xun 鲁迅 tried to be understanding of older women:[4]

A bad memory is an advantage to its owner but injurious to his descendents. The ability to forget the past enables people to free themselves gradually from the pain they once suffered; but it also often makes them repeat the mistakes of their predecessors. When a cruelly treated daughter-in-law becomes a mother-in-law, she may still treat her daughter-in-law cruelly.

An unhappy daughter-in-law was quite without help. She could only hope that her husband would come to love her and take her part over his mother's. The developing love between a couple married as strangers is the subject of Pearl Buck's first novel, *East Wind West Wind*. A traditional girl is married by her parents to a foreign-educated young man who at first despises her. She changes to meet his sulky demands – and to both their surprise, they fall in love.[5]

A mother-in-law had the backing of tradition. The emphasis on the male line, on the devotion of sons to their parents, was founded on the concept of filial piety. Chinese lore is full of stories of exceptional devotion and sacrifice of sons to their parents.

A mother-in-law was responsible for implementing the tradition. She could act as she liked, citing the interests of the family and traditional values, interpreted with a great deal of leeway. Sheng Cheng was born in Yichang 宜昌 (Hubei) in the late Qing, into a declining scholarly family. His grandfather

---

Box 3.1 Filial piety

This is one of the fundamental tenets of Confucianism. The ancient *Classic of Filial Piety* (孝經 *Xiaojing*) demanded that junior generations care for older living generations, and provide the necessities of life, respect and comfort. The ancestors were to be given regular respect through care of their graves – and through achieving success in life. Filial piety was instilled by social custom and by the state. The *Twenty-Four Filial [Behaviours]* (二十四孝 *ershisi xiao*), a Yuan Dynasty compilation, presented examples of extreme devotion of sons to parents. Dong Yong 董永 sold himself into slavery in order to pay for his father's funeral (賣身葬父 *maishen cangfu*). Wu Meng 吳猛 kept mosquitoes from biting his parents by stripping naked and sleeping close to them (恣蚊飽血 *cewen baoxue*). These acts were rewarded, by official or divine intervention. Dong Yong got his freedom back when the daughter of the Emperor of Heaven intervened. The filial exemplars had a permanent place in popular culture; generation after generation of sons were reminded how they should care for their elders.

and uncle were opium smokers. His grandmother held the family together with an iron will. He recorded his own mother's view of his grandmother's interpretation of 'tradition', when the boy chafed against the old lady's rule: 'Your grandmother is like the Empress Dowager. She enforces the laws for others but never for herself or her flesh and blood. She herself never obeys tradition.'[6] The tyrant grandmother made the life of her gentle daughter-in-law hell and sent her to an early grave. She turned her grandson into a revolutionary.

There were good mothers-in-law as well as bad. The mother of Qi Baishi 齊白石, the great painter, was welcomed by her mother in law into a poor peasant family in Hunan:[7]

She married my father when she was seventeen. On her wedding day my grandmother, as was the custom, looked over her dowry box. My mother was a little embarrassed because, being poor, there was very little of value in her box. My grandmother said, being herself from a poor family, 'A good girl does not depend on her dowry: a family gets prosperous on its own strength.'

The grandmother of the writer Ye Zhongyin 葉仲寅, from a rich family in Hebei, was kind to her daughter-in-aw. Immediately after the wedding the young husband went off to Japan to study. The young wife was left alone in a strange family:[8]

Seeing that Mother had to live apart from Father so soon after their wedding, Grandmother then gave Mother extra attention and love. Instead of burdening her with household chores Grandmother just let her stay in her own room doing embroidery and needlework while Grandmother herself did all the housework.

The relationship between mother-in-law and daughter-in-law had periodic ups as well as the many downs. The period before the first grandchild was born was a good time. At a frightening time, approaching her first confinement, the young woman could expect support: she was carrying the older woman's hope.

Waiting for the Baby

The purpose of marriage was procreation. A couple's first baby was expected to arrive within a year of marriage. There was one exception: a child should be born in a 'good year', in the context of the twelve zodiac signs of the Chinese calendar. Conception could be calculated to avoid a baby being born in a bad year. Inducement could speed up the birth of a baby so that it arrived in a good year. No one was more interested in the arrival of a baby than grandmothers-to-be. They watched their daughters-in-law like hawks for signs of pregnancy. They prayed intently that they would conceive. They took them to pray at shrines of goddesses who were believed to send sons (送子 *songzi*); the most potent female deity was Guanyin 觀音, 'Guanyin Who Sends Sons' (送子觀音 *Songzi Guanyin*).

Box 3.2 Good years and bad years

Prospective parents hope that their child will be born in a good year of the Chinese zodiac. The year of birth may determine the child's chances in later life, especially in finding a good husband or wife. Each of the twelve zodiac years is assigned its own characteristics, which become part of traditional calculations of 'love compatibility'. The years 2007 and 2019 were both Pig Years; 2007 was particularly special because it was a Golden Pig, the twelve-year cycle combined with the five elements of gold, water, wood, earth and fire (金水木土火 *jin shui mu tu huo*). A Golden Pig is an ultra-desirable match.

There are problem years; a girl born in a Dragon or Tiger Year may have difficulty in the marriage market, because she may be too assertive. There are no really bad years. I have what sounds like the misfortune to be a Snake, but Snakes have many good characteristics. To assuage feelings of inadequacy amongst Snake people, it is sometimes called the Little Dragon Year. Rats (2020) are clever, hard-working and careful with money (stingy). Some people call it the Mouse Year in English, less cringe making than rat; there is no distinction in Chinese between the two.

The grandmother of Yu Chun-fang, the leading scholar of Guanyin, was a devout follower. She knew the sorrow of not having a son – and the joy of having a grandson:[9]

Married on the eve of the Boxer Rebellion (1900) when she was barely eighteen to a widower more than twice her age, she assumed the duties of the matriarch of a large and complex joint family, bore two daughters and then became a widow at the age of thirty.

Deprived of her inheritance by the sons of the first wife, she lamented her bitter fate for failing to bear a son. Marriage could not have been a pleasant experience for her. My grandmother's prayer to Kuan-yin [Guanyin] for a male heir was eventually answered when my mother gave birth to my younger brother, on whom my grandmother doted.

If there were no sign of pregnancy the older woman would want to go to a major site with her wretched daughter-in-law. The pinnacle pilgrimage site to Guanyin is the island of Putuo visited by many awkward mother-in-law and daughter-in-law couples. The search for Guanyin's help has increased in the Reform Era, with the One Child per Family policy. The avant-garde novelist Zhou Weihui 周卫慧 set her novel *Marrying Buddha* on the island. The heroine, Coco, goes to Putuoshan to pray for a child; she has turned twenty-nine, and realises she is getting old to have a baby. The novel, like her earlier novel *Shanghai Baby*, combines social criticism with erotic awakening.[10]

If prayer failed to produce a pregnancy, then a baby would be adopted – within the family. Childless couples would be 'given' one. Yang Buwei 楊步衛, born in

ILLUSTRATION 3.1 Guanyin

1889, was assigned by her grandmother even before her birth to her childless uncle and aunt. Yang's birth mother had already had eight children (five of whom died in infancy). The matriarch decided that the ninth should go to the childless couple. 'My parents were to be my uncle and aunt and my uncle and aunt were to be my parents.' Her birth mother was heartbroken, but had no thought of opposing her mother-in-law's decision. To make the forced adoption even more painful, she had to nurse the baby. As the child grew up, she knew that her 'mother' was her aunt; she saw her 'aunt' every day, in the family compound.[11] Several years later the process happened again: her 'mother' was given a 'son', born to another of her sisters-in-law.

Box 3.3 Orphans

In traditional China children whose parents were dead would be cared for by their wider family, taken in by grandparents or uncles. There was no equivalent of the infant abandoned or adopted anonymously at birth. French missionaries in Tianjin were convinced that many newborn girls were victims of infanticide. They set out to save 'abandoned' baby girls by setting up an orphanage and offering finder's fees to people who brought babies in. Many of the babies brought to them had actually been kidnapped. The furious local reaction led to the Tianjin massacre (1870).

Family adoption broke down in the Resistance War. There were vast numbers of lost children, either separated from their parents or actually orphaned. The Nationalist government set up orphanages, often visited by Song Meiling, the wife of Chiang Kai-shek, and her sisters Song Ailing 宋爱龄 and Song Qingling. The Communists used orphan boys as messengers. The 'little devils' were used as propaganda for the Party's care for the vulnerable. In the 1980s the One Child per Family policy stimulated the growth of orphanages. Girls were left there so that a family could try for a son in the next pregnancy.

There was no equivalent in China to the Western practices of anonymous adoption, where a baby is placed with a family without being told of its origin, and birth mothers do not know what has become of their babies. Orphans scarcely existed.

Once a pregnancy was established, the control of the mother-in-law over her daughter-in-law had no bounds. The expectant mother had to avoid anything that might upset the foetus – spicy foods, bad language, evil spirits. She was banned from doing anything sad; she was not allowed to go to a funeral. She was subject to the many rules of 'gestatory education'. Many of these rules have remained in currency into the modern age:[12]

> She should separate herself from her husband until after the birth.
> While sleeping she should lie on her back.
> She should not laugh loudly.
> Her eyes should not see bad colours.
> She should not look at obscene pictures.
> She should not gossip or listen to improper conversation.
> She should read good poetry and tell good stories.

When I was pregnant with my second child in 1973, my teacher, Professor D.C. Lau, sent me the galleys of his translation of Confucius' *Analects*, so that my son would learn from Confucius in the womb. My daughter Anna has been immune to Confucius.

There was a complete confidence that the grandmothers-to-be knew how to handle pregnancy and confinement. They saw themselves as repositories of wisdom in these matters; their family members, including the mothers-to-be, accepted this conviction. I have come across no references to a young woman's lack of trust in her mother-in-law's supervision of her pregnancy.

The grandmother-to-be tried to predict the gender of the baby. She would seek the advice of fortune tellers, pray again to Guanyin. The frequency of prayer peaked as the birth drew near. The grandmother of the Chang family went into a routine of intensive prayer each time (seventeen in all) her daughter-in-law was in labour:[13]

Every time Lu Ying was in labour she would also be busy at work, paying obeisance, praying to the four directions on her prayer mat until the baby was born. This was an act of empathy, and also the only way she knew how to beseech the Buddha and all the benevolent spirits to grant the mother and her child a safe passage. A bad leg made the efforts strenuous, so by the time the baby was born the grandmother was usually exhausted.

The grandmother-to-be chose a midwife, after discussions with her friends as to which local midwife would be best. The grandmother was not actually in the room while the young wife was labouring, but was hovering close by. The moment the baby was born the exact time of birth was noted. The Eight Characters (八字 bazi) were recorded, two characters each for the year, the month, the day and the hour. They were essential for determining the child's future life, whom it should marry.

The Newborn

The period after birth was very dangerous. Many infants died after birth. Gao Shengtan, the father of the AIDS campaigner Gao Yaojie 高耀潔, was born in 1894, and married at fourteen. His first two wives died in childbirth, one when he was seventeen, the second when he was nineteen. His third wife produced a son and two daughters, then died in childbirth with her fourth child. His fourth wife, Gao Yaojie's mother, had nine children. Her father's wives went through fifteen pregnancies; three died in childbirth. Eleven children survived their births. This terrible toll influenced Gao's decision to be a gynaecologist.[14]

After the baby was born the grandmother and the midwife took control of the infant, following carefully prescribed rituals for the washing and wrapping of the child. The mother's role was to rest and to provide copious breast milk. She had to eat rich porridge, fish soup and hard-boiled eggs, a dozen or so a day. Milk-stimulating foods, galactogogues, exist in every society. My grandmother stayed in bed for three months after my father was born, drinking several pints

ILLUSTRATION 3.2 Gao Yaojie

of Guinness a day, prescribed by her father, an Edinburgh-trained doctor (gold-standard in the late nineteenth century).

The mother and infant were kept apart from the rest of the household. The mother was not allowed to bathe, to wash her hair, to weep – anything that could affect her milk. This regime lasted for a full month, a practice known as 坐月子 *zuoyuezi* ('sitting the month').[15] It has survived today, especially in Hong Kong and Taiwan, where mother and baby spend the month in special clinics. At the end of the month, when the 'month is fulfilled' (满月 *manyue*), she receives friends and relatives, who bring special foods, notably red eggs. The idea is catching on in North America. Heng Ou's 2016 book *The First Forty Days*, a manual on post-partum care, is based on Hong Kong practices.[16]

The grandmother was front and centre in the special events held to mark the birth. She presided over the *manyue* celebrations, much bigger for a boy than for a girl. The scale of the celebrations differed according to the wealth of a family, but the central role of the paternal grandmother did not. She received even more congratulations than the new mother.

The joy in the newborn's arrival brought concern for the child's survival. The grandmother was the repository of a repertoire of measures that could be taken to protect an infant, especially a son. He wore a richly embroidered cap, with auspicious characters, long life and riches (長命富貴 *changming fugui*) and images of the Eight Immortals and other deities. This cap would be the work of the grandmother. The boy might be given a girl's name, or be called 'little nun' (小尼姑 *xiao nigu*), to mislead the evil spirits (鬼 *gui*) that abounded in the Chinese world. The grandmother was locked in battle with them. A detailed list of what she had to do was compiled by Père Henri Doré, a French Jesuit who worked for many years in China.[17] With an unconscious irony he referred to the practices as 'superstitions', ignoring the metaphysical elements of his own faith – virgin birth, transubstantiation, resurrection.

A key intervention was prayer, especially at temples or shrines associated with children and women. Amulets offered protection; various items might be suspended over the infant's cradle or hung round his neck. Burning an old shoe near where the baby slept would produce fumes that would chase away evil spirits. These customs varied from region to region of China; Doré has almost sixty close-packed pages of particular regional customs and deities. What was common was the intensity of efforts to protect a fragile child.

In the Christian tradition baptism was the principal way to protect an infant, a ceremony usually performed within three months of the birth. Protection from God was assured; the baby was signed with the cross in holy water, and given godparents, to ensure that if anything went wrong with the parents the child would have someone to care for it. Formal baptism has declined, but not the role of godparent. I am the secular godmother of three much-loved girls, Jade, Serene and Casey.

If all interventions failed and the baby died, there came a tragic ceremony, 'Calling the Spirit' (叫魂 *jiaohun*). The parents took one of the infant's outfits, and went round their neighbourhood calling on the child's spirit to come home.

Every dead baby did live on, in the family. It was given a number at birth, how the child was known within the family. The number survived. If the first boy, 老大 Laoda (Old Big), died, the second would still be 老二 Laoer (Old Two). Jerome Ch'en 陳志讓 was 老五 Laowu; he had two living older brothers, and two who had died as infants. The writer Pai Hsien-yung 白先勇 (Bai Xianyong) is also 老五, the fifth son in a family of ten children; all survived.

In the Mao Era the dominant position of older women in the management of childbirth was questioned. Midwives were seen as dirty and unscientific, their care of women in labour primitive and shot through with superstitions. The Party criticised midwives and urged pregnant women to go to a modern, trained midwife or to hospital for a doctor-supervised birth. The problem, particularly in the rural areas, was that there were few hospitals. In 1959 over 750,000 midwives were 'retrained' ones, i.e. old-style midwives with some upgrading;

only 5,300 were fully trained 'modern' midwives. Childbirth was still terrifying.[18]

A system of 'barefoot doctors' (赤脚医生 *chijiao yisheng*), young men and women with a smidgin of medical training, was introduced in rural China. The theory had merit – using local people to care for their own communities – but the conviction that childbirth was a female matter did not shift, and most of the perinatal practitioners continued to be older women. This seemed to work; the population boomed in the 1950s and 1960s, much of the growth to do with a decline in infant mortality.

Baby Care

The confidence that older women showed in their ability to manage pregnancy, childbirth and early infancy continued in the care of babies.

Healthy babies, plump and pink-cheeked, were/are the rewards for grandmothers' efforts and proof of their skills. Grandmothers were/are baby worshippers, a universal form of adoration particular to older women.

Chinese grandmothers showed unrestrained joy in cuddling babies, soothing them, hugging them. The happy infant was their greatest treasure, an indispensable part of their life. Here is Pearl Buck's description of Ling Sao,

ILLUSTRATION 3.3 Fat baby

a forty-year-old grandmother and one of the key figures in the novel *Dragon Seed*, set during the Japanese invasion of China in 1937: 'she shouted for the youngest child to be brought to her, for Ling Sao was a woman who never felt herself whole unless she had a child on her knees or across her hip'.[19]

Ling Sao, a tough, uneducated farm wife, adored her grandchildren; they were what kept her going through the agonies of the Japanese occupation. She cuddled the infants; soothed them; fed them food she had chewed herself; gave them endless, patient attention.

The most adorable babies were bouncing boys, especially ones who seemed to have 'tiger heads and tiger brains', a promise of success in later life.

虎頭虎腦

hutou hunao

tiger head, tiger brain

These little treasures were dressed in tiger caps and tiger shoes, sewn by their grandmothers, another tradition that continues.

It is difficult for a young person to understand the worship of babies. What they see as squalling, smelly bundles, likely to be sick on the unlucky person holding them, older women see as beautiful creatures to be petted, kissed, dandled. The German novelist Erich Maria Remarque, writing in the desperate world of Germany after the First World War, saw the adoration of neighbourhood women for a new baby. They gushed and cooed over the infant; the young narrator was left cold:[20]

It was a perfectly normal child but the ladies were bending over it with expressions of ridiculous enchantment, as if it were the first baby the world had produced. They uttered clucking noises, clipped their fingers before the eyes of the little creature and pursed their lips.

This behaviour is true in almost any culture. Older women make great efforts and spend oceans of time to get the baby to smile, and the person on whom the baby first smiles is blessed. Babies are jiggled up and down, soothed, patted on the back. They are held constantly. (One of the most joyous days of my life was in 2004, holding the sleeping infant Mabel, while watching Roger Federer win Wimbledon.) A baby is passed around from one admirer to another, kissed again and again, tickled, chucked under the chin, even pinched. He/she is compared favourably to other babies, his/her beauty exclaimed over. A lot of time is spent working out which parent or grandparent the baby looks like. The baby is scarcely allowed to cry. They are talked to in baby language. In Chinese the word 'treasure' recurs again and again in talking to the baby: 寶寶 *baobao*; 寶貝 *baobei*; 小寶 *xiaobao*. The organisation that sets out to find kidnapped babies (usually boys) is called Treasure Come Home (Baobei huijia 宝贝回家).

Every language has a range of words for talking to babies, usually uttered in cooing, lilting tones.

Chinese grandmothers believed in breastfeeding and continued to do so when formula was introduced. They are right. While Chinese and foreign companies competed to satisfy a new market for formula, tragedy struck. In 2008 China was horrified to discover that some of the local product was contaminated, with melamine. This caused acute kidney problems. Some 45,000 babies had to be hospitalised; six died. The authorities cracked down hard on the manufacturers; two people were executed. The punishments did not reassure consumers. The scandal created a lively trade in milk powder from Hong Kong to China. Foreign producers dominate the internal market, a rare phenomenon in the Chinese marketplace. The trade continues. In 2021 the People's Republic of China (PRC) customs authorities busted a crime syndicate smuggling New Zealand milk powder into China, in couriered packages.

The baby worshippers' fingers were always busy, making tiny clothes and shoes, knitting jumpers and blankets. The work started before the baby was born; the first reaction to news of a pregnancy was to start sewing or knitting. The most beautiful item in a Chinese baby's layette was a long hooded carrying cloak, often made of silk, the hood trimmed with fur. This lavish creation required hours of dedicated work. Another lovely piece was an embroidered apron, covering only the child's middle. Now grandmothers can order baby clothes online, even designer labels (Dior, Chanel), but they continue to knit and embroider.

In the past, summer clothing for infants was casual: as little as possible, in the heat just an embroidered apron. And all year round the infant wore split pants. The reason was simple: convenience. Diapers/nappies have been essential for the Western infant for a long time. Cloth ones were a nightmare. They had to be boiled after each use. They had to be strapped onto a wriggling baby and held in place with huge safety pins. Over them went plastic pants, which tended to leak. A baby's bottom would often get chafed – diaper/nappy rash was sure proof of an inadequate mother. With disposables a baby can go for hours without being changed. They are highly polluting but it is rare to come across a Western mother who does not use them, however eco-conscious they are in other ways. In China there were no diapers. Pieces of cloth were used to catch what a small baby produced. This is Pearl Buck:[21]

for the greater convenience of both child and parents little children went naked in summer and in winter had their trousers bisected, so that when nature compelled all a tiny creature needed to do was to squat.

As for the babies they were simply held outside the door at regular intervals and encourage by a soft musical whistling to their duty.

Split pants (開襠褲 *kaidangku*) were still the norm when I first lived in China (1964–5).

ILLUSTRATION 3.4 Split pants

Split pants were not sewn at the crotch. When necessary the baby was held out with legs apart. An adult had to be on hand at all times, and a lot of the adult's time was taken up with watching for signs of a coming movement. There are questions about hygiene, but the convenience is undeniable.

A baby would never be alone. It would sleep either with its mother or with its grandmother. Many of the appurtenances of Western babyhood – cribs, cradles, perambulators, strollers, play pens – were unnecessary if the baby, asleep or awake, was never alone. The baby would be held constantly, by mother, grandmother, aunt, older sibling. It did not need its own bed or its own means of transport.

Sleeping with infants has been regarded in the West as almost a criminal act. From birth on infants slept alone, in cradles or cribs. Sleeping with an infant was tantamount to infanticide. Isabella Beeton inveighed in purple prose against sleeping with an infant: 'The mother, frequently, on awakening, discovers the baby's face closely impacted between her bosom and her arm, and its body rigid and lifeless.'[22]

The terror of rolling onto the baby and crushing it, or smothering it by cutting off its airways, was instilled so deep that when the trend for co-sleeping arrived I, like many Western grandmothers, was appalled. But I did hold my tongue and luckily the fashion was short-lived.

Decline of the Mother-in-Law

The decline in the power of the mother-in-law has been under way for a long time. Into the early Republic the traditional structure of the family remained intact. Paternal grandmothers still dominated multi-generational families. The wives of the sons were still bullied by their mothers-in-law. Girls were still sent into arranged marriages, in their mid- to late teens. The trend against arranged marriage was painfully slow to mature. Most parents remained opposed. They had arranged the marriage when the child was young; they were under social and financial obligations. Mothers feared, quite justifiably, that if their son married for love, he would put his wife first, his parents second. He would insist that his wife be treated well, and thus deprive his mother of much of her power as a mother-in-law. She would not get the revenge for her own maltreatment by her husband's mother.

As ideas of marriage changed, the mother-in-law's situation was threatened. She could no longer take things for granted. Her son, his wife and his children might not live with her. Or her son might leave home; she would have only daughters-in-law and grandchildren with her. The growing critiques of the miserable lot of young women fostered subversive resistance in 'modern daughters-in-law'. This was a bitter blow for old women who had been bullied by their mothers-in-law, and were denied revenge.[23]

The fate of these old women with modern daughters-in-law is tragic indeed – poor victims of the transitional period. They suffered under their own mothers-in-law and now, when the time has come for them to take revenge and enjoy what they have long desired, the times cheat them of their rights.

The 'modern daughter-in-law' was at first an urban phenomenon, but in the 1930s she started to appear in rural areas. The sociologist Martin Yang described the beginnings of change in his home in Taitou, a village in eastern Shandong:[24]

People of the younger generation have no sentiment for the orthodox family teachings, and do not look with favour on five generations living together, with the hall and chambers full of children and grandchildren. A frequent complaint from younger daughters-in-law is that they would prefer a poor and independent household of their own to a rich and troublesome household. Quarreling about dividing a family is almost

---

Box 3.4 *Fenjia*

The family, and with it land, housing, livestock and movable possessions, could stay united after the senior male died or at his retirement – or it could be divided. Each son was entitled to an equal share, with shares set aside to support the elders (養老地 *yanglaodi* – literally 'land to nurture the old'), to pay for their funerals and to provide a dowry for any unmarried daughters.[1] It was a complex process; distant relatives or local leaders had to be brought in to assess the value of the property and to adjudicate the division. There were laws on inheritance, which changed over time, but in practice division was less a legal process than one of local custom. *Fenjia* could also occur when family members fell out with each other. Then it became a traumatic process, painful, often acrimonious and seldom settled rapidly.

[1] David Wakefield, *Fenjia: Household Division and Inheritance in Qing and Republican China* (Honolulu: University of Hawaii Press, 1998) is full of fascinating details on individual cases.

---

everyday news in the family. Old people have their hearts broken, but young people think it is a matter of course.

This was a huge threat, 'dividing the family' (分家 *fenjia*), the division of assets between the sons and the creation of separate small households, each son with his wife and children. Income earned by each son remained his, and did not go into the family pot. With division went the hope for the ideal 'four generations under one roof'.

Sons who left home to study or work slipped beyond the direct control of their parents. There was no law against bigamy. Sons who were already married might marry again, for love, without reference to the family at home. Departing sons who were not married might forget about the girl to whom their parents had already engaged them. The fate of the abandoned 'village wife' or fiancée was tragic. The man's parents kept her, if she was married, or compensated her family if she was not. This was what happened in Taitou:[25]

Divorces in farm families have been reported in increasing numbers. Most of these recent divorces are the result of discrepancy in education. Many young sons and young daughters of well-to-do families now go to the new schools. After graduation they find jobs in the cities and do not return to farm villages. Away from home modern boys meet modern girls. They fall in love and want to marry, even though many of them have wives in their farm homes.

Abandoned wives had to stay with their parents-in-law, and care for them as they grew older. They were the victims of the evolution of marriage from a relationship dictated by the family to one based on love. This is Mao Xiaodong's family in the late 1930s, from a rural family in Henan:[26]

Both my father and his two brothers had arranged marriages before they joined the revolution. Later they all remarried. In the case of my father his first wife died before he met my mother. But my two uncles' wives were alive when their husbands left them to marry female comrades. The women and their children simply continued to live in the old family home.

The old ways were put under great stress by the Japanese invasion (1937). It brought mass separation of young people from the old, as the young fled to the unoccupied areas or into the armies. The old ways were perilous to those of the young who still put the old first. The smash hit of postwar movies *The Spring River Flows East* (一江春水向東流 *Yijiang chunshui xiangdongliu*) was a tragic cautionary tale against putting family before self.

The war allowed many young women to escape the dominance of their families. Work opportunities in the factories that started to spring up in the cities and towns of the unoccupied areas changed the lives of young women. Interviews in a factory in Kunming in 1940 with over 400 young women concluded that work had liberated them from their families:[27]

In practically every one of the investigator's conversations with the workers one or another such circumstances as the following is mentioned: those who have lost both parents are commonly despised by other near relatives; those whose mothers have died cannot bear the maltreatment by step-mothers; those who live with brothers and

---

Box 3.5 *The Spring River Flows East* 一江春水向東流

The 1947 film is often called China's *Gone with the Wind*. It tells the story of a young couple separated in 1937 by the Japanese invasion. The wife stays with their son and her mother-in-law in Shanghai. Her husband flees to Chongqing, where he lives a dissolute life; his love for his wife is forgotten. At the end of the war in 1945 he returns to Shanghai, but not to her; he has a new wife and a mistress. When the first wife, now a maid, serves him at a reception, he does not recognise her. She realises that she has been abandoned by the husband who once loved her, and throws herself into the Huangpu river.

The story must have been replicated many times in real life. The title could refer to refugees returning to the eastern cities in 1945, 'flowing east'. It has another doom-laden meaning – 'flowing east' is the equivalent of the English 'going west'.

sisters-in-law feel miserable because of the antagonistic attitude of the other women; those who have been betrothed are not satisfied with their engagement; those who have been married have had continuous quarrels with parents-in-law, with sisters-in-law, with husbands or been deserted.

This catalogue of woes meant that working in a factory, with long hours and poor conditions, living in dormitories, was preferable to life at home. These women enjoyed working in the factory, and they enjoyed *not* being part of a family or the family economy. They spent the money they earned on themselves, on snacks, trinkets and movie tickets.

Other women found work in wartime outside the home, in government offices and schools. The taste of freedom from domestic tyranny, the control of the mother-in-law, spread. The tyranny could not be reasserted after the war; the need for women to work outside the home to help their families was powerful. These breakdowns in the traditional order were a precursor to Communists' programmes of social change after 1949.

After 1949 the protective shield provided to older women by traditional practices disappeared. They lost the automatic position of dominance in their families. Multi-generation families were still the norm, but within them the power of the mother-in-law was waning. Young women were encouraged by the new Marriage Law (1950) to marry by their own choice, not through arrangement. They could leave marriages in which they were unhappy. Daughters-in-law could challenge their mothers-in-law, with the Communist Party on their side. The All China Women's Federation (全国妇女联合会 *quanguo funü lianhehui*), which came into being as the new regime took control, campaigned to get young women to break with the past. Most mothers-in-law had no choice but to accept. They could not afford to be labelled 'reactionaries', or to be insulted by their daughters-in-law in the myriad of meetings that accompanied the introduction of the Marriage Law. Their sons were unlikely to openly put their mothers ahead of their wives.

Despite pressure to abandon the past, some continued to bully and even harm their daughters-in-law. A lurid tale from the early 1950s was an example of 'learning from negative example' to enforce the new law.[28]

In Cangshan 沧山 (Shandong) a young peasant woman was tortured to death by her mother-in-law and the mother-in-law's second husband, a local Communist leader. The murderers were arrested, and forced to confess to their crimes. With a confession in hand officials called a mass meeting of several hundred people. The couple were forced to retell the details of their crime. Then a series of speakers talked about how their own attitudes to daughters-in-law had changed, thanks to the Marriage Law. An even larger mass meeting followed, attended by 10,000 people. 'Mass emotion swelled to a high tide, there was a deafening roar in unison for drastic punishment for the brutal murderers.' They were shot on the spot.

The old habits of deference to a mother-in-law did not disappear at once. Xia Dehong, a committed young Communist who married for love, without reference to his or her parents, still 'knelt and kowtowed three times' before her mother-in-law the first time they met in 1950, to the delight of the old woman, who had expected disrespect from a radical 'new' woman. But the young couple did not move into the family home, nor did the old lady live with them. The person who did, and who cared for their five children, was the young woman's mother.[29]

This was a major innovation. The young mothers whose children grand-mothers cared for could be their daughters-in-law – or their daughters. Half of all grandmothers, the maternal ones, previously virtually excluded from the lives of their daughters' children, now achieved equality with paternal grand-mothers. The *laolao* was as much a grandmother as the *nainai*. The need for child care was so great that they were pressed into service. The *nainai* was no longer the only grandmother.

A moving portrayal of the key role of a maternal grandmother came in the 1993 film *The Blue Kite* (蓝风筝 *Lan fengzheng*).[30] The four Chen sisters and brothers lived in a working-class neighbourhood in Beijing. The old life in a *hutong*, a warm, noisy, neighbourly world, was eroded in the 1950s and 1960s by political turbulence. All four of the siblings got into trouble. The older brother lost his eyesight; his girlfriend was sent to reform through labour for refusing the advances of Party leaders. The older daughter, a political activist, did well in the service of the Party but was 'struggled' in the Cultural Revolution. The younger brother was sent to the countryside for life. The younger sister's first husband was labelled a 'rightist' in the late 1950s and sent to the Great North Waste 北大荒, where he died. Her second husband also died. Her third was a senior Party person, whose own downfall brought her down too. Through all these tragedies the old woman, known only as Ma or Laolao, was the still centre of the family, old-fashioned and uninterested in politics. She took every tribulation in her stride, caring for her grandson, worrying about her children, endlessly cooking family meals. Without her the family would have been driven apart; there would have been no refuge for the brothers and sisters as they went through their individual disasters. The experience of the Chen family was not a rare one, but one known to countless families, where the old, less affected by political campaigns than the young, provided comfort and constancy for their children and grandchildren.

The new roles of the *laolao* allowed the emergence of a special relationship, between an adult daughter and her mother, often a loving one. Chen Huiyin, a peasant woman from Jiangsu, was devoted to her mother, who lived with her family.

Her mother's death came at an awful time, when her husband and her father were in political trouble, early in the Cultural Revolution. The extremism of the

---

Box 3.6 Chen Huiyin's story

When her mother died suddenly in late 1968, her daughter was devastated:

Darkness fell over me and I could not imagine how I would live my life without Mother. Mother had been taking care of everything at home. I did not even know where rice was stored. I was able to earn work points to cover family expenses only because Mother took care of the children. At the time my youngest, Shebao, was only seven years old and needed my mother's care. When I was not feeling well, menstruating, pregnant or nursing, Mother would take care of me. She would cook something, sometimes just a bowl of sugar water, and ask one of my children to take it into the fields for me. I worked hard outside but when I returned home I could relax in a loving atmosphere.

I lived my thirty-seven years of life with my mother. We never quarreled, not even once. She only complained about my willfulness, but she did it in a loving way, I was not only practically dependent on Mother, because she looked after the house for me, but I was emotionally dependent on Mother too. I confided everything to Mother. Mother was my strength. Without concrete words Mother cheered me on.

---

period prevented her from giving her mother a proper funeral; the family could not even burn incense for her (see Chapter 12).[31]

Maternal grandmothers' involvement with their grandchildren accentuates the trusting relationship between mother and daughter, in a three-generation triad. Child care by maternal grandmothers has risen from about one in ten families to one in three or more. Paternal grandmothers are no longer in sole charge; either they are cut out or they opt out. Praise for maternal grandmothers is common:[32]

妈妈生 外婆养 奶奶来观赏

Mama sheng waipo yang nainai lai guanshang

Mummy gives birth, her mother raises the child, his mother comes to visit

Sarcastic phrases show some *nainais* as almost feckless, feeling entitled to enjoy their old age without the burden of child care:

奶奶去跳舞 姥姥当保姆

Nainai qu tiaowu, Laolao dang baomu

Nainai has gone out dancing, Laolao is baby-sitting

Beyond the reach of the Communist Party, the old order survived much longer after 1949. In the hardscrabble world of Hong Kong the family economy was the base on which prosperity was gradually created. All members of families worked; the senior generation that counted was the parents of the husband, not of the wife. The sociologist Janet Salaff described the difference in the lives of two grandmothers living in the Lau family in Shamshuipo:[33]

It is customary for Chinese mothers to be supported in their old age by their mature sons. It was natural, therefore, that Paternal Grandmother was given a room in the newly-weds' flat and took charge of shopping, cooking and the household finances. Since there were no sons in Hong Kong who could care for Maternal Grandmother, she was also taken under the family roof.

Maternal Grandmother worked as an unskilled labourer in a blue jeans factory. She pushed a trolley laden with stitched goods from the machinists' area to the pressers and then transported pressed garments on the same bulky conveyance to the packing area. She had to toil at unskilled and very low-paying factory employment in order to pay her own way in the home because of her tenuous household status. She also performed all of the menial tasks in the Lau household.

This maternal grandmother was essentially a servant in the household. She had no status at all. Her daughter accepted this, just as much as did her son-in-law.

The situation of mothers-in-law did not last in Hong Kong, as families became more prosperous, and employed helpers from the Philippines. And on the Mainland in the Reform Era, young women are less and less willing to live in the same household as their parents-in-law, or to share a stove. This is the story of Mingzhu and Baijian, in rural Shandong:[34]

In 2000 Mingzhu and Baijian had been married for less than a year. To welcome her into the family, Baijian's parents had added a new room to their house, for the couple. This did not satisfy her. She had no separate kitchen of her own, and the quite significant income of her entrepreneurial husband was shared by the whole family, including his unmarried brothers. Mingzhu quarreled ceaselessly with her mother-in-law, whose sights were now set on finding brides for the younger brothers, to increase the size of the household even further. The older woman was no match for her daughter-in-law. One day she decamped to her parents' house, causing a major scandal in the village. Her husband wanted her back, and went often to see her. She – and her parents – were firm. Unless the young couple were allowed to live separately, she would not return. After two months, and with a baby on the way, the mother-in-law caved in. Although the couple continued to live in the same compound as his parents, they now had their own kitchen and control of the husband's income. The older women in the village sympathised with the mother-in-law, but there was a lot of discreet admiration for Mingzhu, so much so that her new household was known as Mingzhujia.

There was no going back, as legions of mothers-in-law have found. The peasant women whom Gail Hershatter interviewed made the same plaintive comments as those recorded by Martin Yang in the 1930s three generations earlier 'Having taken dutiful care of their husband's parents they now find themselves as they age abandoned by their own grown and married children.'[35] Their children had left the villages, had gone off to work elsewhere, and were no longer 'dutiful'. Or perhaps the complaints were universal and timeless, expressions of the fraught relationship between mothers-in-law and daughters-in-law.

4   Child Care

心肝寶貝

xin'gan baobei

Grandchildren are 'heart's and liver's treasures' to their grandparents. (The two organs are the sites of the emotions.) This is just as well, because the expectations placed on Chinese grandparents in child care are huge. As Michael Meyer, one of the most perceptive observers of contemporary China, noted, they are expected to take on any role that is asked of them: 'In a Chinese family, grandparents are more than an accoutrement to be visited and nodded over on major holidays.'[1] Above all, they are child-carers.

Child care has expanded over time from care for infants and small children, living in the same household, to sole care for grandchildren for long periods – weeks, months or even years. Lengthy separation of babies and small children from their parents has become a standard part of childhood (see Chapters 9 and 10). The grandmothers of these children are the carers. These are roles played by grandmothers in many societies: if there was/is paid work available for parents they take it and leave their children with a grandmother. Millions of Filipinas work abroad, the mothers amongst them caring for other people's children, while their own children are in the care of fathers and grandparents. The wealthy in the West relied on nannies to care for their children, on the assumption that a nanny did a better job than a mother could. This is the ineffably snobbish Nancy Mitford:[2]

I have seen too many children brought up without nannies to think this at all desirable. In Oxford the wives of progressive dons did it often as a matter of principle; they would gradually become morons themselves, while the children looked like slum children and behaved like barbarians.

For most families, grandparents were/are the ones who helped with the children. There are plenty of them. In the USA (2014) one in five of the population was a grandparent; in Canada (2015) the proportion was closer to one in four. Many are involved in child care. In the UK the 'grandparents' army' plays a huge role in child care. China has a massive 'army'.

Box 4.1 Baby talk

Grandmothers talk to their treasures in baby talk. Baby talk is simple, delivered in sing-song tones, often without much meaning: 'Who's a pretty girl?' 'Who's a good boy?' Baby talk seems to match babies' own babbling. The experts have taken against baby talk. I have annoyed my own daughters by talking in this way to my treasures. The advice today is to replace baby talk with a new form of language, Parentese. This involves an adult speaking to a child slowly and clearly, never verging into baby talk. This seems to me a new version of how my father talked to non-English speakers. He believed that if he spoke in English slowly and clearly, he would be understood. To the fury of his daughters, who spoke between them French, Spanish, German and Chinese, his method often worked, notably on his one visit to China.

In China, grandmothers' care for infants and small children was gentle, permissive. There was little in the way of schedule. Children ate the same food, mashed up or masticated by an adult if necessary; special foods for children were unknown. Little ones were fed constantly; snacks (candy, sugar cane, peanuts) were popped into open mouths between meals. Small children slept when and where they fell asleep, often in the arms of their grannies. They were held almost all the time; the aim was to keep the child happy and quiet. Grandmothers talked to them constantly.

They told them stories (see Chapter 8). They taught them rhymes and riddles. Here is a Beijing one:

馬四眼而
開茶馆而
一個茶壺
兩個碗而

Ma siyan er
Kai chaguan er
Yige chahu
Liangge waner

Four eyes [i.e. wore glasses] Ma
Ran a teahouse
One teapot
Two tea bowls

They taught them tongue-twisters (繞口令 *raokouling*), plays on words based on the tonal nature of Chinese. This is an example, in which the sound *ma* appears in different tones:

媽媽騎馬
馬慢
媽媽罵馬

Mama qi ma
Ma man
Mama ma ma

Mummy is riding a horse
The horse is slow
Mummy curses the horse

They sang them folk songs. They gave them simple, durable toys, often made of wood or clay. They were designed to keep children quiet, not to stimulate their brains.

Grandmothers trained children in the day-to-day rules of life – how to treat elders with respect, how to use chopsticks, how to say thank you. They instilled social etiquette by constant repetition of gentle commands. I hear my own voice repeating over and over again what my grandmothers said to me: 'What do we say?' – i.e. 'please' or 'thank you'.

Grandmothers were gentle with little ones; they did not discipline them. Very few subscribed to the view that children should be beaten to develop their talents.

不打不成才

Bu da bu chengcai

This is almost word for word 'spare the rod and spoil the child'. It was for parents, not grandparents. Grandmothers did not beat; in fact they could protect a child against the rages of their sons. The Lady Dowager's fury at the beating of Baoyu is the most famous example, but not an isolated one. The writer Ye Zhongyin remembered her grandmother protecting her against the violent rages of her father:[3]

Mother was never brave enough to criticize what he did or said. [Once] having heard Father's uproar Grandmother hurried over and cried 'You're upsetting the child. Why are you so nasty to such a young girl?' She took me away in her arms.

The girl escaped to her grandmother every time her father started to beat her, and became, in his eyes, 'spoilt'.

Love and Affection

Given the Confucian demands on parents to be strict with their children, grandparents could be the loving figures in a household. The writer Xie Bingying 謝冰瑩, born in Hunan in 1906, was the child of a tough mother and an often absent father, both strict disciplinarians. The child turned to her grandmother for comfort every time her mother beat her. The mother's ferocity helped to turn her daughter into a rebel, one of China's first woman soldiers.[4]

ITINERANT TOYMAN.

ILLUSTRATION 4.1 Toys

The common and expected relationship between grandparents and their grandchildren was/is one of mutual love and affection. This was not equally shared. Favouritism was accepted. A woman who had many grandchildren focussed on her favourites, usually grandsons. Grandson-preference was shared by both paternal and maternal grandmothers. The economist Chen Hansheng 陳翰笙, born in 1897, remembered that one of the happiest days of the year was going to see his maternal grandmother, on the first day of the New Year. The old lady lived in a mansion in Wuxi 無錫 (Jiangsu). She received all her descendants, including a crowd of grandchildren. Each child bowed low to the matriarch and was handed a red envelope (see Chapter 5). In the boys' envelope was a shining silver dollar, in the girls' fifty copper cents.[5]

The bond of love between grandmothers and grandchildren stretched from top to bottom of Chinese society. The last emperor of the Qing Dynasty, Puyi 溥儀, had a doting grandmother. She was a tragic woman. Her first child, a daughter, died young, and her third and fourth children, both boys, were ordered adopted out by the terrifying Cixi, the Empress Dowager. The son of her remaining child, Prince Chun, was especially precious to her:[6]

I had been brought up from my earliest days by my grandmother, and she doted on me. According to my nurse, she used to get up once or twice every night to come over and look at me; she did not even put shoes on for fear that the noise of their wooden soles would disturb me. Having reared me for more than two years, she fainted at the news that Tzu-hsi [Cixi] was taking me in to the palace. For the rest of her life she was very liable to fits of insanity.

The emotional bond was as strong lower down the social scale. Martin Yang described the relationships between young and old in Taitou, in the late 1920s:[7]

The relationship between grandparents and grandchildren is a loving one, expressed with a tenderness similar to that between a mother and her child. The happiness of having a grandchild is the goal of all middle-aged parents, and the greatest pleasure of an old man or woman is to hold a grandchild in his arms.

Affection came not only from actual grandmothers, but also from older women who had lost their own children. There was an assumption that all women should have a grandchild, adopted (informally) from within the family. Chang Ch'ung-ho (Zhang Chonghe), daughter of a rich Hefei (Anhui) family, was transferred to a great aunt who had lost her daughter and granddaughter. Ch'ung-ho's mother had given birth to a boy who had died (her fourteenth birth) and was depressed, unable to care for the girl. The child lived a charmed life, in a rich and beautiful house, with a devout old lady who gave her undivided attention. She did not rejoin her birth family until her mid-teens, after the old woman had died.[8]

Gao Yaojie was indulged by an old lady who was not her grandmother. She lived with her elder uncle's wife (大伯母 dabomu) whose own children had all died. By age her aunt could have been her grandmother because she was already forty. She treated the girl with tenderness and love (嬌聲觀養 jiaosheng guanyang). Anything the little girl wanted was done for her. The

adoptive mother had no name – she was just Madam Xu 徐氏; she left the
future AIDS doctor an indelible memory of love and warmth.[9]

The pattern of grandmother love was the same in emigrant communities.
Jade Snow Wong's father owned an overall factory in San Francisco's
Chinatown. Her home was inside the factory. Life was tough and serious.
The parents were very strict, and beat their many children as they felt necessary.
There was little affection from them to the children:[10]

> The one older person who seemed most understanding of a little girl's failure to do the
> proper thing was Mother's mother. Grandmother was little and stooped and always wore
> a loose black Chinese coat and trousers. Her hair was fastened in to a knot at the back of
> her neck by a gold brooch set with pretty jade stones. Sometimes she tucked a narcissus
> or a tuber-rose blossom in to the edges of the knot. If Grandmother happened to be
> visiting when Mother spanked Jade Snow she would always snatch the child away and
> scold Mother instead. To Jade Snow it was remarkable that she should have such power,
> especially since Grandmother was frail while Mother was strong.

Jade's grandmother was the one who talked to her about China, who made
her understand that although she lived in a foreign country, she was still in
a Chinese world.

Activist Communist parents in the 1950s were immersed in political work;
grandmothers provided love and care. Zhang Rong's parents were senior Party
officials in Sichuan, so devoted to their work that they had little time for their
five children. Child care devolved to their maternal grandmother, Yang Yufang,
at first with the help of a maid, later without. Yang provided all the love that the
children received. When the parents were caught up in a political movement,
she was the sole carer for the children for months on end. When she was away
for a while, she returned to find that the children had been sent to nurseries. She
was horrified and set about bringing them home one by one. She accused their
parents of being 'heartless', not knowing that her daughter was in detention,
suspected of 'Rightist tendencies'. The Zhang children loved and respected
their grandmother. She was fierce in protecting them, particularly her favourite,
Xiaohei. The boy sometimes enraged his father, who would beat him. The
father got tongue-lashings from his mother-in-law.[11]

Jian Ping had a happy childhood, in the government compound in Baicheng
白城, a remote railway junction in Jilin. Her parents were filled with zeal for
socialist construction, and scarcely saw their children. The child was with her
nainai all day long, in a warm and loving world, from which her parents and
their harshness were remote:[12]

> Nainai was my constant companion and accomplice. She wanted all her grandchildren to
> be happy, and she allowed us to run free.
> As a child I was always afraid of Mother. She had high expectations of us and was
> always very strict. But Nainai set no rules and passed no judgements.

Box 4.2 Liu Simu 刘思慕

Liu Simu is the star of the Marvel movie *Shang-Chi*. He is one of the new 'Asian' film actors, along with the actors from *Crazy Rich Asians*, who are establishing an Asian presence in the film industry. Liu's best-known role to date is as a young Korean Canadian, in the sitcom *Kim's Convenience*. He was born in Harbin, and raised by his grandparents when his parents went abroad to study. When his father arrived to pick up the five year-old in 1995, he was a complete stranger, as was his mother. In Canada his strict parents kept his nose to the grindstone. He got into the University of Toronto Schools, the most prestigious school in the city. The warmth and undemanding love of his grandmother in China was replaced by high demands and constant criticism. 'It felt like they regarded me as a defective product.' He longed for the love and warmth his grandmother had given him. He became an accountant, but within six months he was sacked for non-attendance. He took up acting, a decision that led to a two-and-a-half-year breach with his parents. He told students at his old school in 2018, 'You've got to do it your own way. Don't be afraid to follow your passion.' The family is now reunited, and the son is earning enough to allow his mother to retire early. Liu is a role model for young Chinese Canadians, for his 'decency, earnestness and charming self-depreciation'. He is a hero to all grandmothers.[1]

[1] *Root*, Spring 2019, p. 23; *Globe and Mail*, 26 July 2019.

   Thirty or forty years later, work and migration rather than political zeal have led to grandmothers caring for grandchildren while their parents are away. Liu Simu 刘思慕, the actor named one of Canada's most beautiful people in 2018, was left behind in Harbin, shortly after his birth in 1989; his parents moved to Canada to study. He was brought up by his 'gentle and patient' grandparents. The person who means the most to him, 'always and forever', is his grandmother, who loved him and cared for him from his birth on.[13]

   A particular pleasure for grandmothers was caring for grandchildren's hair, a delicate and time-consuming process. Little girls had elaborate patterns of bunches and braids, often tied with coloured threads and ribbons. In the late Qing boys' hair had to be combed and braided so that it would grow into a pigtail (queue), required of all Han males to show their subjugation to the Manchu Qing Dynasty. This is Tan Shihua:[14]

My hair was shaved above my forehead but it was long behind my ears. She [my grandmother] braided my hair on each side of my head. The length of these braids was a great satisfaction to both of us. When I grow up the long braid of a man will hang down my back. My grandmother took good care of my hair, washing it with hot water every third day.

ILLUSTRATION 4.2 Liu Simu

The male coiffure died with the Qing Dynasty. After the 1911 Revolution, queues were cut off, a sign that China was no longer subjected to the alien Qing. Boys' hair now grew freely and often wildly, but girls kept braids for decades more. Even in the Mao Era, when pretty clothes were taboo, girls still had elaborate braids, twisted with ribbons and coloured plastics. Their grand-mothers, the hairdressers, gave them a tiny sense of adornment.

For all their kindness to their grandchildren, grandmothers were major figures in the cruel process of binding the feet of their granddaughters.

Foot Binding

The historian of foot binding Dorothy Ko explains the significance of the procedure:[15]

The daughter's foot binding took place in the depths of the women's quarters, under the direction of her mother, sometimes assisted by grandmothers and aunts; no men were

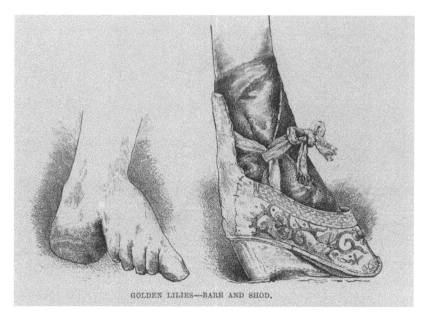

GOLDEN LILIES—BARE AND SHOD.

ILLUSTRATION 4.3 A bound foot

privy to the ceremonial process. It was a solemn occasion, marking the girl's coming of age, the first step of her decade-long grooming to become a bride.

Bound feet were the ultimate symbol of female submission. The practice that young girls in rich or less affluent families who wanted to arrange good marriages for their daughters (hypergamy or marrying up) should have their growing feet contorted by tight binding now seems an extreme form of child abuse. The practice may have had economic causes as well: it kept girls at home to work in handcraft production, as Melissa Brown and her colleagues show in a meticulous study.[16]

In the early Republic the practice came under attack from modern-minded people; girls in the coastal cities were unlikely to have their feet bound. In the interior and in rural areas the practice declined, but when I first lived in Beijing in 1964–1965, I often saw elderly women with tiny feet hobbling along; shoes for bound feet were sold in shoe shops. Their feet must have been bound in the 1920s or 1930s.

Grandmothers shared the belief that with big feet their granddaughters would not find a good match. There was a horrible conflict between love for a child and inflicting pain on her, knowing that the process would end with the child crippled. Gao Yaojie was not spared the pain and misery of foot binding. When she was four the process started; she was in agony for months, and screamed almost constantly. Soon she could not walk at all. Then came an unforeseen interruption: she was one of the few beneficiaries of the Japanese invasion in 1937. The foot-binding process stopped when the family fled westwards ahead of the Japanese armies. Damage had already been done to her feet. Gao has suffered throughout her life from pain in her feet; they never grew beyond a size two.[17]

Evolution of Grandmother Care

In traditional China child care for infants and small children by paternal grandmothers was taken for granted. Then it began to expand, as society and the economy changed. Factory employment boomed in the coastal cities in the late Qing and early Republic. In the cotton mills, one of the major industries, women made up 70 to 80 per cent of the workforce. They lived in dormitories; hours of work were long, weekends unknown. Factory girls often married later than other girls. This was a matter of parental calculation. Unmarried daughters gave their wages to their parents; married ones gave their wages to their parents-in-law. This was the thinking of the mother of an eighteen-year-old girl about her daughter's marriage: 'Oh wait for another two years. Nowadays girls marry later than before. Some families will give their daughters away early but most do not. Since they can earn money we don't want them to get married very soon.'[18]

Once a woman was married it was inevitable that she would become pregnant. The mothers returned to work as soon as the baby was weaned; the woman's mother-in-law, the grandmother, took over the child care. The sadness of women separated from their children was usually ignored, though the compassionate sociologist Chen Da 陳達 recognised the pain:[19]

Who does not hope that they and their children can live together but since caring for children brings so many difficulties, some people say that workers had better not have children, since they will not be able to educate them.

Young men who left home to study, in China or abroad, were already married and fathers by the time they entered university. They left their wives and children with their parents for years or forever. The politically progressive amongst them regarded their families as backward and conservative, but this did not prevent them from leaving their children to be raised in the traditional society they despised. Being 'single' gave them the freedom to pursue their own careers – and to meet a modern woman with whom they could fall in love. The left-behind wife and her children were kept secret from the 'modern' family. Friends of mine born in China but raised in North America only discovered in adulthood that they had half-siblings in their father's home village. The half-siblings knew only too well that they had a father abroad, and suffered greatly for it.

During the Anti-Japanese War many young people fled from the parts of China under Japanese occupation, leaving the old people behind. Grandmothers were sorely missed by the parents of the children born away from home. This is a sad young mother in Chongqing. She and her husband, an 'ideal modern couple', married for love. When their baby was born, there was no grandmother to care for the child; the mother had to care for the infant herself, what would now be called 'the mummy trap':[20]

Because of the problem of finding a reasonable solution to the problem of bringing up their children, thousands and tens of thousands of capable, educated women have lost the opportunity of having a job. From the perspective of the individual or of society, this unquestionably is lamentable.

After more than ten years in school, once a woman gets married, because of the problem of bringing up her children, she has no opportunity to devote herself to society and benefit others.

In the Communist-held areas in the north-west and Shandong the Party expected mothers to put their commitment to the revolution above care for their babies. In the communities of young people cut off from their families there were no grandmothers around. The children were either put in crèches (保育院 *baoyuyuan*) or boarded out with local families. The number of children in crèches was small. A 1949 report showed that in one large base area only 1,700 infants had spent time in its crèche between 1938 and 1948. This low figure implies that most infants were *not* in the crèche.[21] Many children were placed with peasant women; others were sent to their parents' family. Xi Jinping's two half-sisters and one half-brother from their father's first marriage lived with their grandparents in Shaanxi.

After 1949 the human losses of twelve years of war fuelled the conviction at the top of the Communist Party that China had to produce more people, to replace those who had died and to create the workforce that would build socialism. Young women's prime work was 'reproductive labour', producing babies.[22] Proposals for population limitation from the demographer Ma Yinchu 馬寅初 were savagely criticised; he was disgraced. During the Mao Era the population of China almost doubled, from about 550,000,000 to about a billion. Some of this growth can be put down to reduced mortality, but much had to do with the high birth rate. The baby boom of the Mao Era led to the overpopulation against which Beijing has waged war with the One Child per Family policy.

After 1949, in whatever part of China older women lived, whatever class they belonged to, their prime role was to be carers for their grandchildren, to make it possible for young women to work. The stigma against 'respectable' young women being out of the house had gone. In the liberation of young

---

Box 4.3 Bicycles

For four decades from 1949 on China was the kingdom of bicycles. Cars were unknown, except those carrying officials. Buses were creaking and crowded. Most people rode bicycles, one brand only, the Flying Pigeon 飞鸽 Feige, an exact copy of a Raleigh. It was a sturdy boneshaker, without gears, always black. Rush hour in Chinese cities was a tidal wave of bicycles, ridden at sober speeds. In 1986 my daughter Tanya got a speeding ticket on Changanjie in Beijing, riding a ten-speed; the policeman who clocked her at twenty-five kilometres per hour was impressed. In rural China the Pigeon was a passenger and a transport vehicle for livestock and vegetables. Bicycle maintenance was a huge industry, as were bicycle parks. The Pigeon has disappeared; private bikes are streamlined numbers, and ubiquitous bike-share programmes use more utilitarian models.

---

women, grandmothers filled the yawning gaps in child care, and took on even greater responsibility than before.

The addition of *laolaos* to the army of grandmothers must have been welcome for many mothers, who would rather consign their children to their own mother than to their mothers-in-law. It was 'a weakening of patrilineality', the decline in the absolute authority of the paternal line, a fundamental change in the structure of society.[23] In rural areas, where girls still married out of their villages, a new technology made it possible for maternal grandmothers to care for grandchildren – the bicycle. This vehicle could be used to ferry children from their home village to their *laolao*'s village, most likely not on a daily basis but a weekly or monthly one. In my childhood our mother pedalled her daughters round town on an adult tricycle, Vicky in the basket at the front, Polly and me clinging on at the back.

Grandmother care was not the form of child care promoted by the state. The official socialist vision was that small children would spend their lives in crèches, nurseries and kindergartens. In political posters, happy, healthy children, their pink-cheeked faces wreathed in smiles, were shown living without parents or grandparents. The policy worked for a small minority of children, in new factories and in the upper echelons of the Party. Those at the very top of the Communist Party put their children into the 'Revolutionary Cradle' (革命摇篮 *Geming yaolan*), near the Beijing homes of the Party leaders in Zhongnanhai 中南海. Xi Jinping's mother, Qi Xin 齐心, left her four children for extended periods while she studied at the Marxism–Leninism Institute and then worked at the Party School. She stayed at home only until a baby was weaned; after that she came home at most once a week. Their father, Xi Zhongxun 习仲勋, had little time for the children. They were weekly boarders in the Revolutionary

Cradle with other 'red' children. Bo Xilai 薄熙来, the now disgraced and imprisoned rival to Xi, was there.

Nursery spaces were reserved for children with good, red backgrounds. Children with indifferent class backgrounds, or, even worse, with black backgrounds were excluded. They were in the care of their grandparents. The role of grandmothers was omitted from official policies, though they provided most of the child care for urban working mothers:[24]

Many, perhaps even most, working mothers relied on the help of a relative. Though this might be a sister, sister-in-law or cousin, it was most likely to be a mother or mother-in-law who shared the home of the working couple. Ageing parents might even be brought in from the countryside to join the household after the birth of a child.

In rural areas it was taken for granted that paternal grandmothers would care for infants and small children. In villages in Shaanxi in the 1950s the authorities thought of providing child care only to parents without one: 'Not every household had a mother-in-law available to watch the children.'[25] The meaning was clear: a *nainai* had to care for her grandchildren.

To enable grandmothers to be child-carers, the age of retirement for urban women was set at fifty – an age by which many women would be grandmothers. No thought was given to rural women; they did not retire but added child care to their work. As the age of marriage was gradually raised, eventually settling at twenty-five for women, twenty-eight for men, the age at which women became grandmothers rose, with fifty still a likely age for grandmotherhood.

The care for grandchildren came with an unstated reciprocity: the younger generation would care for the older one later on. The firestorm of change in the early 1950s seems to have produced a complete 'turning over' of society, the elimination of the old elite and of large families. But the three-generation family survived, and provided the necessities of life that might someday be provided in a socialist utopia, but had not been in the 1950s. The family was the pension, health insurance and unemployment insurance of its members.

The elderly destitute, without families, were caught. They could no longer get help from temples or the old community charitable organisations – victims of the campaigns against feudalism and superstition. The state was aware that social services might have to be provided for the destitute. In 1956 the Five Guarantees were announced; they promised food, clothing, housing, medical care and burial (五保: 吃穿住医葬 *wubao: chi chuan zhu yi zang*). A pamphlet published in 1960 showed happy elderly people living in a 'home of respect for the aged' (敬老院 *jinglaoyuan*). 'People who are too old to work and have no families can spend the rest of their lives in these homes in happiness.'[26] These homes were thin on the ground, and a last resort. In the early 1980s I visited a home for retired railway workers in Liaoning, with a group of Ontario teachers. One teacher asked the old men how often they saw their children.

The question was translated but there was no answer. She pursued the question. I kicked her under the table; she gave me a black look. I explained in Chinese that the Canadian friend did not understand that these men might not have children. That was the case; they had either been too poor to marry or their children had died.

Besides child care, older peasant women took over more household tasks. As young women went to work outside the home, there was a role reversal. Grandmothers now did many of the menial tasks – fetching water, washing, cooking – once done by their daughters-in-law. The reversal of roles was tough. The older women were part of an 'unlucky generation of middle-aged women'; they lost status as matriarchs, and had to work much harder than before.[27] The household load increased as rural China rocketed through radical changes in the 1950s – land reform, to co-operatives to collectives to communes. Grandmothers took on more and more of the domestic load to allow daughters-in-law to work and get work points, the source of family income.[28]

The point system was shot through with discrimination. Young women were assigned to light work that brought fewer work points than men got. Pregnancy and infant nursing cut into the hours they could work and contribute to the family income. The head of a co-operative in Jianshi 建始 (Hubei) scolded his wife for not working enough hours, for 'living on [by] the exploitation of men'.[29]

The demands on grandmothers as caregivers intensified even further during the Great Leap Forward (1958 on). Peasants spent long hours in the fields, in the vain hope of dramatically increasing agricultural output. A policy of abolishing household tasks was instituted, at the most extreme stage of the commune system. This was the theory:[30]

In the days when each family did its own cooking women were tied to a multitude of trivialities around the kitchen stove or the grind-stone, fussing about the oil, salt and firewood and spending most of the time doing heavy household chores. With the setting up of the community dining rooms in the communes, people can get plenty of tasty, nourishing food, either to eat in the dining room or to carry back home.

This was cloud cuckoo land. People felt entitled to eat as much as they could. Ultra-socialism taught 'to each according to his needs', or in a Chinese version, 'eat in the big household' (吃大户 chidahu), i.e. at a bountiful buffet, more than you need. I understand well. As children our greatest treat was an all-you-can-eat at a Lyons Corner House. My favourite delicacy was a baked bean tartlet; too many carried the danger of being sick in the car on the way home. In China the outcome was tragic. The policy was one of the key factors that precipitated the Great Famine in the early 1960s, in which at least 30 million people died. In one commune in Dongtai 东台 (Jiangsu), not a very poor county, 15 per cent of the population died between 1959 and 1961.[31] Though the famine was

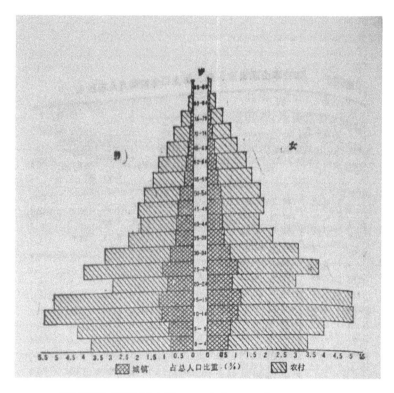

ILLUSTRATION 4.4 The population pagoda

exacerbated by bad weather, its root cause was political extremism. For that reason it is known as Mao's Famine.[32] The high death rate of the elderly is reflected in statistics from the 1982 census for Shandong. Only 7 per cent of the peasant population was over sixty.

Those over eighty (in their early sixties during the famine) made up only half of 1 percent.[33] The expression *chidahu* lingers on, to mean spongers, looking for something for nothing.

Urban grandmothers became yet more important in the chaotic Cultural Revolution (1966–1976). They were the protectors of the grandchildren as the parents were caught up in radical politics, forced to leave home for the countryside or into reform through labour (劳改 *laogai*) (see Chapter 9). The departures were often sudden, without any idea of when they might return. As the schools closed, children were at home all the time. Grandmothers might find themselves in charge of a whole brood of children. One woman, wife of a professor at Peking University, found herself sole carer for a host of young grandchildren, the children of her own six children, all of whom had been sent to cadre school (五七干校 *wuqi ganxiao*).

The Reform Era has changed much in Chinese society, but not the assumption that young mothers will work. The concept of maternity leave has arrived, and was extended in 2012 from ninety weeks to ninety-eight weeks, but it is only available in a limited number of jobs. A great deal of the care of infants passes to the grandmothers within a few months after the birth.

The custom of grandmother care has been cited as a way in which Chinese culture is superior to the West. Chinese grandparents look after small children, allowing parents to focus on their careers, while in the West working parents, without 'available' grandmothers, are obsessed with finding good child care. The unselfishness of Chinese grandparents, who do not expect a carefree retirement, is contrasted to the self-indulgence of Western grannies. This is not a Chinese but a wistful American view, in an article by Kelly Yang that comes perilously close to portraying American grandmothers as hedonistic and self-indulgent:[34]

many young couples [in China] take it for granted that their elderly parents will look after their children when they work. And most grandparents assume their duty, which means they bear a heavy responsibility and have to devote huge amounts of their time and energy to child care.

The burden of work involved depends on the grandmother's age. Grandmothers in their early fifties, with only one grandchild, will be fine, but ones fifteen or twenty years older will be running out of steam. As the age of marriage has risen in modern China, so too has the age at which grandchildren appear. The age escalation of grandmothers happened in my family. Our mother was forty-seven when her first grandchild was born. My sister Polly was in her late fifties, I in my early sixties and my sister Vicky in her early seventies.

Child Care Methods

For child care today's Chinese grandmothers rely on their experience of bringing up their own children. They share the self-confidence of earlier generations of grandmothers. Their methods may be out of date by the standards of their daughters and daughters-in-law – but though modern-day mothers are more likely than earlier generations were to challenge the older generation, they have to be careful; they are indebted to the person who cares for their child.

Grandmothers feed a small child adult food, not food specifically designed for children, often traditional porridges and pickles. They make their own meals, and those of their grandchildren. Western baby food in little jars (now ghastly suckable tubes) does not appeal. The fast-food industry does its best to get children to eat food laden with fat, salt and sugar. Chains such as

McDonalds, with 3,500 outlets, do huge business in China; it is the parents who take the children there.

Grandmothers may have some responsibility for the epidemic of childhood obesity; they give their treasures too many treats.[35] Our mother took the same line. She kept a supply of treats for her grandchildren and great-grandchildren. Near the end of her life she woke to see the golden-haired Misha, aged two, standing beside her bed, his eyes on her biscuit tin. 'I thought I saw an angel,' she said.

The care of grandchildren in China is obligatory but does not have to be hands-on. Yan Hairong found that many better-off urban grandparents had no intention of caring for their grandchildren full-time. What they were prepared to do was to contribute financially to hiring a nanny (保姆 *baomu*). Grandmothers may still supervise their grandchild's *baomu*, hover over the child or drop by unexpectedly.[36] Non-participating grandmothers may also be working. Chen Huiyin did not give up her factory job to care for her grandson. 'When Chen Li was born I continued to work in the factory dining room. I told Xiao Xie [her daughter-in-law] that I would rather help pay for a nanny than quit the job in order to help with the baby.'[37] She recognised her obligation to care for her grandchild, but translated it into a cash payment.

A nanny is not the norm, nor is day care. A 2019 report said that in Shanghai there was licensed day care for only one in ten infants between two and three years old. The fees were high – 30,000–50,000 RMB per annum (US$4,200–7,000). Parents who use licensed day care may share the dismissive opinion of the State Council that 'elderly people can't keep up with the latest in infant care knowledge'.[38] Most parents cannot take such a high-minded stance. Grandmothers have to be used for child care. They give the care because they are expected to, by their children and by society at large. They also get great pleasure from caring for their treasures.

5   Ruling the Roost

作威作福

Zuowei zuofu

Act powerful, bring prosperity

The Household Manager

A Chinese (paternal) grandmother dominated the economy of her household. She was the household manager, the 管家 *guanjia*. This was a job without term, to be handed over (to her oldest son's wife) only when she was no longer capable.

In a charming book about his childhood, published in 1887, Lee Yan Phou (Li Yanfu) described how his grandmother, in a gentry family in Guangdong, ran her household:[1]

She had always the management of the minor affairs of the entire establishment. She it was who assigned the duties and superintended the work of the servants and the employments of the daughters and the daughters-in-law. We had a hired cook, several maid servants and a man servant, so that there was never a need that the ladies of our family should soil their dainty hands or weary their delicate feet. My grandmother, however, had her own ideas about work, and used to arrange that her daughters should not be idle or ignorant.

The old woman was in charge of everything within her household; her husband and sons managed affairs outside the family. She made all decisions, personal, domestic and financial, within the family. She kept track of income and expenditures, at whatever level of wealth or poverty; she managed relations between family members; and she led the observance of rituals and ceremonies. A successful manager ran a tight, harmonious household. Harmony was a proof of her success as a manager. Lee Yan Phou noted how successful his grandmother was:[2]

My grandmother's was a character that drew respect, so she had little trouble in the management of her large family. She had administrative talent of a high order and therefore a fair share of household happiness fell to our lot.

This book was written a little later than Isabella's Beeton's *Mrs Beeton's Book of Household Management* (1861). This massive tome, still in print, deals with every aspect of household management. The indefatigable Isabella compared the mistress of the house to the commander of an army. Her book was directed to relieve 'the discomfort and suffering brought upon men and women by household mismanagement'. She provided recipes for every budget and every occasion. She covered the management of servants. She gave instructions on laundry, furniture polishing, needlework, hair washing (before shampoo). She held forth on infant and child care, from feeding (including supervising a wet nurse if necessary) to treating diseases, to character building. She brought up the oldest of twenty children in a blended family, which explains why many of her recipes are for large numbers. Her own life was short and tragic. She died at the age of twenty-eight, of post-partum fever. Two of her four children died in infancy.

Mrs Beeton wrote for middle-class brides who were setting up their first household; she assumed complete ignorance of household management. Her book was the bible for generations of inexperienced brides who needed a manual to run a new household. A Chinese bride did not set up her own household; she moved into her husband's household, which already had an in-house expert: her mother-in-law.

In households with servants and domestic slaves the job of the household manager was to assign tasks to others and to receive reports that they had been carried out. She kept a watchful eye on the household accounts, and on the honesty of servants, tenants, suppliers and family members. In *A Dream of Red Mansions* the Lady Dowager, ably assisted by her shrewd granddaughter-in-law Wang Xifeng 王熙鳳, had detailed, precise knowledge of all matters in the vast household. Today the two would be running a large corporation.

Management of servants required a range of skills. Unhappy servants had many ways of getting back at their employers, from working slowly or poorly, to gossiping and backbiting, to dishonesty and malice. A shrewd manager averted disruptions. She inspired respect in the servants. She had to know how and when to reward them with gifts or money. She had to know enough about their families to make them feel that there was a personal relationship across the mistress/servant divide. Of course she had the power to punish or fire them, but it was in family's interests to behave benevolently.

In the great majority her of households that had no servants the manager supervised her unmarried daughters and daughters-in-law and allotted jobs. The first job, for a daughter-in-law, was to light the fire in the stove in the morning. Then there was breakfast to be cooked. Bed quilts had to be hung out to air. After the early rush a myriad of daily tasks followed, all supervised by the older woman, who would watch the babies and smaller grandchildren while the younger women worked. They cooked; they fed the poultry – chicken and ducks – kept for eggs and eventually for the pot. In rural areas they ventured outside the house, to pick mushrooms, to gather grass for the stove and wild herbs, fungi and tree barks to make soups, medications and poultices. They did light farm work in the busy seasons – planting out seedlings, weeding growing crops, threshing the cut grain. There were no days off. The concept of a seven-day week with one day of rest is a recent innovation.

Beyond short-term, day-to-day management, the household manager had to plan, on the principle that the household should be as close to self-sufficiency as possible, purchasing few 'outside goods'. Household lighting had to be prepared: wax candles, until the advent of kerosene lamps; women collected beeswax and dipped wicks into the heated, liquid wax to make the candles. Food supplies had to be stocked for the winter and spring, tougher in north China than in the south. Before a northern winter eggs were pickled in brine; long white cabbages (白菜 baicai) were stored in holes dug in the ground just outside the house in the early autumn. Mushrooms, tree fungi and golden persimmons were dried; pork was salted or cured. In the cities coal dust was pressed into brickettes for heating and cooking.

Basket weaving was a periodic activity, ideal for the off season of agriculture. Reeds, osiers and rattan were gathered, then retted; straw was sorted and graded after the grain crop had been harvested. The women wove baskets for storage and for carrying goods. They made sleeping mats and pillows, and blinds to protect the house from the sun in summer; a household would be expanded outwards with a mat shed. And in many parts of rural China they made straw shoes, coarse, scratchy things only slightly better than no footwear.

Textiles

The household manager was the teacher of girls and younger women in handcraft. Textile work was the most important. Cotton was the everyday textile for the bulk of the population. Men cultivated the cotton plants and picked them; women spun the cotton into thread, wove it into cloth, dyed it and made the cloth into clothing and quilts. Cotton garments had to be repeatedly repaired and patched, to prolong their lives. Eventually they were more patch than original. The last tatters of cloth would be sewn together, layer after layer, to make the soles of shoes, which would be attached to a cotton upper. Hemp, grown as hedges around vegetable plots, was retted and woven into coarse cloth for storage bags. The value of its buds as a light narcotic was apparently not appreciated.

Laundry was ardous, though a less time-consuming chore than it is now; clothes were changed much less often, especially in winter.

Padded jackets, trousers and quilts could not be washed, only the jacket worn over the padded jacket was. The padded items had to be inspected regularly for

---

Box 5.1 Washing

In the past washing clothes was immensely complicated, in China as elsewhere. It made sense to wash as seldom as possible. Washing meant hand washing. It meant using awful substances such as ash and lye to assist the hard hand labour; soap powders only appeared, in a few places, at the beginning of the twentieth century. In China washing was often done out of doors, beside a lake or stream, or in a courtyard with water from a well or a water seller. The water was cold, making the process even harder. Hot water on tap, now universal in urban China, did not arrive in Beijing until the 1980s, and even then was limited. Living in a diplomatic compound I was one of the few to have constant hot water; Canadian students came to my apartment to wash themselves and their clothes.

---

lice, and the vermin picked out by nimble fingers. In the spring quilts and padded clothes had to be taken apart, the cloth washed and the silk or cotton wadding combed out, a time-consuming and unpleasant job.

The rich had silk clothing and bedding. The silkworms were raised by cotton-wearing peasant women. In villages in Jiangsu and Shandong women raised silkworm eggs (育蚕 *yucan*). The eggs hatched into industrious little worms, which spun themselves into cocoons that were sold to workshops for spinning into thread. Raising the eggs involved detailed rituals, all led by the older woman who had the inherited knowledge of nurturing the eggs and worms. They grew in special rooms, the walls of the room papered with pictures of cats, to deter rats. The door had paper door spirits stuck onto it. The words 'death' and 'salt' were taboo in the room. Wine and meat were served to the mystical Green Dragon; a household was blessed if a snake slid into the room, the Green Dragon in physical form. No person in mourning could enter the room, no one was allowed to speak in a loud voice or to quarrel in the room. Failure to carry out these observances was courting disaster, the loss of income from the silkworms (and of the older woman's authority).[3]

Older women taught younger ones many forms of textile work – spinning, weaving, needlework, knitting, embroidering, quilting, darning, patching. They supervised them, encouraged them – and spent hour after hour sitting with them. The work was companionable. Women sat together, each with her piece of work in her hand. The work had to be done slowly and painstakingly, so it was more relaxing than other household tasks. Women could chat to each other, all the while watching small children crawling around at their feet.

Women always had a piece of textile work to hand; some work could be done while walking around – for instance, knitting. Most handwork could only be

ILLUSTRATION 5.1 Working together

done in daylight, but coarser work, such a sewing shoe soles, could be done by the feeble light of an oil lamp, after dark.

After 1949 when political meetings were part of life, women always took handwork with them. When I went to teachers' meetings at my school in Beijing (1964–1965) the women knitted, the men smoked. I could go both ways and did.

All women embroidered. Poorer women embroidered goods for sale, decorations to trim the gowns of the wealthy, banners for temples and for celebrations, as well as clothes and quilts for their own families. Richer women embroidered shoes and made gifts, purses and handkerchiefs. Girls sewed pieces for their trousseaux, which they would take to their new homes when they married.

Box 5.2 Embroidery

In almost every culture women take coloured threads and stitch them onto plain fabrics. Patterns and colours vary widely, but all embroidery is painstaking, careful and loving, an expression of a woman's talents. Every Chinese girl was taught many different stitches by demonstration from older women. In China as elsewhere there were many regional styles. *Mary Thomas's Embroidery Book*, which lists thirty styles of embroidery in Britain alone, belonged to my great-aunt Mary, a skilled embroiderer. It is dedicated to 'all those women who, throughout the long past ages, have contributed to the joys of life through their embroideries'.[1]

Much embroidery in China was for home consumption, decorations on clothes, shoes, bedding, drapery. Some was for sale. Millions of Chinese women embroidered official robes, temple hangings, and goods for export. The most demanding piece of embroidery I have ever seen was a large portrait of Mao Zedong, done in shades from black to white. The embroiderer worked on it full-time for a year.

[1] Mary Thomas, *Mary Thomas's Embroidery Book* (London: Hodder and Stoughton, 1934).

Some of the textile work was for home consumption, some for sale, often at periodic markets that were the regular punctuation of rural life. This is a description of a traditional rural family in Fujian:[4]

As Dunglin was occupied with the store in town, his mother, Grandmother Pan became the matriarch of the household. Although grey hair covered her head and furrows lined her face, she had kept, because of her very experience of hardship, a very industrious spirit. She was an elderly woman who managed her household affairs clearly and in orderly fashion. In company with her two daughters-in-law Aunt Lin and Mrs Hwang she took up spinning and weaving, besides carrying on the household work. The three women made cloth from hemp that was cultivated on the poorer lands. The cloth was sold at the market and added somewhat to the family economy

Textile work took up any spare time women had during the day. It was slow, painstaking and in no way cost-effective, in terms of the labour involved, but, as in many other parts of the world, the textile work of women was a tradition and a pleasure.

Social Control

The formal power of older women might not extend beyond the household, but they were a social force. They sat with other grandmothers on

ILLUSTRATION 5.2 Embroidery

the high doorsteps of houses, minding their grandchildren, doing hand-work. They used gossip to wield social control. No bad behaviour missed their scrutiny. Sinners were quickly brought into line, punished by exclusion or mockery. Criticism fell harder on women than on men. A woman labelled a 'broken shoe' (破鞋 *poxie*), on suspicion of sexual misdemeanours, would be cast out, her only recourse to flee or to kill herself.

After 1949 older women's delight in gossip was valuable to the Communist Party, to keep many eyes on the people, through street committees. The committees had many tasks: encouraging cleanliness, keeping watchful eyes on the treatment of children, making sure public spaces were swept. They were given another responsibility: enforcing political messages. The informal

ILLUSTRATION 5.3 Selling cloth

gossip, the more salacious the better, that had always flowed through dense neighbourhoods took on a formal political role. The state exhorted neighbours to watch each other, to record bourgeois behaviour, to track down immorality, to note visitors and to identify departures from socialist policies; all these 'crimes' had to be reported to the local Public Security Bureau (公安局 Gonganju).

Li Jie described the leading gossip of the Shanghai lanes in which she grew up. Grandma Front Bedroom lived in the front bedroom of a much-divided house. The old lady, a malicious and spiteful person, spent her days keeping watch on her neighbours.[5]

Grandma Front Bedroom could proudly pronounce that every person who lived in this branch of the alleyway since 1953 had grown up under her searching scrutiny. When Little Aunt's boyfriend and later husband came to visit, he always heard a squeak when passing by the second floor on the way upstairs. The next day Grandma Front Bedroom would tell Grandma Zhou, who lived in the pavilion room two houses down, how many hours Little Aunt had spent with her boyfriend the evening before in exchange for gossip about Grandma Zhou's immediate neighbours. This way Grandma Front Bedroom learned something about everyone within a ten house radius, from what their great-grandparents did for a living down to the brawl they had had the night before. With this knowledge she often informed on her neighbours during the Mao Era, whenever it was to her advantage to do so.

Old women played another 'gossip' role, no less political. They passed on 'real' news, the 'news of the little streets' (小道消息 xiaodao xiaoxi). This system distributed information on what goods were for sale, on people who were in trouble with the authorities, on political news not covered in formal channels. Passing news through gossip led to exaggeration and inaccuracy, but it had the ring of authenticity. And since few people had much confidence in the news purveyed by official sources, it usually trumped the formal news.

Another function of gossip was to use detailed knowledge of neighbours and neighbouring communities to find mates for their grandchildren. The prospective mate (對象 duixiang) was sussed out by the grandmothers. If an old woman was good at making matches, she might become a professional. Margery Wolf saw this in practice in a Taiwanese village:[6]

A woman freed from the responsibilities of meal preparation and child care has the time to make the numerous visits, casual and official, necessary for truly successful matchmaking. If she happens to be a woman with an outgoing personality who has paid careful attention to the various rituals of engagement and marriage she may find herself with a lively and lucrative business. A talented go-between is in much demand in the country. Although the majority of her business will have to do with marriages, she may also arrange adoptions, settle disputes between family branches, friends or enemies. In Peihotien there was a very strong-minded old lady in her eighties who hobbled for miles on her tiny bound feet, arranging marriages and adoptions, settling family disputes and negotiating face-saving compromises for quarrels of various kinds. Her age and her personality commanded respect from even the most arrogant of men and her tongue lashed the reluctant into submitting to what she considered the best terms they could expect.

Street committees and social spying died even before the end of the Mao Era. Surveillance did not. It is now done electronically, using the smartphones that we all now carry or through face recognition technologies. But while street committees were run by volunteers the surveillance system has to be run by an army of paid public-security employees.

Financial Contributions

In traditional society an efficient grandmother contributed significantly to the family economy. The unpaid work of the women of the household, under her supervision, saved expenditures on household items that would otherwise be purchased, and the handcrafts produced for sale made money.

Besides the home production of necessities many rural areas had specialised moneymaking traditions.[7] These were once known as cottage industries, later in the Mao Era as 'sideline activities', an unfortunate choice of English words given that in English slang it meant an extramarital affair. Many places had/have a traditional 'special product' (特貨 *tehuo*). Place names are brand names. Shaoxing 绍兴 (Zhejiang) has its Yellow Wine. Jinhua 金华 (Zhejiang) has been producing ham for eons. The fierce liquor Maotai comes from Maotai 茅台 (Guizhou). Other places were associated with one product, and produced the only genuine version of it. In the hills of Anxi 安溪 (Fujian) tea bushes were cultivated, and the leaves plucked and processed, to produce Tieguanyin 鐵觀音, the finest of teas. In Yangjiabu 楊家埠 (Shandong) and Yangliuqing 楊柳青 (Hebei), New Year prints (年畫 *nianhua*) were produced, in the tens of millions.[8]

The special products were cultivated, or made in male-dominated work-shops, or at home, where women played the major role. Marketing was 'outside' work, done by men of the family who had connections to the trade webs that got the products to market.

Busy as traditional women were, the burden of household work increased during the first decades of the Republic. New products became essentials: kerosene lamps and lamp oil, cigarettes, matches. These had to be purchased; that required income. There was an intensified emphasis on handcrafts and cottage industries. New ones developed to produce export articles that could be sold to middlemen who moved the products to trading houses in the ports. From there they were shipped to the West, to be sold in department stores. Ease of maritime shipping and consumer demand in the West saw a great increase in exports of silk underwear, nightwear and stockings, embroidered table linens and bed linens, hairnets, straw braid, matting and baskets, all produced at home.

The income from the work was unpredictable. The producers received only a tiny proportion of the eventual sale price. There were too many middlemen along the way, and too many vagaries within the market. The work was insecure, dependent on demand elsewhere. Tea exports declined, as the taste of tea drinkers in Europe and North America changed from green tea to black tea, produced in plantations in India and Ceylon. With the decline went income from tea cultivation, the work of women in the tea-growing areas. The production of filmy hairnets in eastern Shandong, which until the 1920s brought income to a myriad of families, collapsed, as the result of 'a change of fashion in the distant lands of Europe and America, the adoption of the bobbed hair by women'.[9] Short hair required no nets to keep it in place .The Depression after 1929 destroyed the global market for luxury goods, silk underwear and nightwear. The *coup de grâce* was war; in the late 1930s it put an end to international trade. Production for export did not revive until the 1980s when China re-entered world markets.

Celebrations and Festivals

A family's standing in the community depended on lavish (i.e. more than the family could afford) and meticulously choreographed ceremonies, rituals and celelebrations that were central to family life; they had to be performed properly.

The household manager presided over the celebration of festivals that punctuated the year, each with its special foods and rituals. The major event of the year was the New Year (新年 *xinnian*), also called the Spring Festival (春節 *chunjie*) or the Lunar New Year. It was the only long holiday of the year, lasting at least two weeks. The date changes every year, because it is based on the new moon, but it usually happens in late January or in February. Well before the date, the manager went into battle, commanding the younger women of her household like the general of an army, using the knowledge that she had accumulated over decades to make sure that everything would be perfect for the gathering of the family. Every male member of the family was expected to come home, and stay for a month. This influx of people required large supplies of food, some of it prepared the summer before, some in the weeks leading up to the festival.

The tradition of going home at the New Year continues on an unimaginably large scale as migrant workers go home. Hundreds of millions of people travel at the same time (see Chapter 10). The duration of the holiday has been reduced to two weeks but not the intensity of the need to go home and show family solidarity.

Box 5.3 *Hongbao*

红包 *hongbao* (red envelopes) are an essential feature of the New Year. These small envelopes are given from senior to junior in the family, and from employer to employee in the work place. Inside them is money. The amounts may be nominal, as they were once, but may also be quite significant. There are sub-traditions associated with them: two *hongbao* are given together; only even amounts; no amounts with four in them. There are regional variations and family traditions – but no doubt that this is a universally loved practice.

Table 5.1 *Traditional festivals*

Chinese	English	Time	Activities/food
新年春節	New Year/Spring Festival	January/February	Family reunion, gifts to children (红包 *hongbao*). Fifteen days of special foods
清明節	Qingming	April	Visits to cemeteries, sweeping graves (掃墓 *saomu*). Picnics, food offerings to ancestors
端午節	Duanwu	May	Commemoration of Chu Yuan; boat racing. Sticky rice wraps (粽子 *zongzi*)
中秋節	Mid-autumn	September	Harvest festival, moon festival. Moon cakes (月餅 *yuebing*), lanterns

Besides the New Year the household manager was responsible for the celebration of the lesser festivals that marked the progress of the year. All the festivals were based on the family; all involved major preparations (Table 5.1).

The celebrations brought excitement and feasting – and cemented family and community unity. They formed some of the happiest memories of family life. A young person of thirteen or fourteen 'would have witnessed a few hundred ritual celebrations or ceremonies, and would have participated in a somewhat smaller number'.[10]

Weddings and funerals presented special demands on the household manager. The dates of weddings were fairly predictable; marriages were arranged, and the wedding would take place when the young people reached a suitable age. The wedding could be speeded up or postponed. If necessary it could take place in the absence of the groom, though the bride had to be present since she was moving into her husband's home. The groom's family could take years preparing for the wedding: collecting money for the bride price (to the girl's family), the feasts for family and friends of the groom, preparing a new chamber for the couple. The bride's family, meanwhile, had to prepare her trousseau, and put away money for her dowry. All these details, in both households, were the responsibility of the household manager. Funerals were less predictable as to timing, but, as we will see later (see Chapter 12), old people recognised that their life was drawing in, and that they must prepare for a funeral.

After 1949 the celebration of festivals was turned on its head. Most traditional festivals were celebrated only at home, and very quietly. The new festivals were socialist (Table 5.2).

Table 5.2 *Communist festivals*

Chinese	English	Date	Origin
国际妇女节	Women's Day	8 March	International/USSR
五一劳动节	Labour Day	1 May	International/USSR
八一建军节	Army Day	1 August	Founding of the People's Liberation Army
国庆节	National Day	1 October	Founding of the People's Republic

National Day was put nine days ahead of the Double Tenth (雙十 *shuangshi*), the date of the October Revolution in 1911 and the National Day for the Nationalists. The new festivals were not family events, but political ones, with public speeches and parades. On National Day the leaders of the nation appeared on Tiananmen in the middle of Beijing. Tiananmen Square was carved out of old neighbourhoods in the early 1950s specifically to hold huge numbers of people, who were trucked in and choreographed with minute attention to detail. They held up paper flowers or cards to make giant messages, even portraits of the Great Helmsman. These celebrations were carbon copies of Soviet ones. They survive to this day, though they are haunted by memories of the student occupation of the square in 1989, and the bloody crackdown that followed it. In English the crackdown is often called 'Tiananmen'. In Chinese it is known as Liusi 六四, June 4th. It cannot be mentioned openly.

The one traditional festival that survived after 1949 was the New Year, the only annual holiday for most of the population; otherwise the celebration of the family was dead – or, because it emerged three decades later – in cold storage. All the old festivals have re-emerged.

Women's Money

In traditional China, when brides went to their new homes they took with them considerable dowries, elaborate boxes of possessions – and money. A girl from a rich family would bring a large quantity of goods, money and her own servants with her. Middle-class girls took several boxes and a sum of money. Poor girls would have simpler dowries – bedding, some trinkets and a small amount of money. The cost of the dowries was offset by the bride price that the groom's family paid to the girl's family. There was an underlying reason for a generous dowry: the concern of the parents for their departing daughter. When Lu Ying, mother of the four sisters of Hefei, married in 1906 her parents outdid themselves:[11]

Their splendid display of generosity seems to have pleased everyone in the groom's family. One could say that Lu Ying's grand send-off was her parents' last attempt to look after her. It was their way of making sure that she would start her new life under the most favorable of circumstances.

Wives kept control of the money their parents sent with them as part of their dowry. This was one of the key distinctions between wives and concubines – who did not come with dowries and were entirely dependent on their husbands. If women looked after their dowries carefully, they might have a significant nest egg. They could use it as business capital, or in emergencies. It was not part of the household budget.

Mao Dun 茅盾 described a family emergency in 'The shop of the Lin family' (林家铺子 *Lin jia puzi*). The Lins ran a small store in a country town. As the movement to buy Chinese goods (國貨運動 *guohuo yundong*), as opposed to Japanese, gained ground in the 1930s, the Lin family shop was threatened with disaster – much of its stock was Japanese. Seeing the Lin's precarious situation, the head of the Merchants' Guild proposed that the seventeen-year-old daughter, Lin Xiu, be 'given' as a concubine to the head of the local government, a man of forty who already had a wife and a concubine. Mrs Lin reacted with bitter wailing, then brought out her dowry money, gave half to her husband and half to her daughter, and told them to leave town at once. She ordered her daughter to marry the shop assistant: 'Who knows how many days I have left to live – hic – so if you both kowtow in my presence I can set my mind at ease – hic.'[12] Mrs Lin had chronic hiccups, which made the local people mock her. But she was shrewd enough to save her beloved daughter from being a concubine. She found a simple way to make her daughter safe – a quick wedding to a nice young man whom her daughter liked.

In the Mao Era dowries were considered bourgeois; they almost disappeared, as did wedding ceremonies. The groom's family would be expected to provide a room for the new couple, but little in the way of gifts. A bride took very little to her new home, beyond a set of quilts that she had made herself. The quilts often had a vivid red cover embroidered with symbols of marital harmony. I still have the one given to me by my school, the Second Foreign Languages Institute (二外 Erwai), before I left Beijing in 1965 – I was getting married a month later. It is red silk, with gold mandarin ducks embroidered on it.

Challenging Times

There were recurrent challenges to the household manager – natural disasters, bad harvests, death, illness, economic fluctuations – but these tended to be regional (famines) or particular to a family (death, illness). The fighting that erupted in 1937 brought almost insuperable challenges. Supply chains were broken by fighting. Armies requisitioned food, creating local deficits. Young men were taken for the Chinese armies or for forced labour by the Japanese.

Box 5.4 Wartime songs

The Resistance War brought choral singing to China. Thousands of songs were written to help people survive the miseries of war. The words of the songs were written by national figures, and then sung in the army, in schools and in workplaces. Singing was what got exiles from the north and east of the country through endless dark evenings (no electricity) and through bombing raids. The music was either Western or by Western-trained Chinese composers, notably Nie Er 聶耳 and Xian Xinghai 冼星海. In a collection of 2,300 wartime songs, the most powerful emotions were for the nation and for lost home places. Very few were romantic. There was no Chinese equivalent to the mournful 'We'll meet again, don't know where, don't know when' (Vera Lynn), or 'I'll be seeing you' (Frank Sinatra). Women figured only for their work at home making shoes and clothes for the soldiers, or farming the fields, a version of 'Keep the home fires burning' (Ivor Novello), the First World War anthem to women's work.[1]

[1] *Kangzhan gequ xuanji* 抗戰歌曲選集 (A Collection of Songs from the Resistance War) (Taibei: Xing-cheng yuan, 1997).

Food was an obsession for urban residents during the war; they lived with chronic food insecurity. The terrible famine in Henan (1942) was the worst of wartime famines. The textiles that women made at home – cotton cloth, cotton shoes, embroideries, bedding – were, before the war, made for sale as well as for family use. Now women made clothing and shoes for the soldiers, whether Nationalist or Communist, as patriotic acts, without payment.

Old women could do little to help their families other than to go without themselves. Younger women had slightly more opportunities. They could leave their husbands – a practice that became possible and even acceptable during the war years. Failure to provide for a family might lead a wife to look for a new man with better financial prospects. Zhao Ma's fascinating study of runaway wives in wartime Beiping (Beijing) is based on legal cases brought by outraged husbands. It includes the wives' statements about their husbands' inadequacies, almost always their failure to provide a living income.[13]

Inflation, beginning early in the war and accelerating towards 1945, threatened the very existence of households. The end of the Anti-Japanese War did nothing to stanch the misery. Economic insecurity became totally preoccupying. The rates for the Chinese currency (法幣 *fabi*) and the wholesale price index in Shanghai for June 1946 to June 1947 show how precarious the lives of people in the money economy were.[14]

Inflation bred corruption. Both attacked the upright and rewarded the unscrupulous. Even the previously upright abandoned their moral standards. Late

Table 5.3 *Inflation*

	Rate to US dollar	Wholesale price index
June 1946	2,655	378,217
December 1946	6,063	681,563
March 1947	14,000	1,386,593
June 1947	36,826	2,905,790

payment of bills saved money; hoarding was profitable. The people who did well were black-marketeers and profiteers, greedy people without any sense of social or familial obligation. Inflation shrank the family unit. A worker's wage could only support his immediate family, his wife and children. Families were in such a parlous state that many were willing to accept the Communist Party when it came to power in 1949 so long as it stopped the chaos.

It did. By measures still poorly understood the new government *did* stop inflation. The relief felt by the population at large was enormous. An early PRC publication claimed that the Communist victory had not only brought political and economic security but had improved family relations: 'a warm love for their children' had developed amongst the workers at the Shijingshan Steel Works (石景山钢铁厂 *Shijingshan gangtiechang*) near Beijing. In the socialist utopia even wife-beating would disappear:[15]

It was quite a different story in the old days. With prices of daily necessities soaring sky high a month's pay would not even buy enough food for a few days. Huddling in their hovels with many worries they often beat their wives and scolded their children.

After 1949 the combined effects of the wartime depredations and the new communist policies meant that large multi-generational households were doomed, as was the dominance of the household manager. An equality of poverty was established; inflation was replaced by a new economy in which everyone was more or less poor. Once-rich families lost their property, either confiscated or voluntarily disposed of as a show of loyalty to the new regime. Clothing became drab and utilitarian – out went long gowns, silks and furs; in came blue and black cotton pant suits, for both sexes. Lavish food was outlawed, in favour of coarse grains and vegetables. Cars were for Party officials only; buses, bicycles and feet were the means of getting around. Urban housing was redistributed to accommodate people moving to the cities, almost a flood in the early 1950s.

In three-generation families, still the common form, the seniors lost their dominant roles. The incomes older women had once earned from handcrafts did not reappear; China was cut off from world trade, behind the Bamboo

Curtain. They had no pensions and little in the way of savings; pre-1949 bank savings had been eaten away by inflation and by the change in currency after 1949. Old people from the former elite were vulnerable; they were on the wrong side of the revolution. Their large houses were divided up between multiple families. Shares were useless, since most private companies had passed under state control. People hung on to their share certificates – now a staple at the Beijing market for antiquities and curios, the Panjiayuan 潘家园. The once-rich could not sell their valuables except at cut-rate prices to second-hand stores; there was no market for treasures in a world that demanded abstinence from luxury.

In both rural and urban China the burden of housework, still complicated and time-consuming in the days before electricity, running water or labour-saving devices (electric or gas stoves, refrigerators, washing machines, driers), fell more and more on older women as younger women went to work. There was no technological progress on the home front, except limited electricity in the cities, only for lighting. The bulbs were usually twenty watts, just enough to cut the darkness but not enough to read or sew. To put a revolutionary spin on the drudgery, people were exhorted to live simply, and to take pride in doing so.

坚苦朴素
Jianku pusu

'Endure hardship, live modestly' was the slogan. The simple life was hard and non-stop. A fire had to be lit first thing every morning, for cooking. Water had to be fetched from a well or a pump. 'Night soil' (human waste) had to be taken out of the house and either put to mature in a cistern (rural China), later to be used as a fertiliser, or given to the 'honey carts' that trolled through urban lanes and streets. The house had to be tidied, quilts folded and modest cleaning done. Cooking was from scratch, over a single ring in the top of the stove.

Food shopping was complicated. Each item had to be bought at a different shop, market or street stall. Often there were queues. Grandmothers could spend a good part of their day going the rounds. Peddlers still carried steamed bread, vegetables and fruit round the streets, but to buy these goods someone had to know the schedules and be at home at the right time. This was the responsibility of grandmothers.

Some things were not shopped for. Clothing was still made at home or by a local tailor. Fabric shops sold increasingly drab materials, shades of blue, grey and black cotton, not silk. Knitting was a universal task for women. A favourite knitted item was long underwear. There drabness was not the rule; the glimpse of pink or purple long johns peeping out from under a man's dark blue trousers gave a frisson.

Non-food shopping was limited. There were bookstores that sold authorised literature and political texts, and shoe and hat shops. General stores (百货商店 *baihuo shangdian*) started to appear in the 1950s, but they were few and far between. The Baihuo dalou 百货大楼 in Wangfujing 王府井, the main shopping street in Beijing, was more a monument to socialist ideas than a place where people actually shopped. I first went there not long after going to GUM in Moscow. The Moscow store was beautiful, unlike the cavernous Baihuo dalou, but both had one thing in common: they were staffed by assistants who lounged behind glass-topped counters. In Beijing the favourite response to a shopper was 没有 *meiyou* – 'we don't have it', delivered in a ringing tone that implied that failing to give the customer what they wanted had made the assistant's day. In my many visits to the store my only purchases were hand-kerchiefs and a fur hat.

Many products were rationed, scarce or unavailable. People were issued coupons by their workplace or street committee. The three main coupons were for grain, oil and cotton (粮票油票布票 *liangpiao, youpiao, bupiao*). These goods were generally available. Others were in short supply; rumours of particular goods for sale spread like wildfire.

All Change

Things got worse in the early 1960s; during the famine years shortages were acute in the cities and absolute in many rural areas. The Cultural Revolution brought its own chaos. But at the end of that terrible period households started to change. In the early Reform Era labour-saving devices started to creep in. Refrigerators, tiny at first, became a status symbol. Electricity was still expensive, and some people turned their fridges off at night, with predictable consequences. Dowries came back. The bride came to her husband's house with bedding and clothing, the husband's family provided the 'five revolves' (五轮 *wulun*) – bicycle, sewing machine, radio, watch and fan.

The One Child per Family policy eroded the position of the household manager. Her daughters-in-law were older and less malleable. Her grandchildren were fewer. The young wanted to set up their own households. A bride today may demand an apartment, a car and major appliances, possibly with space for his or her parents, so that they can care for a precious grandchild. But the grandmother is not in charge of the household. The traditional household manager is no more. Her only remaining duty is caring for her grandchildren.

6 Old Age

家有一老黃金活寶

Jia you yi lao huangjin huobao

A family with an old person has a golden living treasure

The phrase implies that all old people are revered and respected. Old age brings wisdom, which means that 'old age deserves respect' (年高德功 *niangao degong*). The traditional Chinese pattern is like the tradition of First Nations peoples in North America, for whom members of the senior generation are 'elders', the repositories of wisdom, the transmitters of culture.

Old people in China could expect to reap the rewards of the care that they had given to their own elders. There was a rolling reciprocity in the relations within a family: each generation was the insurance policy for the one that came before its own. The purpose of raising sons was, in old age, to ensure respect and avoid [misery] in old age.

養兒防老

Yanger fanglao

This is still the formal attitude to the old. Old age has not, in theory, lost its lustre.

In the past few people made it to old age (老年時期 *laonian shiqi*), which started at some not very precise date around sixty. A huge study of rural China conducted in the early 1930s showed that only 14 per cent of the population was over fifty.[1] I have discussed the lives of grandmothers before talking about old age, because many women were not old when their first grandchild was born, and many grandmothers did not make it to old age.

Chinese women have shared with men in enjoying reverence for age. In old age they achieved equality with men. Women could look forward to growing old; age would bring them happiness and respect as their lives were drawing towards their end. Old age brought women an authority they had not had when they were young. Janet Salaff described a Chinese woman's life trajectory:[2]

Women anticipated that when their own sons married and ultimately bore grandsons to further the family line, and they became the eldest generation in the home, they would gain ascendancy. As their star reached its zenith the matriarchs could at last manage the household budget and contemplate retirement from active household labour and drudgery.

This is a striking contrast to the Western trajectory, where women tend to lose power as they get older. They often outlive their husbands. They have pensions, state or private, they are not financially dependent on their children, and they do not expect to live with them. Their relations with them depend on how much love and affection there is in the relationship between the generations. There is no legal or social sanction that requires younger generations to look after the older. Many English terms for old women are contemptuous: 'old wives' tales', 'old crone', 'old bag', 'old cow'. Much of the literature about old women is dismal – poverty, isolation, Alzheimer's. This coverage ignores the happiest part of old age for many women: having grandchildren. The momentous change brought by the arrival of a grandchild was described by Sheila Kitzinger as 'a peak point in a woman's life'.[3]

The ideal of a golden old age was embedded in the Confucian tenet of filial piety. The character is written 孝 xiao, made up of part of the character for 'old', 老 lao, and the character for 'son', 子 zi. The Classic of Filial Piety (孝經 Xiaojing), written two millennia ago in the Han Dynasty, demanded that junior generations care for older generations still alive, provide the necessities of life, and give them respect and comfort. After death they became ancestors, given regular respect through care for their graves. Filial piety was instilled by social custom and by the state. The Twenty-Four Filial [Behaviours] (二十四孝 ershisi xiao), a Yuan Dynasty compilation, presented examples of extreme devotion to parents, most quite improbable.

The upward trajectory of ageing, from oppressed to respected, applied to most Han women. But some lived their lives on a more even trajectory: they were not repressed in youth and were respected in later life. Hakka (客家 kejia) women, living mainly in south China and on Taiwan, have always had greater autonomy than other Han women, their feet have never been bound, and they expect not only to run their own households but also to engage in business. Taiwanese women have a reputation for being feisty, energetic and entrepreneurial: 'A truly successful Taiwanese woman is a rugged individualist, who has learned to depend largely on herself while appearing to lean on her father, her husband and her son.'[4]

In traditional China respect for old women was shown every day. They were first in line for any comforts the family could afford. In a wealthy family a grandmother had her own courtyard, where she often shared her bed with the warm little body of one of her grandchildren. In a family living in a single room in north China the grandmother slept in the warmest place, on the heated

---

Box 6.1 Strong women

The Hakka 客家 (*kejia*) people live throughout southern China and on Taiwan, in Hong Kong and in the Overseas communities. Their contributions in the political and economic worlds have been enormous. Many political leaders were and are Hakka: Hong Xiuquan 洪秀全, Sun Yat-sen 孫中山, Li Guanyao 李官耀 (Lee Kuan-yu), Deng Xiaoping 邓小平, Li Denghui 李登辉 (Lee Teng-hui) and Tsai Ying-wen 蔡英文. Hakka women have always been the equal to men, their feet have never been bound and they work as hard as or harder than men. The work ethic of women is used to disparage/envy men: 'women work, men laze' (女劳男逸 *nülao nanyi*).

Amongst the non-Han ethnic groups in south-west China are other strong women. Zhuang 壮族 women choose their own husbands, in complex courtship rituals that involve singing duets. Yi 彝族 women are tall, strong, immensely hardworking and in charge, socially, politically and economically. Their husbands, often physically smaller, are little more than drones who do no work. The Mosu 摩梭 are a small group living around Lu Gu Lake 泸沽湖. Women are completely in charge; the society is entirely matrilineal, there is no marriage, and men are allowed only very limited roles. Traditionally Tibetan women practised polyandry – more than one husband. The rationale for this is obscure, especially since up to 20 per cent of men were monks and therefore unable to marry.

---

sleeping platform (炕 *kang*) above the stove. She was the first to be served at mealtimes. As her life lengthened, comforts increased. When she went out, if she had difficulty walking, her sons would carry her on their backs, wheel her in a wheelbarrow or pedal her in a bicycle with a chair attached at the back – a striking feature of street traffic in Beijing in the early 1960s.

Respect reached its height in lavish celebrations for decade birthdays, the 大壽 *dashou*. For the eightieth birthday of the Lady Dowager of the Jia family her sons organised several days of banquets. Gifts poured in. The gifts from the emperor (one of her granddaughters was an imperial concubine) were two sceptres, gold and jade, four bolts of satin, four gold and jade earrings and 500 ounces of silver. Before each banquet the guests presented congratulations and gifts to the old lady; after each one there was an opera performance. By the end of the celebrations the clan was exhausted – and in serious financial difficulties.[5]

The lavishness of the Jia clan could not be matched by other families, except in the ratio between means and expenditures: the rule of thumb was that a family lucky enough to have an elder should spend more than they could afford. There was no choice. The failure to celebrate a *dashou* for a parent or grandparent was sacrilege. In early Republican Beijing the seventieth birthday of Old Mr Wu lasted all day, and included a lavish banquet and entertainment by acrobats, singers, drummers and storytellers. Hundreds of guests came. All the junior members of the family made obeisance (磕頭 *ketou*/kowtow) to the old man.[6] In Fujian a less wealthy rural family honoured its matriarch:[7]

> In the afternoon of New Year's Day, Donglin begged Grandmother Pan to dress herself up in special finery, to receive honour from her descendants, because she had now arrived at seventy years of age. The Chinese always count one's age from the New Year rather than on one's actual birthday. Grandmother Pan put on a fine, sweeping, embroidered coat covering her to her ankles and took her seat in a broad armchair covered with a red spread and placed in the centre of the main hall. Before her another red spread was placed on the floor.
>   [The whole family performed three bows before her in order of age.]
>   Happiness reigned in the house. There was no business today, no school, no farming, no routine household work. This was the perfect day of enjoyment, rest, talk and relaxation, all in a flood of warm sentiment.

Widowhood

The good treatment of old women continued in widowhood. The death of their husband made them more, not less, important in the family; they were now the oldest member. There were restrictions. Widows were not allowed to remarry; they remained dependent on their dead husband's family, on their sons. Even a young widow could have no expectation of remarriage; her fate was to mourn her husband for the rest of her life, to stay with his family and raise her children, never to think of herself. 'Chaste widowhood remained the norm for respectable women' well into the Republic.[8] Very poor widows might marry a man who was too poor to make a proper marriage or who was living in undesirable circumstances. Wu Liantian, from Laiyang 萊陽 (Shandong), had migrated to Manchuria and settled there. He could find no woman from home willing to move to live in the dreadful cold, until he found a poor widow with five children; she *was* willing.[9]

Widows had one consolation for their devotion to the dead husband: if their sons could afford it they rewarded their mothers with the erection of a commemorative arch (牌坊 *paifang*) dedicated to a chaste widow.

In the early Communist period there were millions of war widows. Widows whose husbands had fought in Communist armies had some support: they were given land in the land reform and help with farming. Those whose husbands had died fighting for the Nationalists had no recognition; they received no land, nor did women whose husbands were not dead but in Taiwan or in labour camps. Some did not know whether their husbands were alive or dead; only

---

Box 6.2 Beauty trumps custom

Old Madam Yin, the redoubtable heroine of Ida Pruitt's memoir of Peking life, turned out to have a romantic and unlikely backstory. She was a remarried widow. As a beautiful young girl she helped out in her father's small store in a garrison town. A young officer caught sight of her and fell in love in the twinkling of an eye. She was shyer but still felt a pang of love at first sight. His proposal of marriage to her family was refused. She was married off to a pawnbroker; he married a less beautiful girl. Both had children. Then his wife and her husband conveniently died, the attraction between the two was rekindled, they married, had three more children and lived a long life of love and happiness.[1]

[1] Ida Pruitt, *Old Madam Yin: A Memoir of Peking Life* (Stanford: Stanford University Press, 1979), pp. 80–89.

---

after the Mao Era, in the 1980s, was it possible to find out what might have happened to the missing men.

Waning Respect for Age

The tradition of respect for age was alive in the late Qing and the early Republic, but threatened. Revolution was in the air. Foreign influences were spreading. The kaleidoscope of shifting changes created new worlds into which the elderly fitted less well than the young. The mundane roles of old women in the household and child care were still essential, but respect for age was waning. The threat was not missed by those who doubted the value of modern, often Western, ways. Lin Yutang 林語堂, writing in 1935, presented a stark contrast between the life of an old man in China, an 'imposing figure, dignified and good to look at', loved and respected by his family and society, and that of pathetic old men in the West, 'past the period of their usefulness, trying to get attention by claiming that they were still young in spirit'. Traditional Chinese ways of treating the elderly were 'a thousand times better than all the pensions in the world'.[10]

His good friend Pearl Buck took the same view. She wrote about the villages near her childhood home in Jiangsu, in this rather florid view of respect for the elderly:[11]

How often had I come upon a village, anywhere in China, to find sitting outside the door on a bench at the edge of the threshing floor a comfortably dressed old man or woman, dozing in the sun, pipe in hand, idle without reproach, loved and cared for and made much of, merely because he or she was old. Old people were treasured and no one was afraid to grow old. When an old one spoke the others listened, eager for the wisdom of his accumulated years.

Buck counterposed the happy lives of elderly Chinese to the misery of the elderly in the USA, decrepit and lonely, cast aside and living in old peoples' homes. George Kates, an American who lived in Beijing in the 1930s, agreed with her:[12]

The modern Westerner loses enormously by not comprehending what high ranges, both of appearance and conduct, are available to those who have actually cultivated their later years. This single mistake, and the consequent mismanagement of all our possibilities from middle-age on, puts us worlds apart from those Chinese within the traditional system. We wax happily but wane with ineptitude. The last part of life we tend to abandon, even to despair, whereas for the Chinese it is a summit.

Their views could not have been further away from those of the young Chinese intellectuals (whom Buck detested). They railed against the deadening influence of the old. With the May 4th Movement (1919 on) the young, impatient and contemptuous of the old order, made themselves heard. They demanded autonomy from their elders, especially their fathers and grandfathers.

Some elders, recognising the possibility of disobedience, made comprom-ises. Two young members of the Ling family in Beijing were married in the same year. Both marriages were arranged, but the weddings were different. The first was traditional. Everything was red: bridal sedan chair, costumes, banners, candles, lanterns. Four hundred guests were invited to the groom's house. The second wedding was 'modern'. It took place in a hotel, there were far fewer guests, the groom wore a tailcoat. The bride's dress was pink, halfway between Chinese red and Western white. For the bride the modern touches meant little. She was miserable about marrying a man she had never met.[13]

Compromises were the harbinger of what was to come. After 1928 China had a new national government, a new capital and a sense of progress and modernity. Chiang Kai-shek's wife, Song Meiling, was not cloistered, but was a very public figure.

Optimists went so far as to believe that the family system, the bastion of the past, the enemy of change, was dead. The sociologist Tao Menghe 陶孟和, writing in 1930, had no doubt:[14]

It has been in the past the family that is responsible in very large measure for social peace and order, economic development and perpetuation of the nation. Now the system is crumbling at a rapid rate. Not only huge households are disappearing and are doomed to extinction but even the 'small family' seems to be losing its solidarity and cohesiveness.

Box 6.3 Nanjing

In 1928 the ancient southern capital became the capital of China again. The city on the southern bank of the Yangzi was a more sensible place for the national capital than Beijing. It was a transport hub, it lay in the middle of a rich agricultural region and it had been the capital in the early Ming Dynasty and under the Taiping movement. The Nationalist government decided to make it into a new city, fit for a new nation. Wide new boulevards were cut through the city, meeting at a round point that became the centre of the new city, Xinjiekou 新街口. The boulevards were lined with plane trees. Government and commercial buildings were built to fine art deco designs. Many historic structures had been destroyed when the Taipings were put down in 1864, but those that survived – the city wall, the government complex (総统府 Zongtongfu) – were preserved. The city filled up rapidly with incomers working in government, the army and the universities.

Nanjing flourished only briefly. In 1931 a disastrous flood inundated the lower Yangzi valley. At the same time Japan took over Manchuria. The Nationalist government was forced onto the defensive. The death knell came at the end of 1937. The city was occupied by Japanese forces, who committed the terrible Nanjing massacre. After a few years as the capital of the puppet government (1939–1945) it had less than four years as national capital again (1945–1949) before the new Communist government installed itself in Beijing.

Tao believed that the battle against the old ways had been won:[15]

every young man (or young woman) is now renouncing the dictates of the elders; he is to choose his own life-mate, his own career, his independence in life and will by no means be hampered by any responsibility, such as was incumbent on the dutiful son in former days. This sense of individual freedom has undoubtedly been instilled into the minds of all classes. Divorces, desertions from homes and adventures and exploits of the youth, as are disclosed in modern autobiographical fictions and newspapers from day to day, are but a glimpse of this widespread movement.

Tao's research on Shanghai workers in the cotton industry told a different story. Seventy-three per cent of worker families had only two generations; the small size was due not to the triumph of modern individual freedom but to poverty. Workers could not afford to bring their elders with them; they had to be left in the countryside.[16]

Migration contributed to the waning of respect for age. The early Republic saw major migrations, collectively known as 'village leaving' (離村 licun), made possible by four innovations: the growth of transport networks; the mushrooming of jobs in Manchuria, the new cities and abroad; study in new universities; and recruitment in to the burgeoning armies. Most of the migrants were young men. They left their parents, wives and children at home. Their departure changed family dynamics. For the grandmother her son's absence might not affect her control of the household, but took away his daily reinforcement of her position.

The conflict between new and old, young and old, was made almost irrelevant by the catastrophe that came upon China in 1937. The invasion and the brutal behaviour of Japanese soldiers triggered massive refugee movements. Short-distance movements involved flight from towns and cities into the surrounding countryside. Long-distance movements, which included the government and its civil servants, huge numbers of soldiers, and civilians, took millions into the interior (內地 *neidi*).

Scorched-earth tactics used to slow the onrush of the Japanese armies caused terrible loss of life and mass flight. In June 1938 the government ordered the breaching of the southern dike of the Yellow River, at Huayuankou 花園口 (Henan). The waters of the river poured out over the plains. Over the next few months nearly a million died, and millions more were made refugees. This was one of the greatest disasters in Chinese history, and possibly the worst single disaster of what would later be the Second World War.[17] The Henan famine (1942–1943) produced hundreds of thousands of refugees.

The effect of war on the elderly was catastrophic. The refugees were the strongest – younger men, their wives and older children. The elderly and the very young had to be left behind. The Japanese invasion created a new phenomenon in China – ardent patriotism. It could only be interpreted as an assault on the Chinese people as a whole. Loyalty to the nation rose above loyalty to the family, the glue that stuck traditional society together. The government labelled people who collaborated with the Japanese 'traitors to the Chinese race' (漢奸 *hanjian*).[18] The label could be extended to people who did not flee from the occupiers. This was unfair; many in the occupied areas had no choice but to coexist with the enemy, to survive. Some were too old or too poor to flee. Some had too many family responsibilities; the decision to stay did not mean active collaboration. At the beginning of Lao She's 老舍 novel *Four Generations under One Roof* (四世同堂 *Sishi tongtang*) two brothers had an anguished discussion. The younger brother, a student, was determined to leave the city and join the resistance. The older brother, a teacher, could not abandon his grandfather, his parents, his wife and his two children; all depended on him. The younger brother could go if the older stayed. The older brother told him, 'It's impossible for me [to leave Beiping]. It is better for you to serve the country and for me to serve the older generations.'[19]

The wartime losses suffered by the elderly were grievous – deaths of children, departure of children, destruction of property. They lost the world they knew and the future they had expected. The American sociologist Marion

Levy saw their suffering. He based his work on discussions with Chinese sociologists and on his own observations just after the Japanese defeat:[20]

The present aged of China are almost entirely people who have clung to the 'traditional' ways. They have now reached the stage of life at which, in terms of their own institutional patterns, they have every right to expect a maximum amount of honour, consideration and ease. The aged were used to poverty because so many families lived so close to the margin of subsistence but it was a poverty shared by the family, and the aged had first call on whatever goods there were. Now more and more live into old age only to find abandonment and poverty in isolation. The old age insurance of the 'traditional' family is being wiped out without being replaced.

For young people away from home the war brought liberation. They could make their own lives without the interference of their elders. They were independent, and they relished it. The young political scientist Francis Hsu 許粮光 wrote excitedly in 1942, 'Conscription, war, devastations and new opportunities have combined to drive or induce many young people away from home and shatter the last stronghold of patriarchal authority, that is the financial control over the younger generation.'[21]

More and more young women worked outside the home, some in professional jobs. This is the case of Li Shuping:[22]

Thirty-year-old Li Shu-ping carries on quite successfully both in her career and as a mother. Three years ago (1941) she took the State Examination for judges. It was during her pregnancy. It was difficult for her to move about. Immediately after the examination she went to the hospital to have her baby delivered.

She is now a judge in the district court in Meishan, Szechwan [Sichuan] her home town. She sits in the court every morning –, spends the afternoons in writing court verdicts and goes home to take care of her mother, her husband's mother and her seven children.

War upset social conventions. The status of women with dubious backgrounds improved. In flight from the Japanese they left their past behind. These women included 'forsaken girls, unloved wives, refugee women, slave-girls, prostitutes, oppressed concubines'. They used the turbulence of war to 'break loose from their slavery'.[23]

Wartime freedom for women applied only to the unoccupied areas. In the areas under Japanese occupation the situation of young women was precarious, their freedom more restricted than before the war, not less. Many were confined to their homes, for fear of being kidnapped and sent as sex slaves (I refuse to use the insulting term 'comfort women') to Japanese army brothels.

Survival into old age seemed more of an achievement during the war than it did in peacetime. The celebration of the ninetieth birthday (九十大壽 *jiushi dashou*) of Madame Ma, the mother of General Pai Ch'ung-hsi, in March 1944 came at a grim stage of the war.

Box 6.4 Pai Ch'ung-hsi's mother

Pai Ch'ung-hsi's mother, surnamed Ma, had six children. She was widowed early in life, and fell into poverty. She could only afford to send one son to school; she chose her third son, who showed early signs of the ability that was to take him to the top of the Chinese military. His two elder brothers were sent to be apprentices, while his mother sewed shoes to pay for his school fees. This eventually damaged her eyesight. Pai attributed his later success to his mother's care for him, and to the sacrifices she and his elder brothers made for him. The great party for the old lady's ninetieth birthday was a recognition of all that his mother and his family had done for him.[1]

[1] Pai Hsien-yung 白先勇, *Fu-ch'in yu Min-kuo* 父親與民國 (Father and the Republic) (Taipei: Shibao, 2012), *xia*, pp. 204–223.

There were days of banquets and opera performances in Guilin. China's military elite flew in. Chiang Kai-shek was not there but he sent a substantial donation – 10,000,000 yuan – even taking inflation into account still an enormous sum. Many of her ten grandchildren – three granddaughters and seven grandsons – were there.[24]

The war against Japan ended in 1945; civil war started at once, between the Nationalist government and the Communists. Inflation made the situation even more dire. The painter Qi Baishi 齊白石, in his early eighties in 1945, described how the mounting inflation destroyed the chances of a better life:[25]

My hopes for a better China after the Japanese surrendered were shattered. The national paper currency had become almost waste paper. A small loaf cost two hundred thousand yuan and a dinner out ten million. People hoarded up things instead, and my paintings became one of their objects of hoarding. They came with bundles of banknotes for my paintings and when I looked at the pile of pictures I painted I was a little frightened at the sight. Why should I waste my time and energy in exchange for a lot of useless waste paper which can hardly buy enough to keep me alive. So with a deep sigh I hung up a sign saying 'No orders accepted temporarily'.

By late 1949 it was clear the Communists had won the civil war. Few of the elderly had much enthusiasm for Communism, but few thought of fleeing. Nor did their adult children who *were* leaving think of taking them with them. Flight was difficult, dangerous and expensive, not for decrepit elderly people.

Those few elderly who did flee with their families found themselves in strange worlds. They had little in common with Chinese societies in Taiwan or Hong Kong, and did not speak the local language. They could not earn an

ILLUSTRATION 6.1 Pai Ch'ung-hsi's family

income of their own. They were dependent on their children. They seemed
useless – except in relation to their grandchildren.'

A Long Aberration

For the three decades after 1949 respect for age was eclipsed in Mainland
China. The watchwords were 'new' and 'young'. Social engineering decreed
that the family was to be replaced by the collective. Li Jie describes what
happened in Shanghai: 'The Maoist organization of individuals in to collectives
transcended and divided families, handling them like machine parts that could
be dismantled and rearranged.'[26]

Class warfare flourished; the poor and dispossessed came to the fore; the rich
went to the bottom of the social hierarchy. Class status was inherited. It could work
in different directions. The elderly of the old elite became liabilities for their
families; they condemned their dependents to a bad status. Elderly peasants or
workers could help their children and grandchildren to a bright future, as descendants of formerly oppressed people. A class designation was assigned to every
family. In mass meetings members of the old elite were denounced. Some were

ILLUSTRATION 6.2 Qi Baishi at ninety

executed, almost all were expropriated, and their children and grandchildren were labelled one of the 'Five Black Categories' (黑五类 *heiwulei*). Those already committed to the Party were exempt, but had to accept the fate of their families. The father of Zhao Ziyang 赵紫阳, premier of the PRC, was executed as a landlord; his son could not defend him, the ultimate betrayal of filial piety. The intergenerational transfer of class status oppressed all those not born into the lowest levels of society until the beginnings of reform in the late 1970s.

The Party waged war on religion, superstition and so-called feudal practices. The assaults bore down heavily on old women. Many seemed living embodiments of feudalism and the cruel past; their bound feet were a constant reminder of the old society that the Party rejected. Their devotion to the deities who had helped them through the tribulations of life was suspect. Marx's pronouncement that religion was 'the opium of the people' was transplanted to China. Temples and shrines were taboo, some torn down, others turned to secular uses – schools, clinics, Party offices.

The CCP had no specific role for grandmothers. The women's movement was headed by the quite elderly Song Qingling and Deng Yingchao 邓颖超, the

---

Box 6.5 Five Black Categories

The Five Black Categories (黑五类 *heiwulei*) of the population were designated early in the Mao Era. The labels still strike cold fear. They condemned those who were labelled and their families to long-term discrimination and persecution, in descending order: execution, imprisonment, dispatch to remote border regions, expropriation of property, denial of education, denial of health care, denial of jobs. The labelling was often arbitrary, made by Party committees or members, often in secret. There was no appeal against a label.

Dizhu 地主 – landlord. Labelled during land reform.

Funong 富农 – rich peasant. As above.

Fan geming 反革命 – counterrevolutionary – people associated with the Nationalists.

Huai fenzi 坏分子 – bad elements: bandits, religious sectarians, sexually promiscuous people, drug users, petty criminals.

Youpai 右派 – Rightists. Labelled during the Anti-Rightists Movement (1957–1958)

---

wife of Zhou Enlai, both childless, surrogate 'grannies to the nation', without grandchildren of their own.

The Party proclaimed potential equality between men and women. Mao Zedong's much-quoted phrase was '*women may hold up half the sky*'

妇女能顶半边天

Funü neng ding banbiantian

It was a prediction rather than a promise. Mao was talking about young women. For older women the issue was not to shape a new world, but to survive. In the new world old people were too close to a discarded past. They had little to offer their children. Land reform and confiscation of the property of the rich took away the prospect of inheritance; the old system of partible inheritance, in which each son was eligible for a portion of his parents' property, disappeared. The burden of care of the elderly did not disappear; it remained the responsibility of the sons, as a publication in the Great Leap Forward made clear. 'Homes of respect for the aged' were only for those without sons:[27]

People's communes in various places have set up 'homes of respect for the aged'. People who are too old to work and have no families to support them can spend the rest of their life in these homes in happiness. The old people say that in the past if you had no son to support you in your old age life was indeed bitter and lonely. But now we may settle down to spend the rest of our lives in happiness in the homes. With or without a son life is as sweet as nectar.

The duty of most elderly was to be useful as long as they could, then fade into gentle senility, passively smiling and expressing their gratitude for living in the new era.

The Party gave recognition to a few elderly women, the mothers and widows of revolutionary martyrs, presented as paragons of virtue, because they had cared for the children of the heroes. They had no names. The mother of Peng Pai 彭湃, revolutionary hero, was known only as 'Auntie Peng' (not even her own surname). She was the concubine of a wealthy landlord. She helped her three sons make revolution. She personally burnt the land deeds of the Peng family. Two of her sons died at the hands of the Nationalists. She fled to Hong Kong with her daughter-in-law and grandchildren. After 1949 she became a socialist heroine, presiding over her sons' legacy – and a happy grandmother:[28]

And around her are grandchildren who are carrying on earnestly and determinedly the work that still has to be done – the task of building their beloved motherland into a great industrialized nation in which the richness of production, science and culture will be enjoyed by all. Remembering this Auntie Peng feels that her life in its late years is full of warmth and happiness.

Parents of senior officials did well. After 1949 the grandmother of Mu Anping went to live with her eldest son, a senior cadre, in Beijing; she looked after her grandchildren, in a luxury she had never dreamt of.[29] Party members had to be careful about reverence for their elderly. The decade birthdays of the 'golden treasures' of the family were now 'feudal'. Liao Haifang, mother of five sons, was praised for her refusal to let them give her a seventieth-birthday feast: socialism had pre-empted the need to celebrate old age:[30]

Under the old society I suffered to bring you up so that I should not starve in my old age, [but] I have often attended political study sessions on the family and I've come to understand many of the reasons behind it, and my thinking has altered. Provided you obey the Party and Chairman Mao and strive hard to build socialism, this will make me much happier than a birthday feast or feeding me with fish and meat every day.

In the Mao Era the elderly were shifted into the background. They bore the brunt of the famine that came after the Great Leap Forward, the Great Three-Year Famine (三年大饥荒 sannian da jihuang). This is an account from a village in Sichuan:[31]

People were dying at such a fast rate . . . no one had the capacity or energy to care for anyone else . . . Both of my grandmothers died of starvation. Of course my parents were sad about their deaths. But in those days, we had nothing, how could we care for the dead? . . . In those days every family lost a few people. By 1961 most families in our village had only two or three people left. If the situation had gone on for another two years, most people would have succumbed in the end. There would be no one left to care for anyone.

The famine was followed by the madness of the Cultural Revolution (1966–1976). Mao Zedong's edicts drove young people to 'destroy the four olds':

破四旧

po si jiu

The 'four olds' were customs, culture, habits and ideas. The Red Guards, full of zeal and self-righteousness, believed devoutly that whatever they did, however violent, was justified:

革命无罪 造反有理

Geming wuzui zaofan youli

In revolution there is no crime, to rebel is justified

Red Guards roamed the land, searching for 'feudal remnants'. They destroyed temples, shrines, tombs, graves. They burned books and pictures. They attacked individuals whom they identified as 'enemies'. The elderly, as embodiments of the Four Olds, were in danger. Many were attacked; many were driven to suicide. In 1967 Lao She (aged sixty-seven), the great chronicler of Beijing, filled his pockets with stones and walked to Taiping Lake in the west of the city.

The Elderly in the Reform Era

In the early 1980s, after ten years of the turmoil of the Cultural Revolution, an exhausted country sought a new order, one that continues to today. It has been necessary to bury the recent past – with the exception that Mao Zedong is still on the currency (though many now live in a cashless world) and his portrait still hangs on Tiananmen. The Communist Party is still in control.

By contrast to the previous decades, the Reform Era has been a good time for many elderly Chinese. After so much upheaval they live in relative tranquility, in a world where money is king; the Cult of Money has replaced the Cult of Mao. Some elderly people have made their own fortunes in the Reform Era. One of the first people to set up a private restaurant in Beijing, in 1980, was Liu Guixian 刘桂仙. She turned one room of her house in a *hutong* just south of the Museum of Fine Arts into a tiny restaurant. It soon grew in size and reputation; it had a shabby chic that allowed Liu to make enough money to buy houses for herself and her husband and for each of their five adult children.[32]

Such success stories of elderly entrepreneurs who benefit their children are rare. More common are self-sufficient elderly and those who need support from their children. The children are expected to provide this, both by the revived Confucian tradition and by law. The shift in family composition, as a result of rising life expectancy and of the One Child per Family policy, means that the demands are heavier. The 4–2–1 syndrome (四二一综合症 *sieryi zonghezheng*) refers to a family with four grandparents, two parents and one child.

The ideal situation for the elderly is to hold a state pension, and to have several gainfully employed adult children who provide love and emotional support. This situation is not uncommon. A good pension is a perk that almost automatically goes with Communist Party membership. It is almost axiomatic that the 90,000,000-plus members will be in good enough pre-retirement employment to guarantee a generous pension. For many more people pension coverage is limited or non-existent. For urban residents, retirement income used to be the responsibility of work units (单位 *danwei*); pensions were paid out of unit funds. People retired, expecting their unit to provide them with housing, medical care and a small income. In the early Reform Era this seemed possible. A small survey of eighty elderly people in a street in Guangzhou in 1990 found that 75 per cent had some pension income. Though the sums were small the pensioners did not complain; half of them lived with their children.[33] So long as old people kept their expectations low, and had dutiful children, life was fine. Not for long. Work units started to disappear, privatised or bankrupt. With them went the previous benefits. Many urban elderly were left without a pension or medical coverage. Their children were laid off (下岗 *xiagang*) from what had seemed secure jobs and were not able to help. The demise of units coincided with the development of a real-estate market and the sale of unit apartments. Housing security was gone. Those who could afford it could buy their own place, but this was cold comfort for elderly people without savings. Some elderly people were able in the 1980s to reclaim real property expropriated in the 1950s, but this was a long and difficult process, demanding determination and stamina.

The pension shortfall is recognised by the government. The Central Committee determined in October 2015 that at an unspecified later date all old people would be eligible for a basic pension. The date is now more precise. In March 2021, Premier Li Keqiang 李克强 announced at the National Peoples' Conference that 95 per cent of the elderly will have access to a basic pension over the next five years. The cost and the complexity of creating a system are daunting. Some people have difficulty proving their age – they were born before birth certificates were used. For many of today's elderly their pensions are their children. For those without support from their children the situation is dire. From time to time 'care in the community', the idea that neighbours will take care of those in need, is suggested; the slogan is 'Distant relatives are not as good as close neighbours':

Box 6.6 Ye Jiaying 葉嘉瑩

Ye Jiaying was born to an elite Manchu family in Beijing. During the Japanese occupation, the family's large compound was expropriated. When the Nationalists returned to power in 1945, the compound was seized as enemy property. In 1949 Ye and her father moved to Taiwan and eventually to Canada, where she had a successful career at the University of British Columbia. Her father died in Canada. Under his will, his daughter inherited all his property. In the early 1980s she was surprised to learn from the Beijing city authorities that she had inherited the family compound, in which lived nearly ninety people, some of them her relatives. The kicker was that she had to provide housing for all the people living there to gain possession. She dealt tirelessly with relatives and officials, but eventually the property was expropriated for the widening of Changanjie.

远亲不如近邻

Yuanqin buru jinlin

This optimistic idea is no more viable in China than it has been in Western countries that have tried it, for the simple reason that there is often no caring community. Some elderly people may find a place in temples, monasteries or nunneries, the traditional places where those unable to fend for themselves were traditionally cared for, but these refuges are scarce, as are government-run facilities. In June 2015 the Beijing city government announced that a 450-bed home run by the city would be turned over to elderly people in need whose only child was dead, 失独 *shidu*, a contraction of 失去独生子女 *shiqu dusheng zinü*, mainly couples whose only child was born after the start of the One Child per Family policy. There were almost 5,000 such people in the city already waiting for care.[34]

The market economy does look after the affluent elderly, the 'silver consumers'. Children with resources may hire a *baomu* to look after their elderly parents. Expensive private care homes flourish. The Golden Heights retirement home in Beijing offers care for US$2,000 a month (a fraction of what deluxe elder care would cost in North America). Psychological persuasion is applied; elderly parents are advised to move to homes 'rather than live with their children to avoid resentment and blaming them for not taking care of them'.[35] Cheaper homes provide poorer care. Their workers endure 'three highs and three lows: high turnover, high workload, high age; low status, low salary, low education'.[36]

The assumption that the young and middle-aged will support their elders is under threat. Adult children no longer feel obliged to live with their parents.

Family division is accepted. The percentage of rural elderly living with their children has declined, dramatically, from 70 per cent in 1991 to 49 per cent in 2006.[37] Dividing the family was a blow to the older generation, who had assumed that in their old age they would live in a multi-generation family. In better-off rural areas, so many families have built new houses that division is simple – the elderly stay in the old house, the young ones move into the new house. Division may even appeal to the elderly, so long as their children make financial contributions to their welfare. Living with adult children is not always a paradise. There may be constant conflicts. This is an elderly man in a village in Hubei:[38]

I now have much more freedom and some cash too. I have some indulgences. I like to smoke and have two drinks every day. But when I was living with my son's family they were very reluctant to spend money on me. We would quarrel over these matters endlessly and I often ended up not getting my cigarettes and drinks, Now living separately from them, I can get some cash from the chickens I raise and now I can smoke and drink whenever I want.

The state makes the formal obligations of family support clear. Grandparents are protected by law. Children and grandchildren have a duty of care for their parents and grandparents. This is Article 28 of the 1980 Marriage Law:

Grandparents or maternal grandparents who can afford it shall have the duty to bring up their grandchildren or maternal grandchildren who are minors and whose parents are dead or have no capacity of bringing them up. Grandchildren or maternal grandchildren who can afford it shall have the duty to support their grandparents or maternal grandparents whose children are dead or have no means to support them.

The act imposes responsibilities up and down the generational ladder. It requires the elderly to care for the young in the same way that the young must care for the elderly. It goes against the traditional pattern of family relationships in one significant way: it applies equally to paternal grandparents and maternal grandparents. And despite the generous let-out clause 'those who can afford it', responsibility of the young for the old is clear.

The responsibility is reinforced in the 1985 Inheritance Law. If a deceased person dies without a will the law discriminates in the division of property between children who cared for their dead parents and those who did not. The former are entitled to a much larger share than the latter, who might get nothing.[39] This is a heavy message about obligation to parents. Even sterner provisions were included in the 1996 Law to Protect the Rights and Interests of the Elderly (老年人权益保障法 laonianren quanyi baozhang fa). The obligations of children to their elderly (over-sixty) parents were set out in detail; they include providing housing, living costs and health care. The law demanded respect for the elderly; Article IV forbids 'discriminating against, insulting, maltreating or forsaking the elderly'. The aim was crystal clear – and implied that the elderly might be in danger of maltreatment. The looming question is to what extent the laws are upheld, and what recourse the elderly have if their children are negligent.

The legal demands are augmented with emotive, inspirational slogans:

尊老爱老助老

Zunlao ailao zhulao

Respect the elderly, love the elderly, help the elderly

The middle-aged are urged to practise a new code of care for their parents. The New Twenty-Four Filial Exemplars (新二十四孝 *xin ershisi xiao*) differ greatly from the traditional tales of heroic and sometimes extreme efforts by sons on behalf of their parents. The new ones are a list of fairly mundane instructions on how to treat elderly parents.

Box 6.7 The New Twenty-Four Filial Exemplars

These are a radically revised version of the Yuan Dynasty Filial [Behaviours] (see Chapter 4). They contain no excessive acts of devotion.

1. 经常带着爱人子女回家 *Jingchang daizhe airen zinü hujia*	Often take your spouse and children home
2. 节假日尽量与父母共度 *Jiejiari jinliang yu fumu gongdu*	Spend festivals and holidays with your parents
3. 为父母举办生日宴会 *Wei fumu juban shengri yanhui*	Put on birthday banquets for your parents
4. 亲自给父母做饭 *Qinzi wei fumu zuofan*	Cook for your parents yourself
5. 每周给父母打个电话 *Meizhou gei fumu dage dianhua*	Phone your parents once a week
6. 父母的零花钱不能少 *Fumu de linghuaqian buneng shao*	Spending money for your parents should be generous
7. 为父母建立'关爱卡' *Wei fumu jianli 'guanaika'*	Set up a 'concern card' (preloaded debit card)
8. 仔细聆听父母的往事 *Zixi lingting fumu wangshi*	Listen to your parents' reminiscences carefully
9. 教父母学会上网 *Jiao fumu xuehui shangwang*	Teach your parents how to get on to the Net
10. 经常为父母拍照 *Jingchang wei fumu paizhao*	Take photographs for your parents often
11. 对父母的爱要说出口 *Dui fumude ai yao shuochukou*	Talk openly to your parents about your love for them
12. 打开父母的心结 *Dakai fumude xinjie*	Delve into your parents' preoccupations

Box 6.7 (Cont.)

(cont.)

13. 支持父母的业余爱好 *Zhizhi fumude yeyu aihao*	Encourage your parents to take up hobbies
14. 支持单身父母再婚 *Zhizhi danshen fumu caijie*	Support a widowed parent in remarrying
15. 定期带父母做体检 *Dingqi dai fumu zuo ticha*	Take your parents for regular physical check-ups
16. 为父母够买合适的保险 *Wei fumu goumai heshi de baoxian*	Buy appropriate insurance for your parents
17. 常跟父母做交心的沟通 *Chang gen fumu zuo jiaoxin de goutong*	Make frequent emotional connections with parents
18. 带父母一起出席重要的活动 *Dai fumu yiqi zhuxi zhongyao de huodong*	Take your parents to important activities
19. 带父母参观你工作的地方 *Dai fumu canguan ni gongzuo de difang*	Take your parents to visit your workplace
20. 带父母去旅行或故地重游 *Dai fumu qu luxing huo gudi zhong you*	Take your parents on trips or to their old home
21. 和父母一起锻炼身体 *He fumu yiqi duanlian shenti*	Take exercise with your parents
22. 适当参与父母的活动 *Shidang canyu fumu de huodong*	As convenient take part in your parents' activities
23. 陪父母拜访他们的老朋友 *Pei fumu baifang tamen de lao pengyou*	Take your parents to visit their old friends
24. 陪父母看一场老电影 *Pei fumu kan yichang lao dianying*	Take your parents to see an old film

The obligations to parents are without term. Another Confucian saying may have new meaning. There is such a misdeed as living too long:

老而不死

lao er busi

To be old and not die

7   Grandfathers

We have had little to say so far about grandfathers. This is because traditionally and today they play lesser roles in the lives of their grandchildren than grandmothers do, which is a universal pattern.

In the past, men were fathers in their early twenties, grandfathers in their forties. Polygamous men could father children for decades; their youngest children would be younger than their oldest grandchildren. The painter Qi Baishi was in his late seventies in 1940. He had several wives, six sons and six daughters and more than forty grandchildren. Most of them were dependent on him. He lived in chronic anxiety about how he would feed so many mouths, especially since he refused to sell his paintings to the Japanese occupiers of Beijing: he locked his gate and did not go out (閉門不出 *bimen bu chu*).[1]

The number of grandchildren mattered to grandfathers: the more there were, the greater the proof of his success. Rich or poor, a man felt great pride in having grandsons to carry on the family line. Old Wu, in Beijing in the early years of the Republic, developed a 'grandfather-mania'; he took his first grandson in his arms and walked out to see his friends in the local tea house. The outings guaranteed compliments on the baby boy and fuelled his passion for 我孫子 *wo sunzi*, 'my grandson'.[2]

The relationship between grandfather and grandson was reciprocal. This is Lin Yaohua's 林耀華 description of how much a grandfather meant to a boy:[3]

When Dunglin [Huang Donglin] was fourteen, the old man died. It was the first time the boy had experienced grief. He was very much shaken by his grandfather's death. When alive, the old man used to take him to visit friends and relatives, to walk with him across the fields, and to tell him legends and folk stories. The ties between them were very close. The boy learned a great deal of life and of old tales from the old man, and the old man leaned on him as a constant companion, young as he was.

An even greater happiness was to have great-grandchildren, to have 'four generations under one roof'. Lao She gave a lyrical description of a happy old gentleman:[4]

In 1937 . . . Old Grandfather Ch'ien [Qian] was already seventy-five years old. He had long ago given up concerning himself with household affairs. Now his most important work was to water the pots of flowers in the courtyard, tell the stories of olden times, give food to and change the water for the canary in the cage, and, holding the hands of the great-grandson and the great-granddaughter, to wander very slowly out onto the main streets and to visit the Hu Kuo Ssu [Huguosi 護國寺], the Temple of National Protection.

His life was tranquil, interesting, undemanding – the reward for achieving old age.

A Quiet Life

As older women came into their own, as grandmothers and household managers, old men moved into quiescence. By the reversal of two characters, they were shown respect; they were no longer addressed by the casual Old Chen 老陳 (*Lao Chen*) but by the honorific Chen Lao 陳老 (*Venerable Chen*). This was not an absolute rule; some men were never called by the casual term – many did not achieve the honorific.

Old men did not try to look young. They wore padded clothes, the trousers tight to the ankle, often year-round, for fear of feeling cold. They grew wispy beards, which they would stroke gently. They looked dignified and slightly aloof.

The image has survived. ILLUSTRATION 7.1 shows the great calligrapher Li Zhongzheng in his nineties, a few years ago.

It was expected that old men would give up vice – prostitutes, gambling, opium. Those were the activities of younger men. Old men engaged in gentle activities – calligraphy, *taiqi,* keeping birds. They hung out with

---

Box 7.1 Grey hair

Attitudes towards hairstyles for old men have changed over time. When men wore queues, hair colour hardly mattered; the head was shaved and the colour of the hair in the queue was uncertain. What did matter was the colour of the beard: white. The beard should be long and wispy, allowing the old man to stroke his beard with studied reflection. Full beards were taboo for men of any age, associated with bandits, known as redbeards (红胡子 *honghuzi*). After 1911 queues were cut off, but wispy beards continued for old men.

After 1949 Communist Party leaders set a new style: a full head of glistening black hair. The aim, to give the appearance of youth, was no more convincing than the peroxide golden locks of Donald Trump and Boris Johnson. There are now cracks in the black. Though supreme leader Xi Jinping has thick, glossy, black hair on top, there are hints of grey on the sides. Several leading men have gone grey recently. Liu He 刘鹤, the chief trade negotiator with the USA, has a head of silver hair, while the PRC ambassador to the USA, Cui Tiankai 崔天凯, has snowy white hair.

ILLUSTRATION 7.1 Li Zhongzheng

other elderly men to chat (聊聊天 *liaoliao tian*). They hoped through a moderate and quiet life to reach an advanced age.

Elderly men enjoyed tea houses. They sipped tea or wine, ate snacks and gossiped with other old men. Tea houses were like English pubs, but with less serious drinking. Lao She's play *Tea House* (茶館 *Chaguan*) portrayed the warmth and humour of a Beijing tea house. They were noisy, informal places, centres for gossip and rumour. In the Mao Era they were closed down. They have been revived in the Reform Era, though the crowded, lively neighbourhoods in which they were located have gone and bars (coffee or alcohol) compete for customers.

One of the passions of old men was keeping songbirds. This is Chiang Yee's grandfather in the 1920s:[5]

Grandfather Chih-kao, a kind and gentle person, had a passion for birds. He had a lark and two song birds, which he took to a small wooded area near Rouge Hill every morning. Yee often accompanied his grandfather on the excursions. With a dragon-head cane in one hand he would walk slowly telling his baobao [treasure] wonderful stories about birds. When they reached the wooded area Grandfather met with other bird lovers. Their birds then joined with scores of others, chirping tunefully in cages suspended on trees.

The birds lived in elegant cages, furnished with porcelain dishes for water and seed. The cages were covered at night with dark blue padded covers. Their owners talked to the birds, allowed them out to fly around indoors, prepared special foods for them. They took them out for morning walks, to the place where local bird fanciers gathered. The old men would hang up their cages on a branch or set them down close to other cages so that the birds could chat to each other, while their owners chatted to other owners.

When I lived in Beijing in the 1980s I took my dog Lunch – who got his name from where my daughters bought him as a puppy, at a meat stall – out for walks in the early morning. This was a happy time of day for the old men who lived in the little streets close to the diplomatic compound Jianwai gongyu 建外公寓. They strolled around with their cages, chatting to each other, talking to their birds, swinging their cages vigorously. They called out to Lunch. Lunch could be fierce or friendly. He barked at the uniformed guards on our compound, but not at the old men.

Birds were taken by their owners to tea houses, to show off their skills as singers:[6]

The customers sit, engage in conversation with fellow frequenters, watch their pet birds and feed them when in season with live grasshoppers or cicadas, from which the wings and the legs have been pulled off and which are carried in little gauze containers. When these birds are well-nourished and feel good, the proud owners will be entertained by their songsters while covetous fellows cock their ears to listen.

Birdsong was what fanciers most valued; if a bird failed to sing it was replaced. Bird markets were popular places in cities and towns; birds changed hands for considerable sums. The elderly sellers showed off their birds as proudly as they would their grandchildren. Another kind of bird was kept for the eerie sound that came from the whistles as they flew around the city from their rooftop roosts. These were homing pigeons. Their whistles were one of the most evocative sounds of old Beijing.

Old men kept other singing creatures: crickets. They were housed in bamboo or wooden containers, some small enough to keep in a pocket. Old men kept them for the delicate sounds they made. The devotees of cricket fighting were a subset of younger men, who took their crickets to bitter, often deadly, fights, with intense gambling attached. Cricket fighting was like cockfighting in the West – nasty, cruel and deadly.

Teachers

Literate Chinese grandfathers played a major role in their grandsons' education. The lofty rationale was to help the boys succeed in the imperial examination system, to 'become dragons'.

望子成龍

wang zi chenglong

They introduced the boys to calligraphy, teaching strokes and stroke order. The child's first efforts were sketched on a sheet of sand with a stick, or, with water and a large brush, on a tiled floor. Mistakes could be swept away, or allowed to evaporate. The teaching inculcated Confucian values: respect from younger to older, discipline, love of the written word. The ravishing film about the great calligrapher Qi Gong 启功, *The Calligraphy Master* (Beijing, 2015), shows his grandfather, who had passed the highest level of the examinations, teaching the boy. Fu Sinian 傅斯年, a giant of Republican culture, had a traditional education at home, in which the Confucian values were instilled. His teacher was his grand-father, a graduate of the examination system: 'All that constituted my world of thought was from the teachings of my grandfather. He taught me loyalty (忠 *zhong*), filial piety (孝 *xiao*), integrity (節 *jie*) and uprightness (義 *yi*).'[7]

Fu's classical education was followed by a modern education at school and at Peking University. Like other intellectuals of his generation, he was steeped in both traditional and modern culture. He went on to become the leading aca-demic entrepreneur of his generation, founding the Institute of History and Philology 史語所, and spearheading work on excavating China's ancient past at Anyang 安陽 (Henan), then Changde 章德.

Grandfathers took ancestry very seriously. They taught their grandchildren about their forebears and in the telling created the continuity between the ancestors and the grandchildren. They were the keepers of family history. Every family aspired to keep a genealogy, listing the past generations of the family (家譜 *jiapu*). A group of families, a clan, would compile a clan geneal-ogy (族譜 *zupu*).

The tradition of compiling genealogies continues today, after a long break in the Mao Era, when genealogies were burnt by Red Guards as symbols of feudalism. The most famous genealogy, of the Kong family (孔子世家譜 *Kongzi shi jiapu*), the descendants of Confucius, is being updated by a scholarly committee. It lists almost eighty generations.

Compiling a genealogy is an appropriate task for a retired man. Harry Chin, a Vancouver florist, gave himself this task when he retired. He traced his family back to 2318 BCE. The first named ancestor is dated to 1066. The twenty-ninth generation, born in Canada, have the character 加 *jia* for Canada in their Chinese names; since none of them read Chinese, the genealogy is bilingual.[8]

Family records were the only proof of an individual's existence. There were no government birth or death records until recently. There were no baptismal records or birth certificates, the vital documents to confirm existence in the West. My teacher Jerome Ch'en had difficulty with Canada Pensions when he reached pensionable age because he could not prove that he had been born in Chengdu in 1919.

Favourites

It was assumed that a grandfather would prefer the sons of his sons over the sons' daughters, and certainly over his daughters' children. The sons' sons (孫子 *sunzi*) were the ones who carried on the family surname, the ones who would eventually share the family's property. They had to be prepared for their future responsibilities.

Favouring grandsons did not entirely cut out granddaughters or children of daughters. A particular personality might attract an old man. Location made a difference. During the Resistance War family configurations changed dramatically, as people fled from the invasion or moved into the foreign-controlled areas for safety. Yang Jiang's 楊绛 daughter Qian Yuan 錢瑗 spent her early childhood with her maternal grandparents in Shanghai. Her grandfather devoted himself to the little girl. In her father's (Qian Zhongshu 錢鍾書) family a more traditional atmosphere prevailed. The grandparents were entirely focussed on the 'precious grandson' (寶具孫子 *baobei sunzi*), the little emperor of the Qian family (錢家的小皇帝 *Qian Jia de xiao huangdi*).[9] Writing sixty years later, the child's mother still felt a tinge of resentment, that her own precious child had been overshadowed.

Naming

Paternal grandfathers were responsible for choosing the names of their grandchildren, a serious business that required long contemplation and discussion with friends. It was assumed that new parents were not in a fit state to name their children.

Names were not chosen from a roster of names (Robert, Mary, Michael), nor were infants named after relatives, living or dead. The choice of name was an opportunity to show erudition, family pride and (later) loyalty. Generation names were set out decades or even centuries in advance, in a system called 排行 *paihang*. Every boy of a generation shared one character of a two-character given name; the other character denoted the individual. Zhang Zuolin 張作霖, the overlord of Manchuria in the early Republic, had eight sons; all had the character 學 *xue* as the first character of their name.

Naming practices changed in the Mao Era; names had to be politically acceptable. Grandfathers were cut out of the naming process; there was no tolerance for feudal references and names had to suit the new era. The character 紅 *hong* was a godsend; red was lucky in traditional culture and uplifting in Communist thinking. Other 'good' names turned out badly. In the heyday of

Table 7.1 *Revolutionary name changes*

Old			New		
Shebao	社宝	Co-operative treasure	Shedong	社东	Co-operative east
Shezhu	社珠	Co-operative pearl	Shefang	社方	Co-operative place
Shezhen	社珍	Co-operative precious	Shehong	社红	Co-operative red

Sino-Soviet friendship the three children of a Beijing family had the first character 'friend': *Yousu* 友苏 (Friend of the USSR), *Youhua* 友华 (Friend of China), *Youkang* 友康 (Friend of Health). The first child's name was later anathema, after the Sino-Soviet Split. Many children were named for socialist achievements. The economist Hu Angang 胡鞍钢, born in 1953, must have been named for the Anshan Steel Works 鞍山钢铁厂. The Chen family had to rename their children, born in the 1950s. One half of their names was 'progressive'; the character *she*, 'co-operative'; the other half was bourgeois, and had to go. Table 7.1 shows the old and new names.

Together the second parts of the new names spelt out 'Dongfanghong' 东方红, 'The East is red', the anthem of the Cultural Revolution.[10] Wendy Deng Murdoch went the other way, from revolutionary to anodyne. She was born in 1968, at the most extreme stage of the Cultural Revolution, and named Deng Wenge 邓文革, 'Cultural Revolution'. She later changed her name to Wendi 文迪, 'Cultural Stride'. By the time of her marriage to media tycoon Rupert Murdoch she was Wendy.

Accoutrements of Old Men

There is a whole range of beautiful items made for old men. These included canes with elaborate handles carved from precious woods, pipes with jade mouthpieces and pieces of jade to be turned round and round in the hand. Then there were the accoutrements of calligraphy, the four treasures of the scholar's room (文房四寶 *wenfang sibao*): brushes, ink, paper and ink stones. These were as rare, beautiful and elaborate as a man's income allowed. Elaborately carved wooden brush pots held brushes. Seals were collected, and the dishes that held the sticky ink. The stone from which seals were carved mattered; some were expensive – the red-streaked 'chicken blood stone' (鸡血石 *jixueshi*) pieces were exorbitant – but what mattered most was who did the carving, ideally a friend.

Antique and curio shops were haunts of old men. Visits were long-drawn-out, allowing time for tea and conversation. Shop owners knew their customers well; they would let them know when new pieces came in. The business died in the Mao Era, when antiques were 'bourgeois'. Antique collecting is now revived, though in a more impersonal way, often online. Major treasures are sold not in stores but by auctions run by international houses such as Christie's and Sotheby's.

New Grandfathers

In the Mao Era the burdens on grandmothers increased. Young parents left their children with their own parents for six days of the week, or were away for long periods (see Chapter 9). Through these change the roles of urban grandfathers altered only slightly. They no longer enjoyed respect for age, but they did not take on household duties.

Grandfathers in refugee families in Hong Kong and Taiwan did have a new role, the connection between the new place and the old home. They helped their grandchildren through confusion and upheaval by steeping them in stories of the past. Adeline Yen Mah, whose family fled from Shanghai in 1949, found her Yeye 爺爺 a comfort in the strange world of Hong Kong. He distracted her from the insecurity of her childhood not by reassuring her directly, but by taking her back to a distant past:[11]

He told me stories from the Legends of the Three Kingdoms, accompanying the tales with snatches of Chinese opera when he was in a good mood. He taught me the magic and mystery hidden in many Chinese characters, illustrating them with brilliant examples which filled me with wonder and delight.

She comforted him too. He was living through the loss of everything he had in Tianjin and Shanghai. He knew no English or Cantonese; he was too old to make a new business. His world was lost.

In the Reform Era old men have come to share some domestic tasks that were once exclusively women's. The changes may seem small. Li Fengsheng 李逢生 described proudly how much he did for his family. Every morning at 5.30 he got up, left his daughter's apartment, shared with his wife, son-in-law and grandson, and went to buy a bottle of the freshest milk for the precious boy. This and going to buy vegetables later on in the day was the sum total of his contribution to the household; the housework was done by his wife. The rest of his day was given over to chatting with his friends and playing cards.[12]

Rural grandfathers have less time to relax in the new age. The economy of a rural family has changed dramatically since the large-scale migrations began. In a family whose young people are not at home the burden of fieldwork falls on the old men. Some are capable of doing this, with help from their wives and grandchildren, or by working in co-operation with neighbours. Others are too old or decrepit to do much. Their frailty produces a secondary migration. Peasants from really poor parts of China move into areas where the young men are gone. I saw this in a beautiful seaside village in Fujian. Elderly local people and their grandchildren lived on the ground floors of new five-storey homes, built with the proceeds of their children's work away from home. The upper storeys of the new houses were empty, waiting for the middle generation to return. Behind these houses, the old village houses, single-storey red brick houses, were filled with men and women from Guangxi and Guizhou. The men work in the fields, the women in a small clothing factory. There was little contact between the two groups living in the same village. The old people spoke only Minnan 闽南 dialect, the people from the interior only their own versions of south-west Mandarin (西南官话 *xinan guanhua*).

The Perils of Polygamy

One salacious side of the lives of men, often grandfathers, was polygamy. It was once thought to have been outlawed but is now around again in a variant form. Taking a concubine was a common practice for Chinese men. Marriage was for life, for men and women, but monogamy only for women.

别抱琵琶

biebao pipa

This phrase (literally 'embrace another lute') carries the veiled attraction of polygamy. The formal justification was the need to produce sons, to continue the family line. A wife who produced only daughters or only one son was likely to experience the pain of her husband bringing another woman into her household. Sexual desire lurked behind this justification, especially if the principal wife *had* produced sons. The concubine would be younger than the wife, chosen by the husband for her looks rather than her social status – a girl he had met in the flower world or a servant in his own household.

There were safeguards for the first wife. She retained her superior status in the family. A concubine's status was lower, though her youth and beauty might give her power over the husband, which increased when she gave birth to sons. The concubine too had safeguards. She and her children were members of the household, her children bore the family surname.

Dynastic ambitions played a part. Important families needed many children to cement their social and economic positions through marriages. The more children there were, the more advantageous marriages could be made. Zhang Zuolin had eight sons and six daughters, from a wife and five concubines, born from 1898 to 1925. The centre of his mansion in Shenyang was a large, rectangular covered courtyard. Across the top of the courtyard was his sumptuous chamber. On either long side were three smaller apartments for the ladies. One would spend the night with the small but sprightly Zhang. He married his children to the children of supporters and important local people. Anna Chao Pai is the child of Zhang Huaidong, third daughter of Zhang Zuolin, and the son

Box 7.2 Farewell my concubine

Concubines have often been associated with romantic loves, the love denied in arranged marriage. The most famous example is the doomed love of Xiang Yu 項羽 in the second century BC. In the battle to set up a new dynasty after the fall of the Qin, the hero of civility, leader of the state of Chu 楚, was defeated by the crude Liu Bang 劉邦 of the state of Han 漢. In defeat Xiang Yu says farewell to his beloved concubine 虞姬. She kills herself after singing a desolate song.

漢兵已略地
四面楚歌聲
大王義氣盡
賤妾何聊生

Hanbing yi lüedi
Simian Chuge sheng
Dawang yi qijin
Qianyi he liaosheng

Han soldiers are in our land
On all sides the sound of Chu singing
The great king is sunk in gloom
Why should this wretched woman live?

This story is told in one of the most popular of all operas, *Bawang bieji* 霸王別姬 (The Hegemon Bids His Concubine Farewell). Chen Kaige's film *Farewell My Concubine* (1993) uses the opera as a backdrop for complicated political events and personal relations. The film starred the Cantopop star Leslie Cheung 張國榮. Cheung's own tragic fate (he committed suicide in 2003) seemed to mirror the tragedy of the concubine's story. A bench in Stanley Park (Vancouver) has become a shrine to Cheung; there are always flowers there.

of Zhao Erxun, viceroy of Manchuria.[13] Tan Kha-khee (陳嘉庚 Chen Jiageng), the rubber baron of Malaya, had four wives and eighteen children (nine sons and nine daughters). He arranged marriages for the children to connect himself to the most important Chinese families in South East Asia. His sons and sons-in-law held important positions in his network of companies. With so many children it was sad that he spent his last years alone in China; none of them followed him when he went to live in China after 1949.[14]

The polygamous household was seldom a happy one, more likely an enclosed battleground in which the wife and the concubines battled each other for dominance over their husband and for preferential treatment for their children. The family of Ling Shuhua was in perpetual warfare. Her father had a wife and five concubines. The first two 'mothers', 大媽 (*Da Ma*), and the first concubine, 二媽 (*Er Ma*), were dead when Shuhua was born, leaving her with Third Mother 三媽 (*San Ma*), Fourth Mother 四媽 (*Si Ma*) (her own mother), Fifth Mother 五媽 (*Wu Ma*) and Sixth Mother 六媽 (*Liu Ma*). Her father begot at least twenty children. Though few of the boys survived infancy, ten girls did; Ling was Little Ten. The children played together, the mothers played *mahjong* and quarreled.[15]

The polygamous husband/grandfather was a harried man. Besides providing for his wives and children he had to arbitrate their quarrels. A harmonious polygamous household, in which women co-operated to make the husband happy and give him many sons, was a dream but almost never the reality.

The position of the grandmother/matriarch in a polygamous household was tricky. She might have endured the arrival of her husband's concubine. Now she had to deal with her son's desire to acquire another woman. She wanted her son to be happy, and she cared little for the anguish of her daughter-in-law. She was the grandmother of all the children, born to wife or concubine. But if her son was too much taken with a concubine, she faced the loss of his affection and of her control in the household. And if the concubine was extravagant – a standard accusation – she could damage the family.

A true matriarch controlled her sons and his wives and concubines, as the Lady Dowager did, by a mixture of kindness and ruthlessness. Without a powerful figure to nip disputes in the bud, warfare was chronic, likely to erupt into open battles on any pretext. Ling Shuhua witnessed epic fights between her father's four concubines, spectacles that the gawking members of the household quite enjoyed:[16]

Both Third and Sixth Mothers' hair was in a horrible state, their long black hair spread over their faces and necks, some of it even covered their eyes. The powder and rouge had been mixed by tears, a patch white on their faces. If one looked carefully one could see many scratches from fingernails.

This kind of catfight was a symptom of the dysfunction of a world in which women were confined to households full of enmity and competition, where tempers could easily get out of hand. The 1991 film *Raise the Red Lantern* (大红灯笼高高掛 *Dahong denglong gaogao gua*), directed by Zhang Yimou 张艺谋, is set in a claustrophobic mansion within which the lives of a wife and three concubines play out. The third concubine, played by superstar Gong Li 巩俐, was sold to the husband after her father died. Everyone in the household is miserable, including the invisible master. The film ends tragically: after a series of complicated intrigues one concubine is driven to death; the third goes mad.

Why the Confucian system, so focussed on harmony, permitted a family form that was fore-ordained to cause disharmony is hard to get one's head around. There were opponents to concubinage. In the 1850s and 1860s the iconoclastic Taiping rebels opposed it; they were converts to Christianity and believed in the equality of men and women and in monogamy, a one-time marriage blessed by God. Despite their beliefs, the leaders of the movement *did* keep concubines; the rule of monogamy was only for lesser Taipings.

There were similar contradictions in the attitudes of the leaders of reform and revolution at the end of the dynasty. There was little enthusiasm for female emancipation. Most were not as extreme as Gu Hongming 辜鴻銘, the conservative Qing official and loyalist, who recommended for Chinese women a 'religion of selflessness', dedicated to making her husband happy, even finding him a concubine if he showed signs of needing one.[17] Kang Youwei 康有為, the reformer and protagonist of female equality, had a wife and five concubines. Sun Yat-sen, the great revolutionary, was married four times, though he never lived with more than one wife at a time. Only his last wife, Song Qingling, was recognised as his widow.

Polygamy continued into the Republic. Rare elite families in which the husband did not take concubines were regarded with amazement and respect. General Pai Ch'ung-hsi and his wife Ma P'ei-chang 馬佩璋 had ten children, seven of them sons; this was the new ideal of 一父一母 *yifu yimu* ('one father and one mother'). Zhang Wuling 張武齡, the educational reformer, and his wife Lu Ying 陸英 had eleven children, seven sons and four daughters.

The model of 'one father and one mother' did not suit all men. Even modern-minded men, such as the banker grandfather of Ye Weili, part of the emerging westernised bourgeoisie of the 1920s and 1930s, took concubines, in his case two. 'The first concubine was once a maid in an official family and was given by the family as a "gift" to my grandfather. The second concubine had been a local opera singer.'[18] The grandfather could not stand his first wife, and had little to do with her. But she ruled the family, treated the concubines like dirt and supervised their children (she had none of her own). The maltreatment of his concubine mother led the boy, Ye Weili's father, towards socialism.

The tradition clashed with modern ideas when a man with an educated wife took a concubine. In 1936 the British traveller Lady Hosie tried to comfort a young friend whose husband had brought her own cousin into the house as his concubine. For his devastated wife this was infidelity, and the breach of a happy marriage: 'he still thinks that when a man rises in society he should have concubines. He wants us all to live together, just like the old days, and have adjoining courtyards, but I will not do it, no, I will not.'[19]

New marriage forms started to emerge in the Republic. One included two wives but not polygamous cohabitation. A young man in his late teens, already married and a father, left home to study or to work. His first marriage was arranged. Once he was off on his own he could look for a marriage based on love, secure in the knowledge that he had left a wife at home to care for his parents and that he had done his duty to the family line by fathering a child. Tan Shihua was married in 1920 to an ugly illiterate girl from a village near his home town in Sichuan. Both husband and wife were sixteen. He had not been able to withstand the pressure of his elders to marry their choice of wife. He hated his own weakness even more than he hated his wife: 'There were people who accepted marriage but accepted it angrily and regarded their wives as a curse, an abscess. The abscess ached and one was ashamed of it but still it could not be cut out.'[20] Tan was cruel to his wife and contemptuous of her. His wife did not complain: 'It is not for a Chinese girl to cry over the fate that her husband does not love her.' Tan went away to university in Beijing. Though he hardly spent any time with her, he did impregnate her. To compound the disaster of the marriage, the child was a daughter, not the son that his family craved. Tan was a young man of more than average arrogance. He had no feeling for the poor girl he abandoned with his family, sentenced to a life of servitude to his elders, without even being the mother of a son.

Another form of marriage that involved more than one wife was the dual family system. During the late Qing and the early Republic, Overseas communities in South East Asia and North America evolved their own practice of marriage, one that accommodated the family at home and the husband abroad. In the dual family the first wife stayed at home. Her duty was to look after her husband's parents. There was no question of the old people leaving home with their sons. This pattern was reinforced by restrictive immigration policies which made it extremely difficult and costly for husbands to take wives or children with them. The wife would bear children, conceived during her husband's visits home. Since few men managed to get home every year, there might be long gaps between births. If the husband was successful, he would have a concubine abroad, usually a girl from his home community. She had no responsibility for his parents. In 1934 Chen Da surveyed home communities of Overseas Chinese in southern Fujian and eastern Guangdong:[21]

According to an old adage if a man should become rich or distinguished in government service he should return to his home village to receive the admiration of his neighbours. Otherwise his unrecognised distinctions could be compared with a gorgeous costume worn by its proud owner through the streets on a dark night.

The last sentence is a reference to one of the most famous *chengyu*:

衣锦還鄉

yijin huanxiang

returning home wearing brocade

Chen gave examples of three dual families (Table 7.2).[22]

The concubine ran the migrant's household abroad, bore his children and – for the benefit of the first wife – made sure that remittances were sent home.

Table 7.2 *Overseas Chinese families*

	Husband's location	Wife's location	Concubines	Children
Rich family	Siam (Thailand)	Home village	4	13, 6 at home
Middle class	Singapore	Home village	1	7, 2 at home
Lower class	Siam	Home village	0	8, 7 at home

ILLUSTRATION 7.2 Gulangyu

His wife would have the joy of living in a fine home. As the parents aged the wife was de facto head of the family at home, in charge of her own children and of any of the concubine's children who had been sent home. Gulangyu 鼓浪嶼 is a charming island just off the seafront of Xiamen (once Amoy). The small, hilly island became, after the Opium War, an international settlement, separated from the control of the Qing government. It gradually developed as an enclave for foreign consuls and businessmen and as the home of the wives of wealthy Overseas Chinese. They lived in elegant villas, surrounded by wide verandas, cooled by the sea breezes. It remains an idyllic place. No vehicle traffic is allowed. It is a centre for piano playing; the dominant sound on walks around the steep paths of the island is piano music.

These dual families were seldom happy. The jealousies and competition within a polygamous family were not erased by distance. The life of the

---

Box 7.3 May-ying

The beautiful Leung May-ying was one of the few women living in Vancouver's
Chinatown in the 1930s and 1940s; most of the residents were single men. Her
life started in deep poverty. She was born in Nanhai 南海 (Guangdong) in 1907,
sold as a servant at the age of four, then as a concubine at seventeen to Chan Sam,
who had moved to Vancouver in 1913. She worked as a waitress to repay his
expenses in getting her to Canada, and to send money back to his first wife in
Guangdong. She gave birth to three daughters. Two of them were sent back to
China; she never saw them again. The third, Way-hing, stayed in Canada,
married and had five children. May-ying's granddaughter, Denise Chong, traced
her life, as an abandoned girl, an unhappy concubine and a woman scorned by the
few 'proper' wives in the Chinese community. She battled through every turn and
twist that fate threw at her. She never went back to China. Her daughter and
granddaughter were the first to go 'home', in the 1980s; the family, divided since
the late 1930s, was partially reunited.[1]

[1] Denise Chong, *The Concubine's Children* (Toronto: Viking, 1994).

---

left-behind wife was tough; she was burdened by the care of the household, the
children, the land and the old people. She envied the concubine, living a life of
imagined ease. The concubine had no status, no family of her own, no control
over the lives of her own children. If they stayed abroad with her, her children
were deprived of grandparents; if they were sent home she missed their
childhood.

Another new form of marriage was serial monogamy. Mao Zedong had four
wives (one never consummated, one died, one abandoned, one survived); Liu
Shaoqi had six wives, one at a time. Chiang Kai-shek married three times, but
never lived in a polygamous setting. His second wife, Chen Jieru 陳潔如, was
not publicly acknowledged, but she considered herself to be his wife, as the title
of her memoir states: 'I was Chiang Kai-shek's wife for seven years.'[23] The
existence of two previous wives did not prevent his marriage to Song Meiling
in a Christian church in Shanghai.

Chiang's son Chiang Ching-kuo 蔣經國 was caught between modern and
traditional behaviour. In the years he spent in the Soviet Union he married
a Soviet woman, Faina Ipatevna Vakhreva (Chiang Fang-ling). Back in China
in 1936 he reverted to Chinese ways. He took up with the beautiful Chang Ya-
juo 章亞若. She gave birth to twin boys in 1942 and then died mysteriously
when the boys were six months old; many believed that she was murdered.
The boys were raised by their maternal family, and took her surname.

ILLUSTRATION 7.3 May-ying

(They are sometimes referred to as 'illegitimate', though that concept did not exist in China at the time.) In 1949 they went to Taiwan with their grandmother, uncle and aunt; they did not know their father or grandfather. Both boys did very well; one, John Chang 章孝嚴, was foreign minister of the Republic of China. Then technology intervened. In 2002 the brothers used DNA to prove that the uncle and aunt who brought them up were not their birth parents. In 2005 their surname was changed to Chiang.

After 1949 the Communists stamped down on polygamy. It was outlawed in the 1950 Marriage Law. Concubines were encouraged to leave their husbands and find a better life for themselves. Young ones were often eager to do so; they had a good chance of remarrying. Older concubines were less eager; their prospect if they left their marriage was

---

Box 7.4 Terms for 'wife'

There are many different words for 'wife' in Chinese, used at different times and with different connotations.

Taitai 太太 is the most formal term, often translated as 'Madam', now dated.
Furen 夫人 is a generic formal term.
Qizi 妻子 is a generic, less formal term.
Airen 爱人 'the loved one', was used in the Mao Era, and is now used for 'lover'.
Laopo 老婆 is a familiar, rather folksy term.
Wuli 屋里 'the person in the house', was an old rural term, no longer in use.

Box 7.5 Favouritism

As a small girl Ling Shuhua 齡叔華 had winning ways and artistic talent. Her talent gave her father cachet amongst his friends in the Beijing scholar elite, who respected painting and calligraphy more than any other art forms.[1] She was the favourite of his ten daughters, and she basked in his approval and affection, which prepared her for a later life of considerable glamour. In the 1930s she had had an affair with Julian Bell, son of Vanessa and Clive Bell, while he was in China. Julian died in the Spanish Civil War, deeply mourned by his parents and his aunt Virginia Woolf. Ling became a successful writer, eventually moving to England where she was an exotic adjunct to the Bloomsbury Group.

[1] Su Hua (Ling Shuhua), *Ancient Melodies* (London: Hogarth, 1953), p. 85.

---

separation from the only world they knew and probable destitution. However much girls had been driven to becoming a concubine by exploitation in the old society, their lives were more comfortable than if they were married to a poor man. For the family the loss of a concubine was hard too. She might be a key part of the family economy. This was the plaintive story of a polygamous store manager in a town near Shanghai, shortly after the Marriage Law was introduced:[24]

In this movement they want me to divorce a wife. That's really difficult. The older wife looks after the household, so divorcing her isn't right. As for the younger one she works in a silk factory and makes eight hundred thousand yuan a month. Divorcing her would be even worse. What should I do?

For this man, the salacious side of concubinage was irrelevant.

The senior leaders' practice of serial monogamy appealed lower down the Communist hierarchy. The desire for new, more attractive 'trophy' wives spilled down to the lower levels of male Party members, especially those who carried the revolution into the soft southern areas of China:[25]

90% of the cadres sent down to Hangzhou from Shandong to supervise the revolutionary transformation fell for the beauties of the south and divorced their peasant wives – who did, however, continue to live with and care for the man's parents.

This was the battle between *mantou* and *wotou*. In north China the staple food is not rice, but wheat and other grains. *Mantou* 馒头 is a steamed bun made of white flour, which, if eaten as it comes out of the steamer, is delicious. *Wotou* 窝头 is a bun made of coarse grains, a food to survive on, not to enjoy. In the early 1950s Communist cadres moving to the south and to the cities to work for the new regime referred disparagingly to the rural women from their home districts as *wotou*, compared to the luscious *mantou* of the areas where they worked. Many divorced their *wotou* wives to marry a *mantou*. Their brides were willing – their economic and political status rose at once.

In Hong Kong polygamy was legal until 1971, under the British practice not to interfere with local customs that were illegal under common law but seemed relatively harmless to public order. The casino tycoon Stanley Ho 何鴻燊 was a flamboyant example of modern-day polygamy. He had four wives, who gave him seventeen children. This great brood did not make his old age happy. The children engaged in epic and very public battles for control of his empire even before he died in 2020; the battles continue after his death.

The legal prohibition on polygamy is still in force on the Mainland, but it has not prevented the growth of the pattern of 'little wives' (小老婆 *xiao laopo*, or 二奶 *ernai*, 'second woman'). Many men who can afford it keep a 'little wife'. The girl is a status symbol, a proof that the man is successful. For an attractive girl, the conventional wisdom is that she will do better as a 'little wife' than she could as an office or factory worker. Her existence is quite open, the only difference being that she is not brought into the family but is kept in a separate establishment, often in 'mistress villages'. The system is not the same as the old polygamy; the girl has no security. She must keep her beauty and her allure; otherwise she may be supplanted by a third (*sannai* 三奶) or a fourth (*sinai* 四奶) 'little wife'. Her children will not be recognised as part of her protector's family, nor will she be able to marry him legally. The tales of the 'little wives' of important men are a big part of contemporary gossip.

There is a lack of hypocrisy in Chinese attitudes to polygamy, none of the deception and the hole-in-the-corner adultery that have accompanied Western men's desires for more sexual experience. Mistresses, common in wealthier sections of society, were/are kept secret, in love nests, not recognised by their lover's family or friends, referred to by derogatory terms such as 'loose woman', or 'slut'. Their children were illegitimate, by-blows. The only Western society that recognised mistresses was France; the title *maîtresse en titre*, given originally to the chief mistress of a king, later extended to the mistresses of prominent men who kept them openly and recognised their children. This may have been what Prince Charles was seeking when he married Diana. She was a suitable mother of a future king but not the woman he loved; Camilla was to be *maîtresse en titre*. Neither Diana nor the British public agreed. By the coincidence of sharing Lady Di's name I have had some insight into how Chinese see her plight as a mistreated wife: women despise the callous Charles; men find it hard to understand how he could prefer dowdy Camilla to beautiful Diana.

Life for grandfathers in China has changed as much as it has for grand-mothers over the past century and a half. They remain the custodians of family history and the transmitters of culture, but, as their lives lengthen, they make greater demands on their children and grandchildren – a process that will need negotiation. They may have to learn to be accommodating rather than demanding.

8   Transmitters of Culture

傳之後世

Chuan zhi houshi

Transmit to the descendants

Traditional grandmothers transmitted the riches of Chinese popular, oral culture to their grandchildren in the telling of legends and tales, and in repetition of proverbs and sayings (成語諺語 *chengyu yanyu*). There were written versions of the oral tradition (cartoons, comics, operas), but the spoken form was the first that children encountered.

The *chengyu* could be condensed versions of cautionary tales. A favourite is the story of a farmer who saw a rabbit run into a tree stump and kill itself. He downed tools and waited for another rabbit to do the same. The moral, condensed as 守株待兔 *shouzhu daitu* (stay by the stump waiting for a rabbit), is fairly obvious: 'don't expect two miracles'. It was a way to underline the need for a child to work hard. Another favourite is the story of the old man who lost his horse, which explains that bad things can turn out well. The English, 'a blessing in disguise', has none of the history of the Chinese version, which comes from the *Huainanzi* 淮南子, a compilation from the second century BC.[1]

Grandmothers transmitted this culture to their grandchildren, without thinking of themselves as cultural transmitters, as a grandfather might in giving Confucian instruction. They passed on the culture stored in their prodigious memories; most were illiterate. The memories of illiterate people tend to be richer than those of the literate; the illiterate cannot corroborate facts from written sources, they must keep them stored in their memories. When I interviewed illiterate former migrants to Manchuria in 1982 I was struck by how precise their memories were. They could remember exactly how much they had been paid for their work fifty years before, and in what currency. They often expressed what they earned in terms of how much food – beans or wheat – it would buy.

In the Mao Era, when everything traditional was under attack, grandmothers were an unwitting fifth column in the preservation of the popular tradition. Ni

---

Box 8.1 Saiweng shima 塞翁失馬

There was an old man who lived at the frontier (a most undesirable place).
One day his mare ran away, disappearing into the lands held by the barbarians.
He refused to be too overwhelmed by this terrible loss. He was right because
a while later the mare returned, bringing a fine stallion with her. This time he
refused to be too overjoyed. He was right, because not long after, his son, riding
the stallion, was thrown, and broke his leg. Again the old man refused to be
brokenhearted. For the third time he was right. When the barbarians attacked
a while later, every able-bodied man except his injured son was taken into the
militia; most of them were killed.

Ping, a television presenter, remembered the tales her grandmother told her,
when she lived with her in Shuimenkou 水門口 (Shandong): 'Grandmother
always had good things to eat in her hands and had endless good stories to tell.
I heard many stories I should not have heard and remembered many things
I should not have remembered at that young age.'[2]

Years later Ni realised that her grandmother had been telling her stories from the
tradition. Revolutionary stories were missing. The old stories are dramatic and
didactic; for many people they are history. Accuracy is not a major concern. One
story whose accuracy might be open to question is the watchword for 'patriotism'.
A millennium ago, Yue Fei 岳飛 resisted an alien invader; he was done to death by
Qin Hui 秦檜. Details cannot be corroborated. Did Yue Fei's mother actually
tattoo the character 'loyal' (忠 *zhong*) on her son's back? Did he actually write the
anthem of patriotism 'The river runs red' (滿江紅 *Manjiang hong*)? Irrelevant;
what matters is that Qin and his wife betrayed their country; their statues kneel
before Yue Fei's tomb, and (until recently) were spat on by every visitor.

Many stories appear in three novels beloved of all Chinese. *The Romance of
the Three Kingdoms* (三國演義 *Sanguo yanyi*) features Zhuge Liang 諸葛亮,
the greatest strategist in Chinese history. One of his best-known strategies is the
'empty city' (空城 *kong cheng*). The enemy was lured into a walled city whose
gates were open, as if abandoned. Inside the defenders fell on the enemy. Zhuge
Liang was a tragic hero, eventually defeated by the venal Cao Cao 曹操, a sad
acceptance that evil may triumph, in the short run, though history will honour
the good man. There are endless cartoons, films and television series based on
Sanguo. A recent film is *Shadow* (影 *Ying*), full of drama, violence and fabulous
feats of martial arts.[3] *Sanguo* is taught in business schools, the army and
(probably) Party schools.

The *Journey to the West* (西游記 *Xiyouji*) tells the story of the bringing of
Buddhist texts to China by the Monk (玄奘 Xuanzang) and his helper Monkey,

the trickster, a childish, clever creature. Monkey is an ideal exemplar for a wilful child; the term 'monkey' is used in Chinese and in English to admonish children, in a rather admiring way. Monkey defeats enemies by guile and dishonesty – a model for powerless people dealing with the powerful. The novel celebrates the ascendancy of Buddhism, the first great foreign influence, in China.

The Water Margin (水滸傳 *Shuihu zhuan*) is a compendium of stories about a band of hard-drinking, brawling outlaws on the margins of society, often compared to Robin Hood and his Merry Men. They were crude and frightening; they stood up for the ordinary people against officials and the rich. *Wu Song Kills the Tiger* (武松殺老虎 *Wu Song sha laohu*) tells how Wu Song, so drunk that he can hardly stand, runs into a tiger – and throttles it with his bare hands. This is a parable for the weak defeating the strong, with a twist: being drunk is not always bad.

These stories have limited parallels in Western culture. Joseph appears in the Bible (Genesis 37), in pictures, in an oratorio by Handel, in a novel by Thomas Mann, in a ballet, in a Dolly Parton song, in the musical *Joseph and the Amazing Technicolor Dreamcoat* and in an episode of *Seinfeld*. Few people know the details, the bitter battles between him and his brothers, the false claim of rape against Joseph.[4] The Joseph stories give an inkling of how popular an ancient story may be. Chinese stories are infinitely more so.

Chinese grandmothers loved to tell their little ones the stories from the popular tradition. The Communist Party was not sure if these stories were feudal, to be attacked, or mass culture, to be respected. The stories continued in circulation during the Mao Era, more exciting than the Party's own heroes, who lacked the drama of Monkey or Wu Song. The great Communist model hero Lei Feng 雷锋 did not die in a battle with a tiger, but was felled by a telephone pole.

Today there is great nostalgia for traditional culture, almost none for the times when the now elderly were young. The stories appear in films, video games and comics, and on children's clothing.

One 'feudal' element has never been out of favour: the colour red (红 *hong*), which has only positive associations, for Communism and for traditional culture (Table 8.1).

The traditional colour of happiness and respect, achievement and beauty, was also the colour of revolution. In the Mao Era dressing a baby boy in red, and carrying him in a red silk shawl, was traditional *and* revolutionary and one of the few remaining uses of silk, apart from red flags. Red stayed in weddings, not for wedding costumes – such extravagances were frowned on – but as rosettes worn on work outfits.

Table 8.1 *Happy reds*

Chinese	Pinyin	English	Traditional	Socialist
红榜	*Hongbang*	List of honour	X	X
红包	*Hongbao*	Red envelope	X	X
红军	*Hongjun*	Red Army		X
红旗	*Hongqi*	Red Flag		X
红人	*Hongren*	Favourite	X	X

ILLUSTRATION 8.1 Lei Feng

Religion and the Spirit World

Religious observance was/is the preserve of older women all over the world. I am one myself, back in the generous and welcoming Anglican (Episcopalian) Church. Female deities play an enormous role in Buddhism, Daoism and Christianity. Guanyin is the supreme goddess. She cares for the poor and the unfortunate, especially for women and children. She brings sons (see Chapter 3).

Besides Guanyin there are lesser female deities. In southern coastal China and Taiwan two celebrated female deities are Mazu 媽祖, also known as

---

Box 8.2 Colours

Colours come with complex symbolism, important in everyday life. Red is the colour of happiness and success, marriage and boys; there are none of the negative associations with red in Western cultures – blood, danger, immorality or sacrifice. Yellow is the colour of the first emperor (黄帝 *huangdi*) and is associated with all emperors. Yellow is also the colour of the earth of north China (黄土地 *huangtudi*). Each of the other primary colours, black, white and blue-green, has its own associations. White is strongly associated with death, the polar opposite of the Western custom of associating black with death. A terrible faux pas is to send white flowers for any occasion other than in sympathy after someone has died. White skin was once considered creepy and nasty, complicating early Chinese–Western contacts; now skin-whitening products are popular in China.

Box 8.3 Numbers

Numbers have particular meanings. One number is super auspicious – eight; value is added to a house or street with eight in its number. Four is inauspicious and to be avoided, in much the same way that thirteen is in the West. The origin of thirteen is the number of people at the Last Supper, the thirteenth being Judas the Betrayer. In some dialects numerology has to do with homonyms (四 *si* = four, 死 *si* = death). Five is often used as a grouping word, from the ancient Five Classics to the modern Five Loves of the Mao Era:

Five Classics 五經	書經 試經 易經 禮經 春秋	*Shujing Shijing Yijing Liji Yuli*	Documents, songs, changes, rites, spring and autumn
Five Directions 五方	東南西北中	*Dong nan xi bei zhong*	North, south, east, west, centre
Five Elements 五行	金木水火土	*Jin mu shui huo tu*	Metal, wood, water, fire, earth
Five Colours 五色	红黄白黑青	*Hong huang bai hei qing*	Red, yellow, white, black, blue-green
Five Metals 五金	金銀銅鐵鍚	*Jin yin tong tie xi*	Gold, silver, copper, iron, tin
Five Tastes 五味	苦辣酸甜咸	*Ku la suan tian xian*	Bitter, hot, acidic, sweet, salty
Five Loves 五爱	祖国 人民 科学 劳动 公共财物	*Zuguo renmin kexue laodong gonggong caiwu*	Country, people, science, work, public property

Box 8.3 (Cont.)

(*cont.*)

Five Grains 五谷	稻谷 玉米 薯类 麦子 大豆	*Daogu yumi shulei maize dadou*	Rice, corn, yams, wheat, beans
Five Senses 五官	耳目鼻唇舌	*Er mu bi chun she*	Hearing, sight, smell, touch, taste
Five Viscera 五臟	心肝脾肺脏	*Xin gan pi fei zang*	Heart, liver, spleen, lungs, kidneys
Five Mountains 五山	泰山 衡山松山花山 横山	*Taishan Hengshan Songshan Huashan Hengshan*	Taishan, Hengshan, Songshan, Huashan, Hengshan

Tianhou 天後, the Queen of Heaven, who protects fishermen, and the Lady of Linshui 臨水夫人, who protects women and children. Chinese deities have been joined by a foreign one: the Virgin Mary, the mother of Christ, is worshipped by Chinese Christians (particularly Roman Catholics). One deity is explicitly associated with old age, the Wusheng laomu 無生老母, the 'Unborn Old Mother'.

The female deities speak to the universal yearning for love and compassion, for understanding and kindness, something that the material world cannot provide. They help people cope with the sadness of life, and with its inevitable end.

Old women pray at the deities' shrines. They look after them. They go on pilgrimages with groups of other old women. They make donations. Some of the donations are conditional: when asking the deity to send a grandson, the bulk of the money is paid only when the son is born.

The 1911 Revolution and the great changes over the next three decades did nothing to reduce the influence of formal religions. Popular religion flourished, with the avid participation of old women. Local deities such as Third Granny Wang (王三奶奶 *Wang San Nainai*) were worshipped for their power to heal the sick.[5] The healing power of deities, before modern medicine, gave an immediate recourse; when an infant fell ill, grandmothers rushed to pray and make offerings at local shrines. A second recourse for illness was to go to local women known for their healing skills.[6] This two-pronged attack might or might not lead to the recovery of the child. If it did, this was proof of the value of the old ways. Modern-minded men hated them. The anthropologist Francis Hsu labelled women healers 'witches'.

It was hard to abandon the old ways. Pearl Buck's heroine Kwei-lan (Guilan) in *East Wind West Wind*, set in the 1930s, was in awe of her Western-educated husband, who despised 'superstition'. She prayed in secret:[7]

I have taken incense and burned it before Kwan-yin [Guanyin] secretly, dreading my husband's laughter. It is all very well not to believe in the gods when there is no trouble approaching. But when sorrow hangs over a house, to whom shall we appeal? I prayed to her before my son was born and she heard me.

The upheavals of war (1937–1949) robbed Chinese of any security. The capriciousness of life turned many people to prayer to keep their families safe. The young might be animated by patriotism for the salvation of their country; the old had seen too much suffering and violence to have faith in China's ability to win the war. They worried about their coming demise with deep pessimism. Francis Hsu observed their resignation:[8]

there are any number of elderly people, men and women, who are interested only in reading scriptures, becoming devotees in temples, ensuring the quality of their coffins and graveyards and preparing wind[ing] sheets. Their resignation to avoid active life is fairly obvious.

Resignation was often expressed as a belief in fate (缘分 *yuanfen*). The belief that mysterious forces that cannot be resisted determine what happens may lead to the passivity that Hsu criticised. A common expression that conveyed the power of fate was 没有辦法 *meiyou banfa*, 'nothing to be done', 'no way out'. No one was to blame. Only a deity could protect you. Yu Chun-fang's grandmother was a devout follower of Guanyin. In late 1945 the Yu family had been waiting in Wuhan for three months for boat tickets to get them home from west China. When they finally got them the family camped out on the banks of the Yangzi in the pre-dawn darkness to board the ship:[9]

Suddenly my grandmother insisted that we not board the ship because she had a vision of Kuan-yin [Guanyin] standing in the middle of the river and gesturing with her right hand to my grandmother to stay away. My grandmother immediately knew that Kuan-yin was telling her that the ship was not safe. My mother, a product of the May 4th Movement, a college graduate and a history teacher, was at first reluctant to listen. But my grandmother was adamant and my mother eventually gave in. Soon after leaving port the ship ran into mines planted by the retreating Japanese army. It sank. If we had been on board what chance would we have had of surviving the shipwreck when none of us could swim.

Beyond religion was the realm of the spirits. Chinese grandchildren learned from their grandmothers about good and evil spirits. Old women were experts on the spirits, who inhabited every corner of the world around them. They knew which parts of a house were haunted and why: a concubine had committed suicide in her room and her angry ghost was still around. They could interpret strange happenings; they knew how to appease the spirits or to please them. They knew how to protect those they loved, especially their grandchildren.

Spirits came in many forms. Some were benevolent, especially the *ling* 靈, the spirits of the ancestors, always doing what they could to help. The spirit of

---

Box 8.4 Amulets

Amulets to protect people from evil and harm have been used in China since prehistory. The tiny jade pendants from the pre-unification dynasties (second and third millennia BC) were amulets. Later on, Buddhist amulets became very common. Amulets give comfort to those who get them for their loved ones, the knowledge that they have done something to keep those they love safe, a spiritual version of an insurance policy. There are many informal protocols around acquiring amulets from Buddhist temples, having them blessed by abbots, rather like Roman Catholic practices on the blessing of rosaries and crosses.

---

a dead person (魂 *hun*) might still be around, and had to be propitiated. The spirits of the natural world (神 *shen*) could be good, evil or anything in between; some needed offerings. Some spirits were malicious, the *gui* 鬼, against which people had to protect themselves. The wartime evil spirits were the Japanese 鬼子 *guizi* . Some *gui* were tricksters, such as the fox fairies (狐狸精 *hulijing*), who appeared disguised as pretty women. Jiang Qing, Mao Zedong's last wife, was referred to discreetly as the 'white-boned demon' (白骨精 *baigujing*) after an evil spirit in the *Journey to the West*.

After 1949, organised religion was harshly attacked. Temples and churches were commandeered, to be used as schools, factories and Party offices. Other places of worship were destroyed, taking with them not only a sacred space but also a community. Nuns and monks were laicised or imprisoned. Foreign missionaries were expelled. The Communist Party was adamantly opposed to superstition and feudal practices. Campaigns were launched to root out religious practice, especially the activities of what were called *deviant* or *evil sects* (邪教 *xiejiao*). But at the same time as religion and superstition were being suppressed, the Party's desire to get younger women working meant that grandmothers raised children. There was a fundamental contradiction here, between leaving grandmothers to care for grandchildren and creating a new socialist society. Children received a continuous stream of 'correct' propaganda in school; at home their grandmothers taught them 'feudal' thought and practices. The Party seems not to have faced up to the contradiction. It must have seemed impossible to reform the thinking of elderly women – and they were so essential for child care that they had to be left alone.

Grandmothers continued traditional rites for the protection of children, even if they had to be performed secretly. They made arrangements for their funeral and burial, not cremation. They kept to the old ways, whether they were now labelled superstitious or not. Many of these beliefs and practices were diametrically opposed to 'scientific socialism', as purveyed by the Communist Party. Most old women, being illiterate, did not read propaganda materials, and movies were rare events, especially in rural China. They tuned out loudspeaker broadcasts, the ubiquitous background to Mao Era life. They could not understand radio broadcasts in the new national language, *putonghua*. Television did not arrive until the mid-1960s, and when it did it provided only turgid revolutionary fare, not entertainment (see Chapter 11).

The persecution of religion came to a gradual end with the death of Mao Zedong and the start of the Reform Era. The current generation of elderly in China have lived to see the revival of the festivals, family gatherings, weddings and funerals that were almost eliminated in the Mao Era; they reinforce the value of the elders. Religious practice, in Buddhism, Daoism, Islam and Christianity, has boomed over the past four decades. Temples, mosques and churches provide a religious and social world for older women. Old places of worship have been rebuilt, and new ones created; as in religious places everywhere in the world, older women are dominant in congregations and in the bands of volunteers who keep the places of worship alive.

The devotion may be extravagant. In the 1990s Zeng Hen scraped together enough money to build a temple on the site where, as a young girl, she had been saved from certain death by PLA soldiers. Her village, on a beautiful beach on the Taiwan Straits, was shelled by a Nationalist vessel. The soldiers threw themselves on top of her; they were killed, she survived. Zeng never forgot the heroes. She was determined that they be commemorated. She managed, after a long struggle with the local authorities, to acquire the site, and to build a shrine to the soldiers. The shrine, supposedly secular, is only half of the building: the other half is a Buddhist temple. Her efforts have been recognised by the PLA; delegations of soldiers regularly visit the temple.[10]

Her devotion has been deemed acceptable. The work of Falungong 法轮功, the Dharma Wheel, has not. The movement started in the early 1990s in Manchuria, then the rust bucket of China. Its adherents, mainly older people, practised meditation and gentle physical exercises, whose aim was to transcend their worldly problems and heal illness. Falungong was a great success, and was initially endorsed by the government. Its downfall came after April 1999. Some 10,000 people formed a human chain round the government headquarters in Beijing. The police did not know what to do with the gentle, passive people, many of them women, many elderly. The government was thunderstruck by the huge demonstration, so close to its heart. Falungong was declared an 'evil sect' and outlawed. Since then its adherents have been actively persecuted on the Mainland. Falungong continues to flourish in Taiwan and in North America. It runs the highly successful dance troupe Shenyun 神韵, which performs widely everywhere except Mainland China and Hong Kong.

Religion is strongly associated with charity in Hong Kong. Religious-based institutions are ubiquitous. Many of the best schools are religious foundations – La Salle College, Wah Yan College, Maryknoll Convent School – as are the best hospitals – Canossa, Adventist, Baptist. Caritas (明愛 *Ming'ai*), a Catholic organisation, is one of the largest providers of social care. Taiwan has a similar pattern of religious involvement in civil society. One of the largest organisations is the Tzu-chi Foundation (慈濟基金會 *tsu-chi chi-chin hui*), a Buddhist organisation with over 10 million volunteers worldwide. Tzu-chi provides a range of charitable services, from health care to disaster relief. Its disaster relief teams, wearing red coveralls, arrive with amazing speed after a natural disaster anywhere in the world. On the Mainland churches and temples do not perform social functions.

Wise Women

Wise women(神婆 *shenpo*) combined traditional, unwritten knowledge of medicine with love and compassion. They practised healing. In many families a resident wise woman, the grandmother, provided day-to-day medical care, and interceded with the gods when children were ill. Other wise women, with more specialised knowledge, were midwives, who helped young women through childbirth. The universal assumption that older women know the mysteries of birth appears in the French word for a midwife, *sage femme*, 'wise woman'.

Elderly women had a repository of knowledge of herbal medicine. They cooked up concoctions, evil-smelling broths or black pastes. The very unpleasantness of the remedies made them more likely to work: no child would willingly come back for a second treatment. My sisters and I were treated on the same principle: iodine for external injuries, quinine for internal problems. Both treatments were so awful that we seldom complained of feeling ill.

In the Mao Era healers were denounced as repositories of superstition, though they continued to practise underground. They are back today. Some are simply repositories of traditional skills; some are a reincarnation of a local spirit. In Mancheng 满城 (Hebei) a local woman came to believe that she was the latest apparition of the Silkworm Mother. She built a small shrine, where she sat with people in need, not saying much. She claimed to solve problems, to provide cures – and to send sons – for a minimal donation. Her fellow villagers, who would otherwise face a long journey into town to a hospital, and the payment of substantial fees, flocked to the healer.[11] Our mother had healing hands; she was trained in Reiki, the Japanese/Christian form of healing. The warmth and power that came from her hands seemed an innate part of her love for others.

Family Stories

Grandmothers told grandchildren family stories. Rae Yang's grandmother, born to a distinguished Manchu family, told her granddaughter stories about her ancestors. The little girl loved them. Later she came to hate them:[12]

In the sixties when class struggle was emphasized I really wished that I had never heard my stories from Nainai so that the thought reform would not be such a difficult task for me. In fact, in those years I even wished that I had never had such a Nainai and those ancestors of hers. They were blood suckers, parasites, smiling tigers, piles of garbage, cow ghosts and snake demons. If I could erase them from my memory I would become a reliable successor of the revolutionary cause like my classmates.

By the time she wrote her book, Yang had a different appreciation of her grandmother's stories; they are oral history, a family history full of detail, possibly exaggerated, even false, but giving the children a sense of where they come from.

Ancestors are to be remembered and revered. They are present, the most important part of a family in the Confucian tradition. Children should be told stories about them. In modern times remembering ancestors has been complicated. Bad or sad ancestors have haunted families. After the 1911 Revolution and the collapse of the Qing Dynasty, many Manchu families changed their surnames and denied their origins. To be associated with the last dynasty was dangerous. Only in the 1980s was it possible to reveal Manchu ancestry, with the benefit that being an ethnic minority allowed a couple to have more than one child.

An even more difficult past is for those descended from people labelled 'traitors' (漢奸 *hanjian*) after the Anti-Japanese War. Their children, now elderly, have had to hide their parentage as much as possible. Many major *hanjian*, such as Wang Jingwei 汪精衛, either died or left China before the Communist takeover, but lesser *hanjian* did not; they were executed. The children of *hanjian* were never able to escape their past.

The 'bad past' may refer to the Civil War. Yi Zhuoxiong 易卓雄, a retired teacher in Liuyang 浏阳 (Hunan), served as a young man in a Nationalist unit in the early 1940s. For this patriotic service he was named a counterrevolutionary, and spent more than a decade in reform through labour (劳改 *laogai*). His sons suffered for having father in *laogai*. He was released in 1962 but his status was not rectified until 1979. In his old age he refuses help from his sons, on the grounds that they have already suffered too much for him.[13]

Old people can now again pass on stories of forebears, especially distinguished ones. The abandonment of class warfare has led to determined efforts to retell the stories of forebears once regarded as disgraceful, now praiseworthy. Descendants write biographies of them that fill the shelves of the huge sections on biography in bookstores. They depend almost entirely on oral history, the retelling of stories that elderly people heard in their own childhoods. Discretion must be observed about how much will be told. Discovering too much about families can be dangerous. Few families are peopled exclusively by stalwart citizens.

家家有本難念的經

Jiajia you ben nannian de jing

Every family has some records that should not be read

A good place for family stories is at the grave. In the West there is no special day for visiting graves. In China there is the Qingming Festival, when the whole family gathers at a grave, takes flowers and refreshments to the departed. The three bows must be made, and news of the family's successes communicated to the dead. Graves must be swept, either literally if they are earthen grave mounds, or symbolically. After the rites the family settle down to their own picnic, and the telling of family stories.

Language

Grandparents play a huge role in a child's language development. They speak to their grandchildren in their native language or dialect. Until recently most Chinese spoke only their own dialect (方言 *fangyan*). These were distinct spoken languages, unintelligible to outsiders, such as Shanghai dialect, Cantonese or Min/Tai 閩台, the spoken language of Fujian and Taiwan. Or they could be variations of what later became the national language, *guoyu* or *putonghua*, mutually intelligible, but with marked regional accents. A scholarly study of the differences between *putonghua* and the dialect of the Shandong peninsula demonstrates the scale of the distinctiveness.[14]

By the 1960s many young people were bilingual, in the national language and in dialect. The grandparents were not. They were their grandchildren's first language instructors, in dialects that were not taught in school, and could only be learned in the home. This might turn out to be of long-term value. Certain dialects (Beijing, Shanghai, Min/Tai, Cantonese) brought their speakers advantage in the economic boom that started in the 1980s. Young people from Shanghai families in Hong Kong, who had learned Shanghai dialect at home, were in demand by branches of Shanghai companies in Hong Kong. People in southern Fujian were quick to establish connections with Taiwanese businesspeople; they all spoke Min/Tai. In Taiwan grandmothers had taught it to their grandchildren even when the Nationalist government was trying to outlaw it, to force the entire population to speak the national language. The grannies were unintentionally subversive.

Chinese grandmothers could seldom teach their grandchildren to read and write, partly because they were illiterate, and partly because, on the Mainland, the literate elderly could not adapt to the simplified characters that supplanted traditional characters after 1956.

Amnesia

Chinese grandparents are circumspect in talking about their personal past. They may want to spare their grandchildren the painful knowledge of what they suffered in war and turmoil. And some may want to hide their behaviour in the Cultural Revolution. Many Chinese in their sixties and seventies were Red Guards. In the first phase they attacked the 'four olds' – customs, culture, habits and ideas. They destroyed old buildings, particularly religious ones, burned books and smashed antiques. They attacked their parents and their teachers. They were eventually restrained by the Party that had instigated their behaviour, and punished by being sent to the countryside. They have consigned this period to the silence of amnesia; it is hard for them to understand themselves, impossible to explain to younger generations. There is even fear that their juvenile behaviour may haunt later generations.

父債子還

Fu zhai zi huan

The debts of the father must be repaid by the son

Those who were victimised in the Cultural Revolution, children of parents in political trouble, like the current supreme leader of China, Xi Jinping, do talk about their experiences. He spent seven years in a small village in Shaanxi, Liangjiahe 梁家河, after his father was denounced for 'taking the capitalist road', i.e. disagreeing with Mao Zedong.

There are consequences of amnesia. The younger generations know very little of the youth of their parents and grandparents, what they did, what they suffered. They may not recognise the reprise of Cultural Revolution rhetoric in the current political climate.

9   Absent Parents

父母在不遠游

Fumu zai buyuanyou

While parents are alive do not travel far away

This stern Confucian commandment underlined the importance of a family being together. The needs of the older generations came first. It is still alive as an official slogan, but is often ignored in practice by an absent middle generation.

Traditional grandparents had an accepted obligation as the stand-ins for absent, incompetent or dead children. Parents who were away while their children were young did not have to worry about them; the family stepped in. Grandparents took over care from sons who were away for work or study; from delinquent sons (opium smokers, gamblers, bandits); and from incompetent ones, men who were down on their luck, sick, unemployed or indebted.

Care in the family meant care by grandmothers; even when the children's mother was at home, her mother-in-law would be recognised as de facto responsible for the upbringing of the children. The matter-of-fact assumption was that a child was just as well cared for by her as by its parents. This pattern continues today.

There were costs involved. Grandmothers had to spend a great deal of time and energy on child care, while their energy was waning as they aged. For the parents, leaving a child involved loss and pain. They missed the children's childhood, the small joys of meals, bedtimes, outings, holidays and birthdays. The anxieties of parenthood were endured at a distance. They lost the precious early years of their children.

Death

The saddest reason for parental absence was death. Maternal death was common until recently. Birth was often traumatic, and mothers often died; post-partum haemorrhages were common, impossible to stop before modern medicine was available. Even if a mother lived, she might not recover fully from birth trauma. Chiang Yee's mother was permanently disabled after his birth, and died when he was five (in 1908).[1] He was raised by his grandmother and an aunt, kind and gentle women who tried to make up for the loss of his mother. The misery of young women married away from their own family might bring a young mother to take her life. The eminent writer Xiao Jun 蕭軍 was born in 1907, to a wealthy family in Liaoning. His mother was abused by her husband. When her son was seven months old, she ate opium, to end her misery. She first gave opium to her baby, but he spat it out and survived. The child was passed to the care of his grandmother, his unmarried aunts and a wet nurse. They all adored the first-born grandchild of the family, indulged him and spoiled him. His feisty grandmother protected him from his violent father. The love of these women enveloped the motherless child, but could not compensate completely. He never forgave his father, for whom he had only implacable hatred.[2]

No grandmother was more heroic in the care of her orphaned grandchildren than the grandmother of (the later marshall of the Peoples' Liberation Army) Peng Dehuai 彭德懷. He was born to a modest peasant family in Hunan, in 1898. His family – parents, four boys and grandmother – got by until it was hit by a series of calamities. His mother died when he was eight; his father fell ill and could no longer work. The family's land was lost, the youngest boy starved to death. His grandmother put her pride behind her and turned to begging:[3]

Leading two of her grandsons . . . the grey-haired woman who was over 70, went out into the falling snow and bitter wind. With the help of a walking stick she swayed from side to side on her little bound feet.

At the end of a day she returned with enough rice to feed the starving family. This was its lowest point. Gradually the family's situation improved. Peng was a child labourer; at eighteen he went into the army. He never forgot his childhood poverty, or his grandmother who had saved the family. His experiences turned him into a revolutionary.

The paternal family was expected to care for an orphaned child. A maternal grandmother might do so, but only in an extreme situation. The poet Lin Beili 林北麗 was born in 1916, less than a month before her father died. Her mother was prostrate with grief, so the infant was sent off to her maternal grandmother. This was not a happy arrangement. 'Grandmother loved to play *mahjong* and enjoy herself in peace, ignoring all household matters.' The infant was left to the mercies of her nanny.[4]

The death of parents is absolute loss. The Edwardian children's book *The Secret Garden* is about two profoundly unhappy children, the orphaned Mary and the motherless Colin; their wealth and privilege do not touch their misery. Watching the film with my granddaughter Mabel I tried (but failed) to explain that what to her is unthinkable, the loss of a parent, was once quite common.

Politics and War

A common reason for the absence of parents was political. In the turbulence of modern China the departure of parents was caused by events beyond a family's control. In the late Qing Dynasty, the parents of young men who joined rebellious and revolutionary movements stepped in when their sons left home – and their wives and children. If the sons' adventures failed, the grandparents' care became permanent. When (in the late 1860s) the Taiping rising collapsed, its adherents could not go home. They wore the sign of their attachment to the Taipings on their heads: their queues were gone. The hair growing all over their heads made them immediately identifiable and assured of a death sentence. The grandparents of their children were the sole carers for the rest of their lives.

In the last decades of the dynasty, reformers and revolutionaries had to go into exile abroad, when their efforts to bring about change failed. Most of the revolutionary leaders left their children in China or in Hong Kong. Political dangers extended to regional rivalries. In south China in the early Republic there were so many ups and downs that regional warlords maintained homes in Hong Kong, to use whenever they had to flee; their children were left permanently in Hong Kong, under the supervision of grandparents. In Manchuria recurrent feuding forced activists to flee. Chi Pang-yuan (Qi Bangyuan) 齊邦媛 was born in 1924, in Manchuria. Her father was often away, immersed in political agitation, first against the Zhang Zuolin regime and then against the Japanese. Her mother supported her husband's work, and left her daughter with her mother-in-law. More than seventy years later, Chi remembered how her grandmother's care had been the one element of stability and affection in her life:[5]

Throughout my life, I have often thought of my grandmother, who worried about her granddaughter from the day I was born until she herself was old and ill. I often feel that I owe her too much. A few years later, we roamed for quite some time from Hankou to Chongqing, where we received news indirectly that she had passed away. I couldn't believe that that warm body that had held me in the winter could ever become cold.

Political activists on the outs with the Nationalist government after 1927 often had to flee. Young people who joined the Communists had to leave their families behind when they fled with the Party into the hinterland. With the Japanese invasion (1937) came tidal waves of refugee movements. Refugees had to leave the young and the elderly behind – the costs and the strain of the journey too much for them. The writer Lao She fled to the west, to Chongqing;

his wife, the artist Hu Jieqing 胡絜青, and their children were in Beijing, with his mother. In 1943 his wife and children fled from the city, and arrived in Chongqing two months later.[6] His mother was too old to move. She was left behind and died alone before the end of the war.

China had an insatiable need for soldiers during the war. Millions of young peasants left home to serve in the armies. Their wives and children were left behind with the grandparents. Civilians, government employees and students fled to the western regions, most without the older members of their families. Overseas Chinese were cut off from their families at home for the duration of the war. The separations of families were ruinous. The sociologist Sun Benwen 孫本文 wrote about the profound disruption to society: 'Parents, brothers, wives, children are scattered, the family's house and property is ruined, the family head and family members are unemployed, daily life is difficult, the young and the children are out of school and roaming about.'[7]

For those left behind, separations amounted to hardship and destitution. Ageing peasants could not farm their land without their sons. Small business-men could not manage their business without their sons. Elderly people who depended on their sons' financial support were without income. The old social support networks based on the extended family, which had once looked after emergency needs, were in tatters, useless.

The floods of refugees were adrift, filled with sadness and anxiety about their families. Chiang Yee's family lost their home in Jiujiang 九江. Several rela-tives, including cousins and a brother-in-law, were killed in the Japanese occupation of the city:[8]

I have heard that our house and garden are entirely destroyed, but I cannot tell. Recently the members of my family, by whom I was surrounded in my childhood, wrote that they had escaped from Kiujiang [Jiujiang] and were scattered in five different places.

Writing in England, where he was safe, he tried to understand what was happening to his home and to his wife and four children:

Is it because we enjoyed such happiness that we have now to bear such grief? How is it that the invaders do not think of their own cousins and relations? The loss of material things – our house, our garden, our collection of paintings and books – leaves me now comparatively unmoved though we took such pleasure in them. But on what principle is a civilisation based that can destroy happiness and kill fellow-beings in the interests of some unstable dream of expansion and aggrandisement?

He was cut off, almost permanently as it turned out. The Communist takeover in 1949 made it dangerous for him to return. He did not go back to China until 1975, forty-two years after he had left. He met his wife and daughters and his five grandchildren. On his first visit he did not stay long, but was back again in two years. He died in 1977, shortly after his wife, and was buried next to her. He had been unhappy when they were together; she had coped without him for more than four decades. They were reunited in death.

At the end of the Resistance War in 1945 refugees straggled home. The reunions with their families were not easy. Eight years had passed, everyone had suffered, but only those who had fled from the occupied areas could trumpet their suffering. A whiff of collaboration clung to those who had stayed, whether they had worked for the Japanese – a tiny minority – or had simply endured the occupation.

Young Communists could not go home; the start of the civil war made that impossible. Ma Xiaodong's parents met in Yan'an during the war, fell in love and married. Their first son was sent to his grandparents in a village in Henan – where he joined his older brother, born to his father's first wife. A daughter born a little later was left with a peasant family. The family settled in Beijing in the early 1950s. The parents went to look for their daughter, only to find that she had 'died of illness some time earlier'.[9] The terse phrase hides an unbearable sadness; the child died without the parents even knowing of her death. Mu Anping's grandmother was more fortunate. Her son Mu Xiang did come home. This is his reunion with his mother, in 1951. There was a knock at her door:[10]

At the sound of her voice the visitor wept. 'Mama it's me, your eldest son. I'm back.' When she opened the door a man in a woolen army uniform stood there with a little boy. Unable to speak, staring up at the man's face, she recognized her eldest son, whom she had not seen for sixteen years and had missed every day.

Both these families were on the winning side in the civil war. The losers, the Nationalists and their supporters, tried to leave the Mainland for Taiwan. Many left wives and children behind them. This was the beginning of total separation. People on the Mainland were forbidden to receive letters or remittances from abroad. They suffered horribly for having 海外关系 *haiwai guanxi* – overseas connections. People in Taiwan were forbidden to contact relatives on the Mainland.[11]

Women made up a small proportion of the exodus; those who did had to leave their children. Mang Yuqin 莽玉琴, whose husband was already in Taiwan, managed to leave the Mainland in late 1950. The journey from the north of China to Taiwan was going to be so difficult that she and her mother decided that the youngest of her three daughters should stay behind, until she could come back to pick her up. The parting was agonising, the grandmother losing her daughter and two granddaughters, the mother leaving her mother and one of her children. Both expected the separation to last a few years at most. It was permanent; her mother died before she was able to go back to China, thirty-five years after she left her for 'a short while'.[12]

Mang's story mirrors that of the writer Amy Tan's mother and the three children she left behind on the Mainland; they were never mentioned to her

Box 9.1 Daisy Tan

Daisy was brought up in a rich family near Shanghai. Her widowed mother was taken into the house as a concubine. She killed herself when Daisy was ten. In her late teens Daisy married a rich young man. She bore him four children, three daughters and a son who died in infancy. The marriage was miserable. She fell in love with another man. In 1949 she left China, her husband and her daughters to be with her love. The daughters were left to the care of her hated husband and his concubine. The girls suffered at home, maltreated by the concubine, and as children with a bad class background. Daisy was completely out of touch with them. She had three more children in America, one of them the writer Amy Tan. The existence of the older daughters was never mentioned, though Daisy's volatility spoke of deep unhappiness. Decades later, in the 1980s, she was reunited with her first children. By then other tragedies had brought her even greater grief, the deaths of her husband and her son Peter. She always battled to survive, never asking why or blaming herself: 'I never heard my mother express remorse. She expressed resignation in various ways: "Could not be helped", "no choice", "cannot be prevented".'[1]

[1] Amy Tan, *Where the Past Begins* (New York: HarperCollins, 2017), p. 85.

other three children born in America. The theme of abandoned children is the lurking secret in Tan's brilliant novel *The Joy Luck Club*.[13]

Other people, neither Nationalist nor Communist, sent their children abroad or to Hong Kong. Four of the six children of the opera star Zhou Xinfang 周信芳 were sent abroad to study in the late 1940s. He had no thought of leaving; his whole life was bound up with opera. But he wanted the children to leave China until things settled down. Short term turned into long term. The family were never together again.[14]

Some young people were already abroad in 1949 and decided not to go home until things settled down. The great painter Zao Wou-ki (Zhao Wuji) 趙無極 and his wife left their son at home with his grandparents when the young couple got scholarships to study in France, in 1947. The parents never returned; the boy was brought up without his parents, and never saw them again. The sadness of Chinese artists and writers in France at the separation from their families in China runs through François Cheng's novel *Le dit de Tianyi*.[15]

The Communist Party was not magnanimous in victory after 1949. It implemented political punishments for being on the wrong side. Surrendered Nationalist soldiers were sent in their hundreds of thousands to the remote border regions, to prison camps and to the *bingtuan* 兵团 – military agricultural settlements. These men, who less than a decade before had been fighting the

Japanese invaders, had to leave their families behind. Their children were cared for by their mothers and grandparents.

In the political movements that shook China's villages, the Anti-traitor Movement (in areas that had been occupied by the Japanese), followed by land reform and the assignment of class status, some old women were able to express their indignation about the past, in the process of 'speaking bitterness'; others were on the receiving end.[16]

People labelled rightists, after 1957, were exiled to the borderlands, to work on state farms. They included prominent intellectuals: Ai Qing 艾青, poet; Ding Cong 丁聪, cartoonist; Ding Ling 丁玲, novelist; Fang Lizhi 方勵之, scientist; Huang Miaozi 黃苗子, artist; Wu Zuguang 吳祖光, playwright; Chen Mengjia 陳夢家, archaeologist. Most of those banished had once supported the Communist Party, but made open criticisms during the brief Hundred Flowers, when the Party asked for 'suggestions'. They had to leave their families behind when they were sent away. Some brave wives went with their husbands; others divorced theirs, in a futile effort to detach their children from their fathers' grim reclassification.[17] Rae Yang's Second Uncle was condemned as a rightist and sent to the borderlands. For the sake of their children his wife divorced him, but continued to live with his mother, the children's *nainai*. Twenty-three years later he was exonerated and rehabilitated; she remarried him. This might have been the happy ending to the traditional love story of the faithful wife who stays loyal to her husband. It was not. The husband was irritable, the wife explosive. Both were smouldering volcanoes. They could not put the past behind them.[18]

The writer Guo Xiaolu 郭小櫓 was born after her father was sent to a labour camp as a rightist. Her mother could not raise the baby on her own, and she was sent to her father's parents in a dirt-poor fishing village in Zhejiang. Her simple, uneducated grandmother cherished her; her childhood was poverty-stricken but full of love. When she was six her parents suddenly turned up to collect her; her father had been rehabilitated. The child was devastated, her grandmother even more so. Within a few hours she was on a bus going to her parents' home. She missed her grandmother dreadfully. Her gentle father, an artist whose depictions of poverty had got him into trouble in 1957, loved her; her tough mother did not. Guo discovered that she had a brother, whom her mother had kept – an extreme form of son-preference, not unlike *Sophie's Choice*.[19] The memoir is written with detachment, an attempt to understand the pressures beyond her family that so distorted her childhood, but the profound sadness of abandonment comes through.

Grandparents caring for the children of missing or exiled sons and daughters had permanent care of these children – and a guarantee of continuous discrimination. Intergenerational contamination determined that the families of those tarred by a bad political label were 'problematic families'. Suspicion cloaked them; the children were denied educational and employment opportunities.

In terms of numbers, the separation of parents and children reached a new height during the Cultural Revolution. In the madness of the Lost Decade, grandmothers stood in for their absent children. Adults in responsible positions (cadres, 干部 *ganbu*) were sent away to May 7th cadre schools, essentially labour camps. The inmates had to leave their children behind; grandmothers stepped in. They kept house, cared for the children, comforted them and held the remnants of the family together. Jian Ping's grandmother, already eighty, had sole care of five children. They were forced out of the family home in the government compound, into a hovel. Zhang Rong's grandmother took care of her five grandchildren when their parents were detained and sent to cadre schools.[20]

When a grandmother was not available, a household helper (阿姨 *ayi*) might care for the children of the vanished parents. Rae Yang's *ayi* stood by her and her brothers when their parents were in trouble. She gave them the only security they knew for years. She had lost her own two children; one had gone to Taiwan in 1949, the other had died of illness.[21]

Young children could not understand the sudden departure of their parents. Yunshu's parents were taken away in 1966; the child was left with her grandmother, who did her best to comfort the confused and miserable child:[22]

Every night when I went to bed she told me that when I opened my eyes the next morning Mum and Dad would be standing by my bed. Each morning I would ask Grandma where they were. She would say that their train was delayed. She knew and I knew that it was just a hopeless dream, but I never tired of hearing it.

Comforting a child whose parents were gone was a tough task for grandparents. So was controlling them. They were not in school – the schools were closed early in the Cultural Revolution. Some too young to be Red Guards were left to their own devices, to run wild. The 1994 film *In the Heat of the Sun* (阳光灿烂的日子 *Yangguang canlan de rizi*) gives an almost lyrical depiction of the lives of a group of abandoned teenagers as they roamed around Beijing. It has elements of nostalgia, for a time of complete freedom, young teenagers enjoying themselves in a world without adults.[23] It has a totally different feeling from William Golding's dystopian *Lord of the Flies* (1954), in which a group of stranded British schoolboys behave with sickening brutality towards each other.

People in their twenties during the Cultural Revolution, too old to be Red Guards, used the chaos of the Cultural Revolution to travel to reclaim their children. Zhang Zhimei's parents in Beijing were caring for her daughter while she was in Harbin, far away. After she heard that they had been attacked by Red Guards and their house ransacked she joined the surge of young people taking to the railways to 'visit Chairman Mao' to get back home. In fear of more trouble she took her daughter away from her parents and went on to her sister in

Hefei 合肥 (Anhui). The removal was devastating for the grandmother and the grandchild:[24]

Looking after my daughter was the centre of her life. On their last night together she stayed awake holding the sleeping Yan in her arms.

With her back more and more bowed she could no longer carry Yan, but she continued to caress her. While the world around her was going crazy, her granddaughter was her great source of consolation.

Red Guards attacked everything old, including their parents; they were hesitant to go after their grandparents, a stage too far. Every adult in Ye Weili's family was under attack in 1967 from the young generation, except the grandmothers; they were off-limits. Only one cousin turned on her grandmother:[25]

She led a group of Red Guards from her school in Beijing to search the home of her own family in Tianjin. The Red Guards ordered Nainai, my cousin's grandmother, to kneel on the ground. Shortly after the old lady died. The rest of the family has never forgiven the cousin for what she did to Nainai.

Grandparents reacted to the ferocity of the Cultural Revolution with resignation. They hated the return of turbulence, only a decade and a half after the end of twelve years of war, but they were in no position to oppose it – nor were they obliged to join in the ceaseless political activities. The grandmother of Zhu Xiaodi, who cared for her grandchildren when her 'red' daughter and son-in-law were in detention, was disheartened:[26]

She never devoted her life to any ideology or idealistic cause. All she did was respect her daughter's choice to marry a handsome young man who turned out to be a Communist. Before the Communist takeover she had suffered because of this marriage, and she could understand that. But she could not understand why she should suffer again now, twenty years after the Communist takeover.

At the other end of the political spectrum were grandmothers from once affluent, westernised families; they were used to being targets in political movements. They battled on. Lu Minzhan's grandmother, once a *grande dame* of the Shanghai bourgeoisie, kept her family together after her son's arrest, the family's eviction from their home and the loss of almost all her possessions. She fought every day to make the best of a bleak situation. When her grandchildren were attacked as children of one of the Five Black Categories her daughter-in-law sank into depression, but she reinforced her grandchildren: 'She thus reminded us that the Red Guards might take away all the symbols of her good fortune but no one could take away from her the right to labour for her loved ones.'[27]

Few people want to remember the Mao Era. Because it is a forgotten time, the grandmothers who kept their families together have not had the credit they deserve for their courage and their determination during the worst times.

Family separations for political reasons are now largely a thing of the past, with one massive exception. In Xinjiang, hundreds of thousands of Uighurs, especially young men, have been put into concentration camps. Others have been dispatched to work in factories thousands of miles away from home. The actions of the Chinese state have been widely labelled genocide. The maltreatment of the Uighurs has received a great deal of attention outside China, and has been a cause of embarrassment to Beijing and its supporters. Beijing has not been successful in portraying the Uighurs as terrorists – instead their peaceable and colourful way of life and their moderate form of Islam have aroused a great deal of support. Many of their important supporters are in the Turkic regions that stretch west from Xinjiang all the way to Turkey, regions that are critical to China's Belt and Road (一带一路 *yidai yilu*) Initiative.

Chinese beyond Mainland China

Twelve years of warfare (1937–1949) broke the old system of dual families for Overseas Chinese. There were no visits home, and very little in the way of financial support. Children in China with their grandparents were cut off from their parents overseas for the duration. Children abroad were unable to get home. After 1945 some children in China went back to their parents abroad, but ones already abroad did not go back to China. For many the Communist victory in 1949 meant almost total separation, until the 1980s. The home communities of Overseas Chinese seemed lost behind the Bamboo Curtain – and with them grandparents and great-grandparents, first wives and children. These separations were so painful that there was a tacit agreement not to mention the family in China. Denise Chong was born and brought up in Vancouver. Her book *The Concubine's Children* describes her discovery of a large family in Guangdong, and the realisation that her grandmother in Canada had not been her grandfather's only wife, but a concubine.[28]

Families of people who fled from China in 1949 endured the same separation. The Mainland was hermetically sealed off. There were no letters, no phone calls. In 1964–1965, my first time in China, I had to wait seven months to phone home, while on a short holiday in Hong Kong. My father got our black Labrador Tom to bark to me – which must have surprised whoever was listening in.

People abroad did not know whether their family members at home were alive or dead. Children growing up abroad had no idea that they even had a family in China. Their parents could not talk about their families in China. Most decided, with deep sadness, that they had left China forever, that their foreign-born children could only belong in the country in which they lived. Maya Lin, the architect and designer of the Vietnam Memorial in Washington, grew up in Athens, Ohio. Her family in China was never mentioned.[29] When she started her studies in architecture, she had no idea that her aunt, Lin Huiyin 林徽因, had been one of the few women architects in China, co-designer of the Martyrs' Memorial in Tiananmen Square. She did not even know that the aunt had existed.

China could not be forgotten in households that included grandparents, but there was a different divide: the grandparents spoke only Chinese; the children were growing up speaking only English. Leslie Li's memoir discusses the complicated family dynamics of the three generations of the Li family in Riverdale, New York. Her grandmother was completely isolated from her granddaughters who spoke no Chinese, but her pleasure in being with them trumped her isolation; there was deep love, expressed not in words but in food (see Chapter 1).

Until the mid-1980s the Republic of China on Taiwan was an authoritarian state. Mainlanders saw themselves as exiles, hoping to get back when the Mainland was restored (光复 *guangfu*) to Nationalist control. The incomers were not welcome; protests by native Taiwanese in 1947 had been crushed with brutal force, an atrocity known as Ererba 二二八 because it started on 28 February. Taiwan was a deeply divided society. Taiwanese (本土 *bentu*) had multi-generational families, Mainlanders (外省 *waisheng*) fractured ones. Only elite Mainlanders had been able to bring all their relatives with them from the Mainland. Below them in the hierarchy were small families of two generations, parents and children; the grandparents were left on the Mainland. At the bottom were the single men, mainly soldiers, who had had to leave their family at home on the Mainland. They lived in the 眷村 *juancun*, military communities of single men.

In the late 1980s, as Taiwan became democratic and the Mainland opened up, there were family reunions. Some old men went back to their wives on the Mainland, to live a more or less happy retirement. For younger people there were visits to family and to graves, but no return to the world their parents had lost.

Work Separations

Probably the largest form of parent–child separation is caused by a parent or parents being away for work. One of the most famous instances of a grandmother caring for a grandchild whose parents were working away from home is Madelyn Dunham, grandmother of Barack Obama. With his father permanently absent, and his mother working in Indonesia, Barack was in the care of his grandparents for eight years, from the age of ten to eighteen. His redoubtable grandmother, born in Peru, Kansas, raised him in Hawaii. She died days before her beloved grandson was elected president. His tribute to her just before she died was one of the finest ever given to a grandmother: 'She has really been the rock of the family, the foundation of the family. Whatever strength, discipline that I have – it comes from her.'

Sending young men away to work was a standard part of family economic strategies in traditional China. They would go away to work on construction projects, or at harvest times, or for a stretch in the army. They went alone, without wives or children. There was reciprocity. The strategy of young men working away from home to earn money for the family contained the assumption that their parents would care for the wives and children at home. The millions of 'swallows' who migrated from Shandong to Manchuria every spring seldom took their families with them. Young women who worked in the factories of Shanghai often left their children in their villages with their mothers or mothers-in-law. The practice grew by leaps and bounds in the Mao Era, and with it the demands on grandparents.

One of the largest movements was the spontaneous (自發 zifa) migration of peasants into the cities in the early 1950s; they were looking for opportunities and for a share in the joys of the revolution. The migrants left their families at home. The movement was curtailed by the introduction of the 戶口 hukou system in 1958, to prevent free movement (see Chapter 10).

A different pattern of parents leaving their children with their grandparents was government-initiated, in the late 1950s. The job assignment system (分配 fenpei) was intended to spread people with talents or special skills around the country. No consideration was given to the marital or parental status of those being assigned. The one exception was an only son, who was allowed to stay with his parents. Young people who married in their place of assignment often sent their children back to their home towns, to the care of grandparents. The parents saw their children once a year, at most. In 1965 my colleague Wang Zhangli accompanied me on a trip to Shanghai. She was able, very briefly, to arrange a meeting with her mother and her daughter on Nanjing Road, as if by chance. Her instructions before she left Beijing had been to look after me, not to see her child. She was delighted at the brief sight of her child; I was mortified.

The psychological impact of separation of young children from their parents was not considered. A group of earnest American early-childhood specialists who visited China late in the Cultural Revolution reflected that grandmothers were transmitters of outdated, even reactionary ideas, the 'ideologically unsavoury traditions of religious activity and family rituals connected with birth, marriage and death'.[30] They did not comment on the impact that the absence of the parents had on children.

Study Abroad

The early pattern (late Qing on) of young men going abroad to study (留學 liuxue) in the US and Japan was broken off in 1937, and only briefly revived in the late 1940s. In the 1950s students were sent to study in the USSR and Eastern Europe.

From the 1950s on students from Hong Kong and Taiwan made up significant proportions of foreign students in North America, and many settled after graduation. No students came from the Mainland until China opened up to the outside world in the 1980s. The pattern of study abroad was revived. There was a 'fever to leave the country' (出国热 chuguo re). During the Mao Era China had fallen behind in economic, scientific and technological terms. Young and not so young people longed to study abroad. It was not easy to achieve: scholarships were essential. And few aspiring students could speak a foreign language. But the determination was enormous, and ways were found. In the 1980s a sign of spring in Beijing was long lines of students outside Western embassies. These were the lucky ones who had been accepted by a foreign university, with a scholarship, queuing to get visas to arrive for the autumn term.

Some of the early students were in their thirties, people already married and with children. It was impossible for them to take children with them. Western governments were unwilling to give visas to children, for fear that the parents would not return to China. And their scholarships were not enough to cover dependents. In the Canadian embassy in Beijing in the mid-1980s I was involved in sending Chinese students to Canada. The issue of leaving children behind often came up, but the rare chance of going abroad could not be missed. Li Jie was left behind with her maternal grandparents when her parents went to the USA; she was separated from them for three and a half years.[31] The experience was common, accepted as necessary but sad. The parents missed their child's young years. This is Liu Haiming, who went to the USA in the late 1980s:[32]

My parents took care of my son after my wife sacrificed her own promising career in China to join me in America. We did not see our son for a few years until my parents brought him over. Although we missed him dearly, we knew we might not be able to come back to the United States on our student visas if we returned to visit him. Deep in our hearts we still regret this separation.

Not all children left with their grandparents in China were or are born there. They were born abroad and then sent home by their parents to be brought up by their grandparents in China. These children are 'satellite children', infants or pre-schoolers, whose care is time-consuming. They go back to the country where their parents live when they are old enough to go to full-time school. There is a growing number of these children, 10,000 in one city alone, Fuzhou. Most were born in the USA; the 'high cost of child care' there led the parents to send their children home.[33]

The situation of PRC students in North America has evolved over time. In the 1980s and 1990s many stayed permanently. In 1989 almost all the students studying in Canada asked to stay on 'humanitarian and compassionate' grounds. Many later brought in their children and parents. Now many graduates return to China hoping to find good opportunities there.

Adoption

One form of permanent loss of birth parents is adoption. In the past this loss was less than absolute in China; adoptions occurred within families (see Chapter 3). A new version evolved from the 1990s on. Baby girls were adopted from orphanages where they had been placed by their parents, in the hope that during the time of the One Child per Family policy the parents, by giving up a girl, could try for a boy. Tens of thousands of baby girls were adopted by new parents in North America, a smaller number in other countries. In the short run the experience is joyful – childless couples become parents, and babies with very limited prospects in China become middle class. In the longer run there may be issues. Girls raised in North America may have no other contact in China than the orphanage from which they were adopted – and records there turned out to be insufficient to connect a girl to her birth parents. International adoption from China has now been halted; children in need of adoption are placed within China.

Reunification and Separation

The exodus from China in the 1980s and 1990s produced a divide between grandchildren abroad and grandparents at home: there was no common language, and a gulf in standard of living until recently. Grandchildren disliked going to visit grandparents, especially in the torrid summer heat of China. Ann Hui's 徐鞍華 1991 film *My American Grandson* (上海假期 *Shanghai jiaqi* (Shanghai Holiday)) is set in the lane housing of old Shanghai, where people lived close to each other in what now seem tough conditions – communal kitchens, no bathrooms, cramped apartments. Into this world drops Tommy, the twelve-year-old grandson of Lao Gu 老顾, an elderly widower whose son and daughter-in-law live in America. The boy is a spoiled brat, rude and aggressive. He speaks not a word of Chinese. He hates everything, the food, the lack of a bathroom, the rules. The neighbours are critical of how he treats his grandfather. The boy phones his parents and asks them to take him home. Then he runs away. He is returned by the police to his grandfather. Everything turns round. The boy weeps in his grandfather's arms. He suddenly speaks fluent Mandarin. He teaches his schoolmates baseball. And when he leaves everyone exchanges 'American goodbyes' – bear hugs.

The film was set in the early years of reform. Today the trauma would be less. It is much easier to get back and forth from abroad to China. Living conditions there have risen dramatically, and more people in China speak English. Vancouver is a laboratory of contemporary separations and reunions. Within the large 'Chinese' community, divided between Canada-born and Hong Kong, Mainland and Taiwan immigrants, one common feature is reunion of those previously separated, grandparents joining children and grandchildren here. And there are new separations. Better job prospects in China have lured some of the earlier immigrants home. Before COVID the pace of arrivals and departures was frenetic, daily flights between Vancouver and many cities in China, Hong Kong and Taiwan. There were 'drop-in' parents, who left children in Canada and flew back and forth to their work in Asia, and 'helicopter' mothers alone abroad who hovered over their children. The back-and-forth is over for the time being, in the COVID era.

留守儿童
Liushou ertong
Left-behind children
空心的村庄
Kongxin de cunzhuang
Villages with an empty heart

Zhao Zhenghai 赵正海 lives in a village in Jishui 吉水 (Jiangxi). He and his wife have three sons and two daughters, born during the Cultural Revolution. All the sons have gone south to work, in Guangdong and Fujian. The elderly couple have had as many as eight grandchildren living with them at a time. They are compensated; their children send 150 yuan per month per child, and make a cash payment of 2,000 yuan once a year, and pay for taxes, electricity and the phone, but the old people are exhausted.[1]

Jishui is one of the myriad of 'villages with empty hearts' in rural China. The empty heart is the middle of three generations – working-age adults. They are absent for almost the whole year or even longer. They leave behind the oldest generation, their parents, and the youngest one, their children. These are the people who have made China's economic miracle possible, the workers who propel economic growth. Fan Lixin, director of the documentary *Last Train Home*, captured their contributions and their sacrifices:[2]

I used to work at TV stations in China. During those days I travelled to different parts of the county. The sharp contrast between lives in the cities and the countryside always struck me. Submerged under the glamour of the modern metropolis, the poverty in the vast rural area is overwhelming. As I travelled, I started to focus on the migrant workers, whom I believe have contributed the most to China's prosperity but benefited the least. Aside from many hardships in life, they also have to bear constant separation from their families who are left behind.

On a cultural level Confucianism played a big role in Chinese lives. Being away from one's family was never encouraged, but a changing society shifted the value toward a pragmatic approach of bettering one's material life. Parents work away from home; they send all savings to the grandparents and kids. Sadly, providing

---

Box 10.1 *Whose Utopia?*

The brilliant film *Whose Utopia?* by multimedia artist Cao Fei 曹斐 documents the lives and dreams of workers at an Osram bulb factory in Foshan 佛山 (Guangdong). The young workers are driven by demanding machines. They all look tired and sullen. But they have dreams too, and their dream figures – a dancer, a musician – flit in and out of the film. In many ways the film is an *homage* to Charlie Chaplin's *Modern Times*, meant, like that film, as a reminder to consumers of what their cheap goods cost the workers.

The photographs of Chinese factories by Edward Burtynsky convey the same message. His factories are clean and even colourful, but enormous and completely impersonal. The workers are disciplined within an inch of their lives.

---

material comfort alone does not translate into filial affection. Without parental presence and emotional support for the left-behind children, they do not connect or sympathize with their parents, as the gap between them can widen into an irreparable split.

These migrants combine two forms of migration: sojourner migration and labour migration. In the Reform Era a pattern of temporary labour migration has emerged, the short-term movement of people from villages to factories and work sites. This pattern is more like sojourner migration than urbanisation patterns in the West or in Maoist China.

China has a long tradition of sojourner migration, migrants who did not separate themselves from home. This pattern was seen in the *qiaoxiang* 僑鄉 in Guangdong and Fujian that sent people overseas as sojourners. In north China 'swallows' went in the spring to Manchuria and came home in the autumn (春去秋回 *chunqu qiuhui*). These migrants stayed connected to their home villages, where they had a hope of inheritance, where they would spend their old age and where they would be buried.

The Industrial Revolution in the West and in Japan saw vast numbers of people leaving rural areas for the cities. The workers had to live near the factories. The owners built housing for them, often poor quality but allowing permanent settlement. In early Maoist China something similar happened, in the name of creating a new society led by the proletariat. New industrial plants and work units (*danwei*) in urban China provided work, housing, health care and child care, all on the same site. The units were to be the new large family. The migrants left the villages behind and became urban residents.

Cheap, disciplined labour is the foundation of China's economic miracle. It allows the production of labour-intensive manufactures (LIMs) for export. The practice started in China in the early Republic. The goal of those who developed industry in the coastal cities was to make China the 'factory of the world'. After the Second World War Hong Kong manufacturers pioneered LIMs.[3] The reform and opening up of the 1980s brought China back into the world economy; her products flooded welcoming markets around the world.

Migrant workers are cheap and malleable. They are not allowed to change their residence status (*hukou*) from rural to urban; they are commonly referred to as 农民工 *nongmingong* (peasant workers). *The Economist* has calculated that over 250,000,000 of China's 800,000,000 urban residents are not permanent residents.[4] A Chinese government source puts the number of labour migrants away from home even higher: 290,770,000.[5] They have little access to public services such as education, and can be sent home as and when employers or local authorities decide. They are quite separate from local urban residents (本地 *bendi*) with *hukou*. They are outsiders (外地 *waidi*), unable to bring their families to their workplaces.

At the start of the Reform Era, in the early 1980s, only unmarried peasants, usually women, left home to work in the new industrial zones. They lived in dormitories attached to factories, visible but still separate from local populations. Then young men left to work in construction, as China's cities and infrastructure grew at staggering speed. They lived in portable housing units or in tents, made of blue and red striped nylon fabric. They were treated with often open hostility by the locals, who saw them as bringing crime and disruption. The migrants, male and female, were outsiders; they did not speak the local dialect and they had little to do with locals. They spent sparingly; most of what they earned went back home.

As time went on women and men worked away from home year after year, even after they were married and had children. A huge migration industry developed to find work for them, to handle remittances and to ship them back and forth from their homes by train, sleeper buses and minibuses. Traditional local-place associations (同乡会 *tongxianghui*) re-emerged supercharged, to look after fellow natives away from home. Improvements in communication – in succession beepers, cell phones, smartphones – allowed migrants to stay in contact with home.

The demand for labour was insatiable. More and more parents left their children at home. By 2016, the average age of labour migrants was the late thirties; most were parents. According to the 2010 Census, there were over 61,000,000 left-behind children (留守儿童 *liushou ertong*). Across the nation this figure accounted for 38 per cent of rural children, 22 per cent of all Chinese children. Almost one child in four was being cared for long term by their grandparents.[6] The detailed results of the 2020 Census, conducted during the pandemic, may show that with many parents at home – the pandemic struck at the Lunar New Year – the number is down.[7]

A large majority of migrant workers are cut off from their children. In 2012, 66 per cent of the 134,000 registered migrant workers in Panyu 番禺 (Guangdong), a major factory county, had left children behind in their villages.[8] UNICEF China reported in 2018 that a third of Chinese children 'could not live with their parents' (不能与父母双方共同居住 *buneng yu fumu shuangfang gongtong juzhu*). Almost 69,000,000 were designated as left-behind (留守 *liushou*), another 34,000,000 floating (流动 *liudong*). This statistic is the only dark one in an otherwise glowing report on improvement in the state of children in China: declining infant mortality, better hygiene, better education, better living conditions.[9]

Migrants cannot legally settle away from home permanently. Some move without formal permission, to live in chronic anxiety of being evicted from the cities. They have much in common with illegal migrants in the US – except that they are in their own country, and illegals in the USA often have their children with them – the Dreamers.

Box 10.2 Fanxiang

Every year, just before the New Year, tens of millions of workers are given two weeks off to go home to their families – 返乡 *fanxiang*. They travel by air, road and (overwhelmingly) rail. The workers carry huge bundles of gifts for their families. The number of people travelling in past years was huge. Fan Lixin's 2009 documentary about two young people going home, *The Last Train Home* 归途列车 (*Guitu lieche*), gives a vivid and claustrophobic sense of the press of people in the stations and on the trains, their cheerfulness under extreme pressure. Underlying their happiness to be going home is the sadness of knowing that this holiday will be the only two weeks of the year they will spend with their children.

Box 10.3 Zhejiang Village

Some bold illegal migrants set up their own enclaves near major cities. Zhejiang Village 浙江村 was a temporary 'village' north of Beijing where tens of thousands of migrants from the southern province of Zhejiang clustered together; none had *hukou*. Most were peddlers, often quite successful. The authorities tolerated the settlement for a while, but in 1995 tore down its temporary structures and evicted the residents. Other illegal settlements have cropped up and have survived, often on the edges of big cities. The inhabitants create their own communities but must always stay ahead of the authorities. There have been similar communities made up of 'real' foreigners, Russians in Beijing, or Nigerians in Guangzhou.

Box 10.4 The ant tribe

Sixteen-year-old Xie Junwen lived with his parents and younger brother in a sub-sub-basement room, nine feet by sixteen. In these miserable, foetid conditions he studied hard to get into university. This family belonged to the 'ant tribe', the subterranean people who inhabit the bowels of many cities. Xie Junwen's parents were not unemployed or unskilled. They were both in good jobs, earning well, as a chef and a teacher. Their problem was that they were outsiders, from the southern province of Hunan; they had no *hukou*, the formal document that would allow them to live where they work. Their children were not eligible to go to state schools. So the parents used their wages to pay private-school fees, leaving them almost no money to live on – and forcing them into the ant heap. Their alternatives would be to return to Hunan, and much less-well-paid jobs, or to leave their son in Hunan with his grandparents. That would cut him off from a good education.[1]

[1] Doug Saunders, *Globe and Mail*, 22 August 2015.

The *hukou* regulations prevent migrants' children from moving to the cities. Older children may visit their parents in school holidays, but working parents have no time to look after them, or money to pay for activities. The visiting children spend their holidays hanging about, little birds of passage (小候鸟 *xiaohou niao*). Some migrant parents find ways to keep their children with them, but the costs are prohibitive. Paid child care for a small child would eat up most of a parent's income. The families live in awful accommodation, even underground in the warrens of tunnels built under Chinese cities in the 1960s when fear of Soviet bombing gripped China.

The labour migrations have produced a profound change in the thinking of rural people. For at least two decades young peasants, men and women, married or not, parents or not, have assumed that they will leave their villages for work. Migration is so common that there is no stigma attached to it, nor to leaving children and old people behind. The incomes earned in the cities are far above what can be earned at home. *Not* migrating from a poor region is almost a sign of incompetence, as the pioneering journalist Leslie Chang observed: 'The new generation . . . is driven out less by the poverty of the countryside and more by the opportunity of the city. There is no longer any shame attached to migration. The shame now lies in staying home.'[10]

The choices migrant parents make are hard. They miss their children as much as the children miss them. There are no hugs and kisses, no everyday life. They worry about the children and about their education. The path to a good future is education, but rural schools are poor, free education only goes to lower middle school. High school is expensive and seldom prepares a rural student for the Gaokao, the national examination for university or college. Migrant parents must accept that their children will not have successful careers, that there will be no long-term reward for the long separations from their children.

Parent–child separations occur in many societies. British children in wealthy families were brought up in the same house but in separate quarters from their parents, in nurseries behind baize-covered doors, to block even their sounds. They were with their parents only at teatime. Boys were sent away altogether, to boarding schools. They came home only in the holidays. Socialist schemes of communal living separated children from their parents, as in Israeli kibbutzes. Filipinas who work in another country as household help have to leave their children at home. All forms are hard on children and on parents.

Technology has changed dramatically since the mass migrations started. Separations are less absolute. Electricity is almost universal. Communications and transport are vastly improved. Television is ubiquitous. Absent parents talk to their children and give long-distance supervision; there are frequent phone calls and WeChat, Facetime or QQ sessions.

The economy of a rural family has changed equally dramatically. Families depend on remittances, the money sent home by children working away. They are now transferred electronically. Agricultural income is less important. Life is better than it was, but still hard.

Some of the research on left-behind children is optimistic, finding that children will turn out to be resilient and adaptable as long as they get support.[11] Most research is less so. Dexter Roberts, a trenchant critic of the migrant labour system, sees the separations as tragic for the children, leading

---

Box 10.5 Governor General Jean

In 2010 I was part of a delegation to China led by the governor general of Canada, Michaelle Jean. Madame Jean is an advocate for women workers. In Foshan we visited the Guangda Garment Factory. During a dialogue with migrant women I introduced myself as a grandmother who cared quite often for my grandchildren – but only for a few hours at a time. I asked the women who were mothers how their own mothers coped with caring for grandchildren. They were eager to speak. Several said that it was very hard for the old women to look after small children, for fifty weeks of the year. They also told us how hard it was for them to be separated from their children. While they were speaking the representative of the All China Federation of Women kept glaring at me. Later she berated me for asking 'awkward' questions. The grandmothers, she told me, were paid for child care, as if that made everything all right.

to 'psychological problems and learning disabilities'.[12] A recent survey of thousands of rural children by Scott Rozelle and Natalie Hall found that 50 per cent were cognitively delayed. Fifty per cent of babies were undernourished, 25 per cent of children had anemia, a third of children had poor vision.[13] And now parents who leave their children behind are more aware of the problems; they were once left-behind children themselves. Fang Tiantian was left behind in a village in Guizhou as a child; now he has left his own daughter behind with the parents who left him behind – whom he resents. He blames them for his lack of education – only until sixteen – and for psychological damage.[14]

The Grandparents

Few rural grandparents have adequate pensions; their children are their pensions. Two decades ago a World Bank study found that 54 per cent of all rural elderly depended entirely on their children for support, and 69 per cent of rural women.[15] The situation has improved now (see Chapter 13), but not enough to weaken economic dependence on children.

The traditional Confucian concept of family was reciprocity; parents 'reared and nourished' (扶養 *fuyang*) their sons, so that the sons would 'respect and nourish' (奉養 *fengyang*) them in old age. This formula is no longer reliable. The traditional one assumed that the elderly would do less and less work as they aged, while their sons gradually took over. Now, in return for remittance money, the elderly have to work, and they have sole care of their grandchildren, for fifty weeks of the year. Peter Hessler described an old man whom he met in a remote village in the northwest: 'He wore the slightly dazed expression that you find among people who have been through war and revolution and famine and now, in their twilight years, have been assigned the task of raising young children.'[16]

The adult children are different from their parents. Leslie Chang captured the yawning gulf today between elderly villagers and their urban-based children. She went with a young worker, Lu Qingmin, to her home village for the New Year. Min saw herself as having to 'civilise' her family. She belonged to a different world than her parents. She loved them, and felt a sense of responsibility, but had nothing much in common with them.[17] This sense of responsibility means that workers away from home are often meticulous in sending money home. Remittances are as strong a proof as any of the strength of the long-term ties to home, and the sense of value in it.[18]

Across China the family farm is still being tended; the land is less an income source than an insurance policy – a guarantee that a person can live and will not starve. The village is the insurance and the pension for the workers. Leaving it for a period may seem essential, but does not break the tie.

The woodblock artist Gu Xiong made the picture of a peasant grandmother in ILLUSTRATION 10.1 when he was a sent-down youth in the
Daba Mountains 大巴山 (Sichuan). Her face is weathered but strong. In the
1970s she was probably only in her fifties or sixties. Today's grandparents
are in their sixties and seventies. They married at older ages than their own
parents, but still in their twenties. In the absence of birth control, they
often had many children. The number of grandchildren living with a single
couple of grandparents can be quite large. Goncalo Santos described an
overburdened old couple in the village in a poor part of Guangdong. They
cared for up to sixteen grandchildren at a time.[19]

ILLUSTRATION 10.1 Peasant grandmother

The Gaos are the optimum couple. They had only two sons. Gao Longhai 高龙海, from a hill village in Gaoan 高安 (Jiangxi), was the Party secretary in his village. In retirement he is quite well off – he and his wife both have pensions, and they have income from their tree nursery. He prized education for his children – his own was cut short by the Cultural Revolution. Both sons are professors, one in Fuzhou, one in Nanchang. When the grandchildren, one for each son, were born, he and his wife helped look after them, taking turns between the two families. The children come to the village for the winter holidays. Gao has travelled widely in China, and even to America when a son was a visiting professor there.[20] The Gaos were moderate in procreating, had only boys, and had Party connections. Their sons did well and neither had more than one child.

The polar opposite is Long Xianzhong 龙先忠 and his wife, from Dazu 大足 (Sichuan), who collapsed from the strain of looking after seven grandchildren (from their four children), on top of running a small store. Unexpected medical expenses of over 100,000 yuan wiped out their savings. For a long time his children made no contribution to the care of their own children, though eventually one son sent 2,000 yuan each year.[21]

Child care falls heavily on the grandmothers. They may feel too old to look after little ones, but it is their duty. They may be disparaged by their children for being stupid and ignorant. Their children and sons- and daughters-in-laws may complain about how the old people are raising the children. The grandchildren hear their parents' complaints and become less and less respectful of the old people, more and more difficult to handle. They complain about how strict and bad-tempered the grandparents are. The children may be resentful and defiant; they are unhappy without their parents, and they lash out at whoever is closest to them. In one lurid case, a girl of sixteen, Xiaoxue 小雪, actually killed her grandmother. As recounted in court at her trial for murder, the story was tragic:[22]

Xiaoxue was born in a village in Guangdong. When she was four both her parents went away for work. She was left behind with her father's mother. When she was eight her parents divorced. Her father married again and had two more children, including the longed-for son. Her father stopped sending money for her care; her mother was seldom heard from. She was a lonely, unloved girl. Her grandfather fell ill, and her grandmother harried the girl to help or to leave home. Finally during a bitter row the girl pushed her *nainai* over and smothered her.

Families are not stable. With couples living apart, marriages may be more likely to break up. If the parents do divorce, it may lead to a permanent separation from one or other of the parents – often the mother. There are dangers for mothers who leave their children with paternal grandparents. If the marriage breaks down, custody of a boy will go to his father; he will be raised by the father's parents, lost to his mother. Dai Xiaolei 戴晓蕾 left her son Tristan with her husband's parents in a village near Beijing. When her marriage foundered, she was denied access to her child; her husband was given custody of the boy. Tristan is a Canadian citizen, as is his mother. The court that gave her husband custody was unmoved by his citizenship: a son has to stay in his father's family.[23]

The legal and social assumption that adult children support their parents is not a guarantee that that will happen. The children may earn too little, may fail in business, may be addicted to drugs or stricken by illness. Their parents still have to care for their grandchildren. Here are some cases:

Wang Wenzhe 王文哲, a retired cadre and his wife, in a village in Huachi 华池 (Gansu) look after three grandchildren from their two sons. Neither earns enough to send any money for the care of their own children. The old people have spent all their savings on their grandchildren.[24]

Yang Ziping 杨子平, from Dongguan 东莞 (Guangdong), had a successful career, and he and his wife have generous pensions (3,800 yuan per month). Their son became a drug addict, and lost his job. The grandparents support his child, and pay for treatment for their son. The son cadges money from his mother, while people who have lent him money to buy drugs come after the father for repayment. Old Yang is so upset that he has left home, for an old peoples' facility, leaving his wife with the son and grandson.[25]

Huang Guangliang 黄光亮 and Liu Xuemei 刘雪梅, an elderly couple from Hunan, followed their two migrant sons to live in a village near Dongguan. They look after four grandchildren, one of whom has pernicious anaemia. Their son descended into depression after his daughter fell ill. His wife left, and the grandparents ended up in sole care of the much-loved girl. Over ten years her medical expenses came to over 100,000 yuan, mostly paid by the old people, from their savings. Their despair hinges on their anxiety that the medical costs will soon be too great for them to bear.[26]

These sad stories of derelict or delinquent children can be replicated in many societies. What stands out in China is that the old people have little in the way of social services to fall back on. The crippling costs of a for-profit medical system mean that financial disaster often lurks close. The social-security net that the family is supposed to constitute has many holes in it. Most at risk are the elderly who have no sons.

Zhu Yingge 朱英歌, in a village in Liuyang 浏阳 (Jiangxi), is a widow in her mid-seventies. She and her husband had a tough time early in their marriage: he was labelled a rich peasant in the land reform. Their four sons should have been a great joy, but three died, two as infants and one in an accident. Her remaining son went away to work a long time ago, and is apparently doing well, but never comes home nor sends money. She is utterly alone and desolate.[27]

Problem Children

Despite the huge responsibility taken on by grandparents, and the daily effort of looking after children for fifty weeks a year, they get little credit. There is a lofty assumption that being raised by grandparents is not good for children. There is a dismissive tone in official and academic accounts about the capacities of the older generation and about the limitations and risks they pose to the left-behind children.

Concern over left-behind children has been growing. In a survey on 'differentiated childhood' (别养童年 *bieyang tongnian*), conducted by the Chinese Academy of Agricultural Sciences in Anhui, Henan, Hunan, Jiangxi and Sichuan, researchers interviewed 400 children. Seventy per cent of them were living with their grandparents.[28] The findings of the report were grimly negative. The elderly were looked at with cold eyes, without even lip service to the wisdom of age: the grandparents had a low cultural level, many were illiterate, they lacked empathy or affection for their grandchildren. The physical care was adequate, but there were few extras – no sports, no out-of-school activities except television. The children had to work: household chores for the girls, fieldwork for the boys. Their educational achievements were minimal. The children were in daily contact with their parents by electronic means but they felt their physical absence. The children wanted more affection from their grandparents, less beating and cursing. This is the plaintive comment of one child: 'Sometimes he beats me or swears at me. I wish he wouldn't be too fierce' (他有时会打骂我们;希望他不要太凶 *Ta youshi hui dama women; xiwang ta bu tai xiong*).[29]

In 2016 the Ministry of Civil Affairs set up a special office to protect left-behind children. The All China Women's Federation (ACWF) has sponsored schemes to improve the lot of the children: substitute parents, 'happy schools', volunteer stints in villages, official visits, summer camps. A very large study was conducted jointly by the Ministries of Education, Civil Affairs and Public Security. The participation of this last ministry reflects an anxiety that children with a poor education and few prospects may be dangerous; they may turn to a life of crime or to rebellion. The Communist Party knows well that young men with little education or skill are often angry, ready to rebel against a society that they feel has short-changed them. These were the 'bare sticks' (光棍 *guanggun*) who became Boxers in 1900, violent youths who joined a messianic organisation that claimed to be able to throw foreigners out of China. The Communist Party got many early recruits from disaffected rural youth – who were only too willing to protest against a society that did not value them.[30]

The ACWF has kept up a drumbeat of warnings about the dangers to vulnerable left-behind children: sexual assault, human trafficking, accidents, becoming runaways or street children. Most important is that without parental supervision, children run wild, their grandparents unable to control them. A tragic story came from a village in Yichun 宜春 (Jiangxi):[31]

Five cousins went swimming in a pond that they had been explicitly ordered not to go to. Four of the boys got into difficulties; the fifth ran to the village to get help, but there were no able-bodied men left in the village to pull the boys out. All four drowned.

Some of the left-behind children are horrors, violent, even murderous. A fourteen-year-old girl surnamed Deng 邓 lived with her grandparents in a remote Guangdong hill village. Her parents, uncles and aunts were all working away. The girl was overburdened with child care; as the oldest in a group of cousins she was charged with looking after the younger ones. She had to drop out of junior high school; she became more and more desperate, and one day killed a six-year-old cousin. In the court proceedings that followed the judge came down hard on both sets of parents for leaving the grandparents with a load they could not sustain.[32]

Changing Times

There is a diminution of trust between parents and grandparents. Today's parents have lost the old, unquestioning confidence in the child-rearing skills of a grandmother. The old people know only traditional ways; their children have been exposed to material on modern parenting – magazines, advertisements, television programmes. Mothers do not give babies sugar water; they do not chew food themselves before feeding it to an infant. They use disposable diapers, not old-fashioned split pants, to deal with the child's 'production'. They find their parents' ways backward.

The sociologist Jun Jing tells a poignant story of what happened when a migrant couple living in Beijing took their son home to visit her parents, in Dachuan 大川 (Gansu). The baby cried constantly. The father wanted to take the baby to a doctor of Western medicine (西医 *xiyi*). The baby's aunt suggested putting the baby on formula. The grandfather made a concoction of roots, dates and millet to feed the baby. The grandmother went to the temple to burn incense. The mother tactfully went along with everything:[33]

Country doctors have cures for my baby. Deities can protect him. Milk powder is a good supplement for breast milk. My father's food therapy could invigorate the baby's health. But I could not figure out how to do all these things with the baby crying in my arms. Finally I decided to take him to the county hospital first and then visit the local deities temple with my mother. And now I am using milk powder and my father's traditional food recipe.

The respect for the elders shown by this young mother is a credit to her sensitivity. A series of interviews by the intrepid journalist Peng Xiaoling with elderly peasants, most grandparents, found that many were anything but happy with how their children treated them. Table 10.1 gives some of the titles of the interviews.[34]

Table 10.1 *Gloomy old people*

我宁愿早死	*Wo ningyuan caosi*	I would like to die soon
想找个人一起流泪	*Xiang zhao geren yiqi liulei*	I am looking for someone to weep with
我是没有明天的人	*Wo shi meiyou mingtian de ren*	I am a person without a tomorrow
年老是个可怕的病	*Nianlao shi ge kepa de bing*	Ageing is a fearful disease

Table 10.2 *Ways of coping*

在酒里可以找到安慰	*Cai jiuli keyi zhao anwei*	You can find comfort in drink
信了耶稣心里会好受些	*Xinle Yesu xinli hui haoshou xie*	Believing in Jesus makes my heart feel better

Table 10.2 gives other titles suggesting ways of coping with sad situations. The same problems recur again and again in Peng's stories: adult children seldom come home, failure of adult children to earn a good living, adult child's divorce with the virtual abandonment of the grandchildren to their grandparents. The cost of health care, their own and the grandchildrens', preyed on the minds of the elderly, who had little or no health insurance.

The work of grandparents of children whose parents have left China illegally is even more demanding than that of grandparents whose children are still in the country; these parents can seldom come back. Those who leave legally can return to China without problems. Those who are channelled – i.e. helped by migration brokers, snakeheads or people smugglers – cannot.[35] Being channelled seems worthwhile for people who want to make their fortune abroad but lack the formal qualifications to do so, but it is financed by debt, expensive and dangerous. The brokers supply bogus papers. One comic but cruel example was a work permit issued by the Republic of Edinburgh, England, which guaranteed the recipient entry to the United Kingdom.[36] If the migrants make it to their destination they are sure of continuing exploitation. There is no question of regular visits home; without valid passports the parents are condemned to legal limbo, unable to cross international borders. The only thing that comes home is money. New houses built with remittances are a sign of prosperity and often too of permanent family division: 'hard-earned income [used] to buy a big house of no use is a widely existing and popularly accepted phenomenon'.[37] The old people and the grandchildren are also in limbo. The parents are not legally away – neither present nor absent – but for their children very much missing.

Left-Behind Elderly (留守老人 *liushou laoren*)

Left-behind children eventually grow up and become self-sufficient. They will probably leave home too, perhaps to join their parents, perhaps to make their way to the cities, into the army, or to working on a government project. Hundreds of thousands of young men work abroad on contract with the government in various countries, on projects that are part of the expansionist Belt and Road Initiative.

The left-behind parents of migrants are burdened down. Physical frailty is a problem; the elderly need more care as they age. Without adequate pensions they do not retire, but the amount of physical labour they can do winds down, their incomes from farming dwindle and they are more and more dependent on their children. The rewards of old age that people hoped for when they were younger may turn out to be ephemeral.

China's remoter villages are going through a process that happened earlier in Europe and North America. Villages in the Scottish Highlands, in Calabria, in the Pyrenees, in the outports of Newfoundland have hollowed out; the young people went away to work and never came back. The elderly were left behind. The process may be an inevitable part of modernisation, but it is a painful one.[38] The *hukou* system has prevented permanent departure from the villages; it has left strange, distorted village communities. Fei Xiaotong dreamt of taking industry to the villages and small towns. The last work of the great anthropologist, done after he was rehabilitated after almost three decades in political disgrace, recapitulated programmes promoted in the 1930s by progressive intellectuals.[39] Fei's prestige gave the project considerable visibility, and in some parts of China it has worked, but it could not prevent the hollowing out of many villages.

When economic growth did not involve migration, the prospects for family unity were much higher, and the demands on grandmothers were real but not overwhelming. In 1989 the anthropologist Ellen Judd surveyed three villages in northern Shandong. Two were doing well; as a sign of the new prosperity most of the village houses had been rebuilt. One was still struggling, and still had old houses. The difference: the first two villages had established small factories, one a weaving and dyeing plant, the other making felt mats. The third village was still primarily involved in farming. The new factories gave employment to the young women of the village, provided they had one or other of their children's grand-mothers to give child care:[40]

grandmothers are a mainstay of childcare and of many other forms of domestic labour in rural China. Some form of domestic labour is a constant in their lives, although it may be reduced in later years, to come to consist largely of (usually) daytime care of young grandchildren.

Without such child care the young women could not work in the factories; the kindergartens were only open during the day but the factories worked on shifts through the night. This was an amicable arrangement. The grandmothers enjoyed looking after the little ones, while the status of the younger women rose with the income they brought into the family. Other rural households found ways to prosperity by setting up their own small entreprises. Judd lists these: running a shop, restaurant or inn; raising chickens, pigs, bees; making false teeth or mirrors. Most were run by women – and they relied on the collaboration of younger and older women to manage the household and run the entreprise.

There are possibilities for village producers in specialised products. In 1986 we stayed in a village near the end of the Great Wall at Shanhaiguan 山海关. The family was producing strawberries, a once-a-year crop that made enough money to allow them to give up other farming and focus on developing an inn. The living room of a house in their compound had been turned into a guest room, where the four of us stayed. It was spartan but comfortable. Some villages can make good incomes from gathering 'mountain products' (山货 shanhuo) – mushrooms, fungi, herbs, birds' nests, parts of wild animals.

Some of the hollowed-out villages recover and come to life again – in new ways. So many people take vacations that mountain villages attract tourists looking for fresh air and closeness to nature. Any village by the sea can turn itself into a resort. Those within reasonable distance of major cities become weekend retreats for the affluent. The village of Mutianyu 慕田峪, on the Great Wall near Beijing, was once run-down, half-empty. The old stone houses have been converted into charming vacation cottages, part of the Brickyard, a sustainable village project brought to life by Jim Spear, an expatriate American, and his wife, Tang Liang, daughter of a distinguished revolutionary. Her father, Tang Kai, was my boss at the Second Foreign Languages Institute in 1964–1965, a deeply committed Communist who had studied in France. He was pleased to see me; I could speak French.

Villages with a shrine or temple may become pilgrimage destinations. Historic sites have become places of secular pilgrimage. There are battle sites from the Resistance War and the Civil War, and Mao Era pilgrimage sites, such as Dazhai 大寨 (Shanxi), once the model for collectivisation; they were ghost sites for decades but are now benefiting from 'red tourism'. A fictional 'red' site was created by Yan Lianke 阎连科 in his novel *Lenin's Kisses*. The novel is a satire about the creation of a monument in a mountain village to commemorate Lenin's 'visit' to China (it never happened). The village becomes a pilgrimage site.[41]

Rural industrialisation and entreprise demand energetic and resourceful leaders, a supply of raw materials, access to markets and good luck. Otherwise villages must continue to rely on the export of labour to cities and factories elsewhere to bring in extra income. Many villages are too far from major centres to attract visitors, or too lacking in scenery or charming architecture. The myriad villages on the monotonous North China Plain will never attract visitors. It is impossible to tell if the hollowing-out process will be reversed, if there will there be grandmothers left in the villages to look after the next generation of children. The reforms have not been going on long enough to tell with certainty that the present generation of migrant workers will actually go home to the villages once they are too old to work in the cities, or whether they will find means to stay away.

Long-term solutions for rural China are hard to foresee and even harder for a government, authoritarian or not, to implement. Some observers assume that China will go the way of North America, where a tiny rural population farms great tracts of land in a highly mechanised way. Another possibility is that innovation and technological change will make living in rural areas so attractive and even lucrative – organic foods, premium livestock, handcrafts – that peasants will be able to stay in their villages and do well from farming. They will advertise and sell their products online. These solutions are not pipe dreams. In the months before the New Year the barren karst hills about the Li river near Guilin (outside the protected scenic zone) are covered by glistening plastic bubbles, each a little glasshouse for an orange bush, to be sent to Guangzhou and Hong Kong.

Help from richer parts of China will come. The Ice Boy, living in rural Yunnan with his grandmother, was so poor that he had no hat. He arrived at school with his hair frozen in a halo round his head. His parents were working away, and sent next to no money home. Once the story was spread by the *South China Morning Post* donations poured in; the local government provided a new house. The parents returned and rekindled their relationship.[42]

Beijing claimed, in November 2020, to have reached its goal of eradicating poverty, a claim slightly pared down by Xi Jinping; on 25 February 2021 he said that *extreme* poverty (极端贫困 *jiduan pinkun*), an income of less than US$2.30 a day, had been eradicated. The current labour migrations have created huge inequalities between rural and urban China. The old inequalities that Maoist policies claimed would be eradicated are back, the gaps even wider than before. The gap extends to the younger generations and to the semi-abandoned elderly. Left-behind children have far fewer opportunities than urban children. The rural elderly are worse off than the urban elderly. The Communist Party is still in power, preaching both socialism and Confucianism.

11 The Pleasures of Old Age

Two Russian words uttered every day with deep sighs by my grandmother-in-law, Maria Nikolaiovna Boborikina, were *staras niradas* ('old age is no joy'). An English equivalent is that old age is 'better than the alternative' (death). Gloomy sayings are far less common in Chinese worlds. Life for Chinese old people has never been all gloom, especially not for old women. They knew/know how to enjoy themselves. There were/are special pleasures to be had.

Plants

One delight for old women was/is growing flowers, not in the earth but in pots. The growers tend ornamental blooms (orchids, lilies, hyacinths and narcissi). White narcissi (水仙 *shuixian*) are grown to flower at the New Year. The bulbs grow in flat dishes with low rims. The most prized narcissi dishes are the pale-blue 汝 *Ru* dishes of the Song Dynasty, the most valuable of all ceramics. At a recent sale in Hong Kong a *Ru* dish realised HK$290,000,000 (US$38 million).

Orchids (蘭花 *lanhua*) are more demanding than narcissi. They need precise temperature and humidity. They demand patience; they take their time to bloom – months or even years. They reveal their beauty slowly; the buds fatten and gradually open. They are the ideal plant for the elderly, who have the time to nurture them and admire them. There are common orchids and rare ones. The most prized are collected in tropical forests in South East Asia, or cultivated by individuals or institutions. The Shenzhen Nongke orchid (深圳农科兰花 *Shenzhen Nongke lanhua*), a delicate pink, green and cream orchid, was cultivated at the Shenzhen Agricultural College. A single plant was sold in 2014 for 1,600,000 RMB (US$250,000).

Narcissi and orchids were grown indoors, chrysanthemums and peonies out of doors, in huge pots, to bloom as autumn came on. Even modest houses would have flowers outside the front door. Growing flowers out of doors required skill and patience – and protecting them from children, cats and pigeons. Gladys Yang 戴乃迭, the great translator, had a tiny, beautiful garden, which she protected zealously from human and natural enemies. Her daughter Yang Zhi has continued the tradition, at Gladys' Garden in Beijing.

Paying Calls

Paying calls and receiving visitors at home was a great pleasure for old women. While elderly men went out to teahouses to meet their friends or strolled around the neighbourhood, older women visited each other. In poorer homes this might mean visiting near neighbours, chatting with them and sharing tea, peanuts and candies. In richer families the ladies of the house rode out in sedan chairs to visit relatives and friends.

Chinese households were always ready to receive visitors, and to welcome them with tea, served with ceremony and courtesies. Speciality teas (名茶 mingcha) were kept for visitors. Hot water was waiting in a kettle on the stove or – more recently – in a thermos bottle. In England the phrase that greeted guests was 'I'll put the kettle on'. In China hot water was always to hand. No one drank unboiled water. Cold water was cold boiled water (凉開水 liangkaishui). The thermos has been replaced by machines that supply hot or cold water.

In wealthy homes visits were within the household, from one courtyard to another. Younger members of the family – children, grandchildren and great-grandchildren – visited the matriarch in the morning to pay their respects. In *A Dream of Red Mansions* the Lady Dowager received a string of relatives each morning. She kept a virtual roll call; she worried if someone did not show up. She seldom made visits herself, but her maids visited other maids and brought back to the old lady the intelligence that she needed to run her household.

The Victorian/Edwardian equivalent of family visiting was dinner. In affluent families all adults were required at dinner. A gong sounded in the early evening, a signal for the members of the family to go upstairs and change into evening wear. They soon came down, resplendent and bejewelled, and met in the library for a drink. The butler came in to announce that 'dinner is served'. After the last course the ladies withdrew to the (with)drawing room; the men stayed in the dining room to drink port. These rituals have been lovingly re-created in *Downton Abbey*. Less affluent people had supper as a family. In all but the wealthiest homes dinner did not survive the Second World War; dinner morphed into supper, at which adults and children ate together.

Gossip

Intelligence gathering was a key activity for old women. In the days before newspapers, telephones or social media, a 'good gossip' was the chief means of

---

Box 11.1 Gluttony

Gluttony has emerged in different places and different times, perhaps nowhere more so that in late nineteenth- and early twentieth-century England. Victorians and Edwardians ate constantly. In wealthy families morning tea with biscuits was brought to the adults in bed. Then followed breakfast in the dining room; chafing dishes on the sideboard held bacon, sausages, eggs, kippers, kedgeree. Once recovered from breakfast they had morning coffee with more biscuits. Luncheon was usually only two courses, but tea was serious, with sandwiches, scones and cake. Dinner was at least four courses, each with a different wine. For those who were still hungry before bed a cold supper was laid out on the sideboard in the dining room.

---

passing on news. Some of it was ill-intentioned, some fallacious. Content was distorted with repeating. But gossip served a real need and it gave real pleasure.

In pre-device societies gossip had currency. It conveyed status; possession of the latest gossip demonstrated insider knowledge, of the neighbourhood or of one's own family. The person who had hot gossip to pass on had distinct social capital, was respected so long as not caught out in too large a falsehood or inaccuracy.

Gossiping in China has similarities to other countries. It is associated with women more than with men, with old women more than with younger ones. The Yiddish *yenta* is an old busybody who collects information about everyone around her. *Yentas* exist in most societies. Older women are influential in the gossip sphere because they have the time to devote to it – and because they see themselves as the guardians of moral order and of high standards of household and child care. As a young woman in a stern Scottish town, Inverary, my mother lived in fear of the local 'biddies' who kept eagle eyes on the housekeeping of younger women. She was incapable of keeping her doorstep white; her laundry, done in a copper in the basement of the tenement in which we lived, was seldom spotless – and almost never dry. Even though she was an outsider, a Navy wife, she was not spared.

Gossip may not require leaving home. In communities with narrow streets lined with houses with balconies, news is shouted across from one house to another. When I was with my sister Polly in Cazorla in southern Spain I saw the local gossip leader in action. Juana's strident cry, aimed at each balcony as she walked down the narrow street, was 'the alcoholic is dead'. She headed off to the cemetery, only to discover that someone else was being buried. She did her rounds in reverse and shouted out the correction, 'the alcoholic is not dead'.

Person-to-person gossip has been partially replaced by social media. This is a sad diminution. Posting hot gossip online is not restrained by fear of prosecution for libel or by exposure in one's community as mean-spirited and unreliable. There is no possibility of nuance, of suggestive phrases that tail off and allow the listener to supply their own ending, no gasps of shock and horror. And the malicious have the protection of anonymity.

Social gossip is limited to communities of people who know each other. Political gossip is not. In the closed world of Beijing politics insider information was/is sparse. Spreading it can be labelled 'revealing state secrets', a serious criminal offence. When I first lived in China (1964–1965) political gossip was dangerous, but at a time of shortages and rationing, gossip about prices of various items, where they were available, how many coupons they needed, was not (see Chapter 5). By the 1980s, when I lived in Beijing again, everything had changed. There were few shortages; political gossip was open, full of lurid tales of corruption. The sums of money corruptly acquired by senior political figures were enormous. I argued against an old lady who told me that Deng Xiaoping had 30 billion dollars in California; it seemed too much. The love lives of senior political figures were another popular topic, as were the activities of their children, the 'princelings' (太子党 *taizidang*).

The rise of the Internet put political gossip online. Whatever means the authorities used to censor it, the netizens for a long while were ahead, coming up with ever more inventive ways to avoid the censors. That time seems to have passed, with the authorities declaring victory.

Entertainment at Home

For respectable Chinese women in the past, home entertainment was limited. There were musical instruments; the *pipa* 琵琶 and the *guzheng* 古筝, both associated with women. There was tradition of family singing; songs were either religious chants or folk songs, sung outside to relieve the drudgery of fieldwork. Women did not go out to theatres or opera houses, the preserve of men and 'professional women'. Rich women enjoyed opera productions in their own houses; itinerant troupes were hired for special occasions, such as birthdays. The Lady Dowager loved to commission operatic performances in the Jia household. The Empress Dowager Cixi had an opera theatre built at her new summer palace, the Yiheyuan 颐和园 (the first summer palace, the Yuanmingyuan 圆明园, was destroyed by British and French forces in 1860). The vibrant nightlife that developed in Shanghai in the late Qing and the Republic was exclusively for men.[1] The pleasure houses gave Shanghai the salacious reputation that brought generations of foreign men to the city, to compete with the local men for the services of courtesans.

Evening life was limited until the past half-century. Traditional Chinese homes had small oil lamps, using vegetable oil. More efficient kerosene was introduced in Republican China. Alice Tisdale Hobart, wife of a Standard Oil executive, wrote several novels set in oil depots in China. One, *Oil for the Lamps of China* (1934), was turned into a romantic film. For the great majority of the population, before electricity, darkness meant sleep. I spent parts of my first decade in a house without electricity, lit by oil lamps and candles. They were dangerous; children were not allowed to touch either. When Granny blew out the candle in my room, it was total blackness, pressing in on me; I was so scared that all I could do was go to sleep.

One form of recreation that grew in China from the late Qing on was mahjong 麻将. It is a woman's game and a very noisy one, accompanied by clacking of tiles, shouts and exclamations. It is played at tables for four. Mahjong parties involve many tables, with five players assigned to each table; players rotate so that none collapses from exhaustion or hunger. A party in a wealthy home in Shanghai, attended by the inveterate traveller Lady Hosie in 1936, went on from four in the afternoon 'to the wee small hours'. The matriarch of the family stayed up until after eleven.[2]

Mahjong is not a game of luck; the players are strategists. In the movie *Crazy Rich Asians* (2018) Rachel (Constance Wu) challenges Eleanor (Michelle Yeoh), the mother of her lover Nick. Rachel, with a Ph.D. in game theory, defaults on the point of defeating the steely matriarch; she announces that Eleanor can have her son back (have a Kleenex or three ready for the happy ending).

For many women mahjong was an addiction that ate up time and took precedence over domestic demands. One of Jerome Ch'en's earliest memories, in the 1920s, was playing underneath his mother's mahjong table while she and her friends were at the game, ignoring the children. Much of the intensity of the game comes from its intimate connection to gambling. The game has been regarded as a social scourge. It was banned early in the Communist period. The ban was easy to implement. The game cannot be played quietly; the noise easily attracted the attention of the authorities. In the Reform Era it is back.

Shopping

One of the great joys of older urban women was/is shopping. Women from poor households stepped out of the home early in the morning to shop. Traders set up their stalls or carried their goods round on poles, shouting out calls to advertise their wares. The old girls came out to inspect each item, to complain about the quality, to exclaim in mock horror at the price, to offer their own ridiculously low price – and eventually to make a purchase. The bargaining was loud and energetic; other people joined in, on one side or the other. If she did well, the old woman went home delighted. If not she returned the next day to berate the seller.

In wealthier families shopping took place at home. Peddlers came and laid out their wares for the ladies of the household. Items could be bought or orders could be placed with the peddlers for their next call. Tailors came, bringing fabric samples with them. They took measurements and returned in days with the made-up item. In England home shopping for clothing was limited to corsets, measured in the privacy of the home by the Spirella lady.

China missed one stage of shopping: catalogue shopping. North American women pored over the Sears Roebuck, Eatons or Montgomery Ward catalogues, planning their future shopping – or dreaming of what they would like to have. In their day they were bibles of consumer information. The catalogues have gone, replaced by online shopping. There China leads the way, with an intense online consumer culture, the largest in the world.

A new breed of women of 'a certain age' (not necessarily old) has launched itself into the online shopping world, the 中国大妈 Zhongguo dama ('Chinese Aunties'). These sprightly, energetic women follow every trend in prices and products. They eagerly purchase goods, shares and properties online. They are not unlike their sisters in Hong Kong and Taiwan, who have long since been shrewd and well-informed consumers and investors.

Neighbourhoods

The lives of urban women once revolved around neighbourhoods. Shanghai led the charge in breaking out of the limits of neighbourhoods. The new cityscape of the 1920s made it easy to move around, using public transport, cars or rickshaws. Older women could think of recreation outside the home, other than visits to temples. They could go to the homes of relatives and friends; they could go to movies. They could shop in the new department stores, rather than wait at home for peddlers to call. Sincere (先施百貨 xianshi baihuo), opened in 1900, was one of the great department stores that lined Nanking Road.

The Beijing hutongs, the lanes that bordered the courtyards where the bulk of the population lived, were filled with rich, colourful life, constant interaction between neighbours, hawkers, children, peddlers, beggars, craftsmen. Old women, out early to shop, could plug into the stream of gossip and rumour. The narrow hutongs prevented much vehicle traffic. When I drove around Beijing in the 1980s I lived in fear of being 'hutonged', caught in a hutong that got narrower and narrower until reversing out was the only possibility. I would draw a crowd of local volunteers, who with much shouting got me out. This vivid street life of Beijing survived into the

1980s. Since then it has largely been destroyed. Dilapidated courtyard houses have been torn down, and the life that went with the neighbourhoods erased, in favour of isolated living in high-rise apartments. City officials said that 500,000 people were evicted from the centre of town between 1991 and 2003, though unofficial estimates ran higher. The loss of this world is described in painful detail by Michael Meyer, who witnessed the destruction of Dashalan 大厦蓝, the area just south of the Front Gate (前门 qianmen), in the run-up to the 2008 Olympics.[3] Demolitions were preceded by the appearance of the character for demolition

$$拆$$
chai

stencilled onto walls.

In the 1950s Beijing's Ten Great Buildings (十大建筑 *shida jianzhu*) were Soviet-style edifices, with curly eaves here and there as a Chinese element. Now the new buildings that have erased the old Beijing are anonymous marble, brass and glass towers, with a smattering of 'signature' buildings, such as the Opera House or the Bird's Nest, that carry no cultural reference to Beijing or to China. Too late the city government has realised that, unlike other world capitals, it has placed no premium on preserving the old, except for the most famous sites – the Forbidden City, the Temple of Heaven. The great losers are the elderly, confined to apartments, dependent on elevators, deprived of the neighbourhood life they once loved.

Shopping in China is less entertaining today. The emphasis is on speed, not on spending time in an agreeable way, giving full rein to bargaining. The decline has been gradual. Stores gradually replaced street sellers, then supermarkets replaced stores; now online shopping has almost taken over. Groceries are delivered in minutes – but without any of the exhilaration of marketing and bargaining.

Handcrafts

Handcraft work was once a major activity for grandmothers, making practical items for family use. That work is gone. Shoes and clothing are manufactured in factories. Worn clothes are no longer darned or patched. Sweaters are machine-made, the vivid hand-knitted long johns of the Mao Era replaced by factory-made long underwear and tights. Padded jackets have given way to factory-made down jackets. People sleep under factory-made duvets, not under home-made quilts; duvets can be machine-washed and do not have to be unpicked and remade each spring, as the old quilts did.

Handcraft has survived, however, as embroidery and knitting for pleasure rather than practical use, knitting beautiful baby clothes or elaborate sweaters from expensive yarn. These are ways to pass time and to show love and care for the recipient.

New Home Entertainment

Before electricity arrived, the old went to bed once darkness fell. Now they spend their evenings watching television. There are national and regional channels, in Mandarin and in regional dialects. There are endless series. The most popular with the elderly are historical stories from the great novels – *Journey to the West*, *Three Kingdoms* and *A Dream of Red Mansions*. Other series are based on famous individuals – the Rongzheng Emperor, the Qianlong Emperor, the Song Dynasty corruption fighter Judge Bao (包青天 *Bao Qingtian*). These are lavish productions, with brilliant costumes and huge casts; some go into hundreds of episodes. The gritty socialist realism of late Mao Era programming (television arrived in the mid-1960s) has gone.

There are television channels dedicated to opera. Traditional opera was almost destroyed in the 1960s, replaced by turgid revolutionary opera, which did not survive. Beijing opera (京剧 *jingju*) has been revived, as has southern opera (昆剧 *kunju*), brought back from the brink by the efforts of Pai Hsien-yung. His most famous production is *The Peony Pavilion* (牡丹亭 *Mudanting*).

In the 1980s and 1990s karaoke was popular home entertainment; it has lasted longer with the elderly than with the young. It has been a mixed blessing for me. I have never come across a karaoke disc that did not have 'Diana' on it. I have had to sit with a fixed smile while a singer wailed out 'Oh, please stay by me Di-an-na'.

Public Recreation

In the Mao Era a lot of time was dedicated to political meetings and to collective, organised public activities such as parades and demonstrations. Old women played only small roles in these activities, but they did have to take up the slack at home to allow their daughters-in-law to participate.

The urban elderly now have access to very different forms of public recreation. Local authorities sponsor activity centres for the elderly (老年活动中心 *laonian huodong zhongxin*), where they can spend as much time as they like. Public parks are people-friendly; for the elderly entrance is free, as are bus tickets to get there. In the parks the elderly sing in choirs and play chess (象棋 *xiangqi*) and every form of card game. The grounds of the Temple of Heaven are always packed with spritely elderly, singing, dancing, practising martial arts and chatting.

The elderly dance. The dancing is Western ballroom dancing, performed outdoors to the music of boom boxes, often on an asphalt floor. The dancers are extraordinarily skilled and serious. There is a lightly disguised reason for dancing. The dance floor is an ideal place for elderly singles to find a match. Rather than rely on websites, as younger people might, those seeking love or companionship can meet on the dance floor.

Dancing has become so popular in the city parks that the government has felt the need to crack down. In 2015 the city authorities of Beijing announced that only twelve dances at a session were permitted, and that the 'dancing grannies' would have to restrain their exuberance.[4] The restriction has not prevented the All China Women's Federation from encouraging dancing and other physical exercise to keep elderly women fit. In 2016 the organisation headlined the 'Keep-Fit Granny' from Xi'an, Jia Yuxiang, and 'Hip Hop Granny' in Beijing, Wu Ying, aged seventy-two.[5]

New Careers and Past Times

Old women have launched out in new directions over the last few decades. Chang Xiufeng, from rural Henan, started to paint while looking after her grandchild, sharing the child's crayons and paints. She developed a style that blends Van Gogh with Chinese peasant painting. She was known as 'Granny Van Gogh'; she died in 2019. Zheng Suzhen, an eighty-five-year-old great-grandmother from Xiamen, developed a successful career impersonating Queen Elizabeth. The 'fashionista grandma with a young, wild heart' makes appearances dressed in regal outfits, her hair curled in the queen's classic style. The lack of a real resemblance did not prevent Zheng, whose working life was as a pig farmer, from doing well out of her new career.[6]

Matchmakers, almost always older women, once played a key role in Chinese society, helping families find suitable partners for their children. The tradition was considered by the Communist Party the essence of feudal family control and was replaced in the Mao Era by having Party members suggest matches for the young people under their supervision, a practice now obsolete.

Marriage is still almost universal, but young people want to choose whom they marry. Finding 'the one' is not easy. Many young women have high expectations of their future husband: graduate degree, good income, good looks. Love matters, but not as the sole basis for marriage. They are not prepared to marry down, to someone less well qualified than themselves. For young men the pressure is different. Their family will bear much of the cost of the wedding. And their families feel the need for a grandson. Parents would still prefer an arranged marriage. A World Bank study in 2015 proved this, with complex mathematical equations: parents believed that an arranged marriage would secure their old age, even if the marriages were loveless.[7]

For young people who do not meet 'the one' at school or at work there are professional matchmakers, many online. The online sites are less than satisfactory: they encourage exaggeration and lying, especially about financial issues, and looks. As time passes, the situation gets serious, especially for women, in danger of becoming 'left-over women' (剩女 shengnü), unmarried at thirty. Grandmothers troll their connections to find suitable partners for their grandchildren, ferreting out the income and character of a possible mate, arranging meetings – embarrassing for the young people.[8]

Some old women have found an alternative to matchmaking for the young: matchmaking for their own age group. Elderly widows and widowers long to find companionship and love with members of their own generation. Remarriage for widows used to be forbidden, but times are changing. Zhou Shuhua is known as the 'number one matchmaker in the world' (天下第一红娘 tianxia diyi hongniang). She is always dressed in red, the colour of happiness – and of weddings. She sets up widows and widowers with each other. Zhou observed how many lonely old people there were in her home town of Shenyang, a gritty northern city, and decided to do something about it. She is now in her early eighties, with twenty years of matchmaking behind her. Her work is voluntary, but the grateful new couples find ways to express their thanks. Their children and grandchildren have more mixed reactions. If the elderly newlyweds spend money on travel it may threaten their inheritance prospects.

Remarriage of widows is given official endorsement, for example the rather far-fetched but well-publicised story of an eighty-year-old widow, Liu Xingfen, marrying Yu Hunhe, aged 103, in a joint wedding ceremony with her granddaughter.[9] Adult children are barred by law from preventing the remarriage of elderly parents, but that is a long way from encouraging it; there is still opposition, especially in rural China.

Old-age romance seems to be a universal theme. There is a whole subgenre of British film and television: charming old people behaving in slightly nutty ways – *The Last of the Summer Wine*, *Waiting for God*, *The Best Exotic Marigold Hotel*, *Last Tango in Halifax* – always ending in late love.

Weddings

One pleasure for the elderly is diminishing – weddings. The grandparents of the groom were traditionally the honoured guests at weddings. There were no vows; instead the couple bowed to the closest representative of the ancestors, the senior generation of the groom's family. For old people it was the clearest proof of their success in running a good family. In the Mao Era that all changed.

Weddings were moved out of the family, and became simply a visit to the local police office to register a change of address. This could be perilous for foreigners who did not speak Chinese. Andrew Condran, a Scottish marine who was captured in the Korean War and chose to go to China, went with Jacqueline Xiong to an anonymous office, without realising that the visit was a wedding ceremony. In 1985 a young Québécois student went out with a girl in Shanghai twice, and then went with her to an office whose name he did not understand. He discovered through a friend who interpreted for him that he was married and that his wife and six family members were eager to leave for Canada at once.

At the start of the Reform Era, weddings were celebrated again, with family banquets, at which the elders were the honoured guests. These were not expensive or elaborate occasions, but strong liquor was served. Through the diplomatic store, located for an impenetrable reason in a pavilion of the Temple of the Sun (日坛 *ritan*), I had access to the most desirable of spirits, Johnny Walker Red Label. I donated bottles for several weddings.

The simple family wedding was a transitional fashion. Lavish wedding practices are now firmly entrenched in China, from dresses to flowers to photographs. Many couples follow a pattern from Taiwan, of going to a 'wedding palace' for a whole day, to be photographed in a range of outfits – traditional Chinese, modern Western, Qing court costumes, *Gone with the Wind*-style – in front of backdrops of famous places. After the shoot they get beautiful albums, full of pictures of themselves. The picture wedding saves the expense of inviting guests; instead of feeding their relatives and friends the couple spend all the money on themselves. The presence of grandparents is not needed.

The fashion for expensive weddings is worldwide. In some respects the Chinese are restrained compared to the West. There are no bridesmaids, in identical outfits that seldom suit any of them, no cute flower girls or page boys and no groomsmen, in ill-fitting rented suits. The mother of the bride is not expected to wear an outlandish outfit. In China the focus is on the couple. Destination weddings are very popular, opportunities for endless photographing. Grandparents are not likely to play a role in them.

Holidays

In the past annual vacations were virtually unknown in China. The rich might move to the hills or mountains to escape the heat (避暑 *bishu*) but the only trips away from home for most people were pilgrimages (see Chapter 8). Foreigners living in China in the early Republic brought new ideas. They built villas in the mountains, like Lushan 廬山, near Nanjing.

Chiang Kai-shek made it a tradition for Chinese leaders to summer there, continued by Mao Zedong. It was here in 1959 that Mao ousted Peng Dehuai, the last senior Communist to criticise him. Another resort developed by foreign residents in the 1920s and 1930s was Beidaihe 北戴河, on the coast north-east of Beijing. In the Mao Era the villas were taken over by the leaders of the Party, who spent part of every summer there, and held discussions and conferences. Mao Zedong swam in the sea. The Party also built resorts in major beauty spots – Hangzhou, Taihu, Qingdao – where its members could rest and recuperate. These were off-limits to the general population. One of Qiu Xiaolong's brilliant murder mysteries is set in such a resort above Taihu – *Don't Cry Lake Tai* (2012).

Now holidays are for all. In the 1980s holidays started with day trips for groups of work colleagues, in spring and autumn (春游秋游 *chunyou qiuyou*). Day excursions have expanded, to longer visits to beauty spots or historical sites – possibly some that the elderly had visited in their youth, as Red Guards. 'Red tourism' is a new fashion.

There is international travel. Thailand combines the opportunity of a pilgrimage with a beach holiday. Older people are not keen on one aspect of a beach holiday, tanning, 'burning black' (晒黑 *shaihei*); having a sun-darkened skin is associated with field labour. Vancouver is a popular destination, with 750,000 visitors from the PRC in 2018; the number plunged in 2019 because of the Meng Wanzhou affair and Beijing's bitter attacks on Canada. In 2020 COVID killed it dead.

Travel may be a sign of independence for older people. Su Min, a fifty-six-year-old grandmother from Zhengzhou, set out on a round-China road trip, driving herself, in part to escape from having to care for her twin grandsons.[10]

Advancing Age

Westerners often try to seem younger than they actually are. They seek the fountain of youth, applying creams and lotions to prevent wrinkles; an advertisement for a new serum is 'look younger longer'. They colour their hair, they have plastic surgery, they wear 'young' clothes, they exercise, they even lie about their age, they risk looking like 'mutton dressed up as lamb', in my grandmother's phrase. In China the opposite is true. Old women expect to age beautifully. In ILLUSTRATION 11.1 Sarah Tsang Ngo is dressing the hair of her grandmother Beatrice Yu.

Old people are proud of their advancing age, and never lie about it. Wrinkles are proud proof of experience, not hideous signs of decay. A cane is a signal that young people should help an elderly person, not a symbol of incompetence. Life has got better for many elderly women. There has been no major

ILLUSTRATION 11.1 Loving couple

turbulence for a long while, they are better off financially than they were, there has been no famine since the 1960s, technology has opened their worlds. They have lost too – a comfortable, slow-paced world of respect and warmth, which will never come back.

12   Leaving This Life

民不畏死奈何以死懼之

Min buwei si naihe yi si juzhi

If a person does not fear death, how can you make it a threat?

One lurking pressure in old age is the need to make arrangements for leaving this life. For many in the West this is difficult; to accept that death is in prospect and to make pre-need arrangements seems morbid. Elderly Chinese have been more sanguine about death: it is inevitable and must be treated with respect. In traditional beliefs the proper fulfilment of end-of-life rituals was essential. If things were done badly, or not at all, the ghost of the dead would haunt the living.

Chinese women, as mothers or grandmothers, achieved equality with men in death. The period of formal mourning for them observed by their sons and grandsons was the same length as that for their husbands: three years. Elderly women left as little as possible to chance over the way in which they would leave this life. In their fifties or sixties, their thoughts would turn to making preparations for a fitting departure. There was much to be done, complicated and detailed arrangements to be made.

Emperors started the arrangements for their tombs in middle age, if not before, and spent vast amounts of the state's money on them. The first emperor, Qin Shihuang 秦始皇, started planning his massive tomb near Xi'an even before he became emperor. The tomb, still not opened, is guarded by the Terracotta Warriors (兵馬俑 *bingmayong*), terracotta replicas of horses, chariots and 8,000 soldiers. Later emperors had massive tombs built, though none quite as grand as Qin Shihuang's. Even after the Qing Dynasty came to an end in 1911, the second president of the Republic, Yuan Shikai 袁世凱, ordered a splendid tomb in Anyang, almost identical to an imperial tomb except that the roof tiles of the tomb complex are green rather than gold. The first president, Sun Yat-sen, who died in 1925, was the exception. He wanted only a simple tomb, but his wife's brother-in-law Chiang Kai-shek insisted on creating a grand tomb for him on the Purple Mountain that towers above the new capital, Nanjing.

Ordinary people followed a similar principle in preparing for death – to spend lavishly, more than they could afford, on their grave, their coffin, their funeral and their memorials. These arrangements were not thought of as morbid but as practical and enjoyable. They ensured a good funeral and a good burial. Their children and grandchildren did not object; it took the burden off their shoulders.

Today things are more complicated. Reluctance to confront the inevitability of death has crept in. The movie *The Farewell*, set in contemporary Changchun 长春, hinges around a family's decision not to tell the grandmother that she has advanced cancer; since a diagnosis of cancer seems fatal, the Chinese title of the film is *Don't Tell Her* (别告诉她 *Bie gaosu ta*).[1] In her acceptance of her Golden Globe award for Best Actress (January 2020), Awkwafina thanked her own grandmother, 'who brought me up'.

The Grave

The first task in preparing for death was to establish that there was a grave site. There were no public cemeteries or churchyards. In traditional China this was not an issue for wealthy families; they maintained their own graveyards over many generations. The Wu family in early Republican China maintained their cemetery in the country to the east of Beijing: 'Like all typical Peking grave-yards theirs was a spacious piece of land many acres in size . . . surrounded and thickly shaded by rows of tall poplar trees and cedars planted several gener-ations back.'[2] These were once prominent features of the rural landscape, walled and shaded with thuja trees; on the flat North China Plain these were often the only trees. If a family did not have its own graveyard, finding a grave site meant finding a plot, in a place where the spirits of the wind and water (風水 *fengshui*) were in harmony, often on a hillside. A *fengshui* expert was hired to identify a good site. Plots for rural burials were quite easy to come by, but for urban residents the task was complicated; burials could not take place inside the city. It was profoundly unlucky to keep the dead within the city walls. The continued presence of Mao Zedong's embalmed remains in the dead centre of Beijing is a breach of this tradition.

The grave site was not only a place for burial, but also a place where the dead could be commemorated. Every spring families tended the graves of their dead. This festival, the Qingming (清明, 'Pure and Bright'), at the beginning of April was as much a social occasion as a commemorative one; above all it was a symbolic act of family unity. The entire living family would gather at the grave, tidy it (literally 'sweep it', 掃墓 *saomu*), pour libations of wine on the graves, lay out fruit and other offerings of

ILLUSTRATION 12.1 Three Bows

food, and then spend time sitting beside the graves reminiscing and chatting with each other and with the dead. Each member of the family
performed the Three Bows (三拜 *sanbai*). Hai Chi-yuet, whom my parents
cherished, performed the bows at their grave in an English churchyard
(ILLUSTRATION 12.1).

Many family cemeteries on the Mainland were destroyed in the 1950s, as
were grave mounds in fields. A prestigious new cemetery, for ashes only, was
created at Babaoshan 八寶山, in the western suburbs of Beijing. In the imperial
era this was where court eunuchs were buried. After 1949 it became the burial
site of revolutionary leaders.

The state encouraged cremation, in the evocative phrase 'transformation by
fire' (火化 *huohua*). Ashes might be scattered at a place the person loved.
Dr C.C. Ch'en (陳志潛 Chen Zhiqian) directed that his ashes be scattered at
Dujiangyan 都江堰, the head of the irrigation system that turned the Chengdu
plain into one of the most fertile parts of China two millennia earlier. It
represented to him one of China's finest achievements.

Cemeteries have appeared in the Reform Era. Most are commercially run.
These are crowded places, with very little room between graves or urn niches;

they have pictures of the deceased on them. Niches are now the most costly form of real estate, more expensive, per square foot, than a luxury condominium. Michael Meyer describes his wife Frances's efforts to acquire a suitable place for her father's ashes:[3]

At the privately run Eternal Garden Cemetery in Shenzhen, a saleswoman explained to Frances that 50,000 yuan (US$7547) would secure her father's ashes in a one-square meter hillside plot for twenty years, with an option to renew for fifty years after that, provided the cemetery had not been evicted by a building site.

'If you want the grave to face the pond and valley, which has the best fengshui, it will cost 70,000 yuan. They are selling quickly; I suggest you buy today. The price will not go down'. Frances quickly chose the tomb with a view.

Babaoshan has been expanded to accommodate less famous people who can pay huge sums to have their remains placed there.

The Coffin

In the past a person's coffin and burial clothes had to be prepared and kept ready for the death day. The wealthy might order a coffin from Liuzhou 柳州 (Guangxi), a town whose economy was based on camphor and sandalwood coffins that promised to preserve the corpse. Ordinary people used the best wood available in their area. The decision to order a coffin was a recognition that death was foreseeable. Carpenters would be hired, wood purchased. The making of the coffin was carried out in a courtyard of the house of the future occupant, who would supervise the process. This public activity demonstrated not only that a person was prepared for death, but also that they would leave in style:[4]

Usually an elderly person had a coffin made and stored in the clan temple long before death. The quality of the coffin is of as much importance as is the quality of a set of clothes or of a house.

Besides the coffin, suitable grave clothes (壽衣 shouyi) had to be prepared. Making them ahead of time spared relatives the macabre decision after someone had died of what clothes to put on the corpse. In the early Republic the grandmother of the Chang family started her planning in her early sixties, more than a decade before she died. When death came everything was ready:[5]

The deceased was dressed in the burial clothes she herself had gotten ready more than a decade before. (She had slept in them one New Year to formally establish that they belonged to her.) Her coffin was completed around the same time her burial clothes were made. Its material was yellow nanmu, the best money could buy for a coffin. The family had it stored in a funeral home in Shanghai. Every year an employee of the undertaker would apply an extra coat of lacquer to the coffin.

The clothes could be as lavish as the person ordering them wanted them to be. This is Old Madam Yin, a rich Beijing matriarch, in the late 1930s. She had intimations that her death might not be far away. She showed off her grave clothes with pride:[6]

She was like a bride showing off her trousseau. She took up the red silk underwear – long trousers and a short coat that would be next to the skin ... There was a pair of padded silk trousers and a knee-length padded coat to go on next. Then there was the formal pleated skirt of many colors and gay embroidery and the red silk formal coat ... To go over all these was the long sleeveless coat of embroidered black satin.

The turbulence of wartime (1937–1949) nullified these preparations. Wartime casualties, soldiers and civilians, often had no graves, let alone coffins. After 1949 the Communist Party's opposition to burial as a feudal practice led to the destruction of coffins. In a village outside Jinan the elderly wife of a former landlord saw her coffin smashed. She felt its loss as much as the loss of the family's land. Large coffins were not seen again until the 1980s.

The Funeral

Beyond preparing the coffin and the burial clothing the future dead person had to set aside money to pay for the priests who would lead the funeral ceremonies, and for professional mourners, women who would wail throughout the ceremonies, to spare the family members from having to wail ceaselessly themselves. Money also had to be set aside to pay for feeding the family and neighbours who would gather for the ceremonies, which might last several days. The procession to the burial ground and the catafalque bearing the coffin had to be financed – money for musicians, for the catafalque and for its bearers. The white hemp robes that the family would wear during the ceremonies had to be prepared.

When the death did occur, the preparations were put into action. Geomancers were consulted to find the best day and hour for the funeral. Summonses were sent out to family members, except pregnant women, who were excluded from funerals. The family mourners were issued with their robes. The catafalque and the procession to the grave were assembled. Musicians and professional wailers were hired. Priests, both Buddhist and Daoist, chanted during the procession and at the grave site.[7]

After the coffin had been lowered into the grave the mourners burnt paper versions of everything that the deceased would need in the afterlife. These included paper food, books, clothing and effigies of human beings who would wait on the deceased or entertain him or her in the afterlife (ILLUSTRATION 12.2). These are the descriptions of the human effigies burnt at the funeral of old Mr Wu, in early Republican Beijing:[8]

paper servants, full-size effigy of the cook carrying a market basket and a cut of meat, and the maid-servant with the face basin and a towel, and a dish containing a cake of

ILLUSTRATION 12.2 Paper servants

soap etc., all made of paper and each bearing on the back a paper label with a name on it so the spirit of old Mr. Wu would be able to address them by their names.

The practice of taking day-to-day items to the grave goes back millennia. The archaic bronzes and jades from the Shang and Zhou Dynasties were made not as works of art to be displayed publicly, but as objects to accompany the deceased into the afterlife. Skeletons found in ancient graves reveal that servants were buried alive with their masters. In the Han and Tang Dynasties terracotta replicas replaced human servants.

Paper money – ghost money or joss (金纸 *jinzhi*) – was burnt at the funeral, so that the deceased would have the wherewithal to look after their needs in the afterlife. New paper offerings would be burnt in subsequent years at Qingming. It was a comforting feeling for the living, to be able to look after the needs of their dead.

The funeral rites could stretch over long periods. Temporary burial was permitted by custom, until a suitable time could be found for interment. Sun Yat-sen was not buried for several years after his death, the time that it took to build the tremendous mausoleum for him. Until then he rested in the Temple of the Azure Cloud (碧雲寺 *Biyunsi*) outside Beijing. Tan Kha-khee 陈嘉庚, the most famous Overseas Chinese, was not able to go home for his mother's funeral in Fujian until two years after she had died, 'due to business commitments in Singapore'. Her burial had to wait until her beloved son could get home.[9] Overseas Chinese who died abroad were buried there, with the understanding that the burial was temporary, and that their bones would later be exhumed and sent back to their native place in China. The Harling Point Cemetery in Victoria (British Columbia) faces west across the sea to China. For a long time it was the temporary burial place for Chinese who died in British Columbia. It became permanent after 1937, when it was no longer possible to send remains home.

In the Mao Era funeral practices were transformed. The Communist Party was strongly against lavish funerals and prolonged mourning. A Soviet form of commemoration meetings emerged, run by a special committee; the dead person was represented by a photograph. Huge paper wreaths were displayed. The bereaved wore black armbands.

These proceedings were inadequate to express grief; for many the desire to give a loved one a good send-off could not be suppressed. In 1966, Zhang Buwang, a local cadre in Ruian 瑞安 (Zhejiang), invited hundreds of people to his mother's funeral, and put on a lavish banquet after the ceremonies. His actions were approved by most of the local people. She was a mother, a grandmother and a great-grandmother, the embodiment of 'four generations under one roof'. Those above Zhang in the political hierarchy did not feel up to disciplining him. They had bigger things to worry about as the Cultural Revolution got under way.[10]

The Maoist attack on traditional ways of treating the dead caused great anguish to the elderly. Graves sited on arable land were dug up and moved to unproductive land. The disturbance of the graves and their dead was a grim prediction of what would happen later. Zhang Buwang was lucky in his timing when he buried his mother in 1966. Even a few months later this would not have been possible. At the depth of the Cultural Revolution Red Guards took joy in desecrating graves, symbols of the feudal past. The most famous example was the Kong Lin 孔林, the Cemetery of Confucius, which covers over three square kilometers near Qufu 曲阜, Confucius' native place in Shandong. The cemetery houses the graves of over a 100,000 descendants of Confucius. Along with the Confucian Temple (孔庙 *Kong miao*) and the Confucius Mansion (孔府 *Kong fu*), it had been the symbolic heart of Confucianism, maintained by successive dynasties. In 1966 Red Guards from Beijing set about vandalising the sites. In the cemetery they went to work, desecrating individual tombs, smashing the stele that stood above them and performing gross indignities on human remains. The Red Guards left after they had destroyed about 2,000 graves. Then came grave robbers, looking for the precious objects buried with the deceased. No grave was left untouched. Another band of Red Guards desecrated the tomb of the Ming Wanli 萬曆 Emperor, the Ding Ling 定陵. This was the first of the Ming tombs to be excavated in 1959; seven years later Red Guards poured in and smashed the emperor's skeleton.

Disturbing the dead is a universal taboo. In Western countries Halloween and all the creepy costumes that go with it stem from the fear of upsetting the spirits of the dead. In China, where respect for the ancestors was a fundamental pillar of society, the disturbance of the dead hit even harder. But there are precedents. Tombs with valuables in them have always been targets of robbers. Many of the ancient artefacts on the antique market today come from looted tombs. The tomb of the Empress Dowager, the Dingdong 定東, was looted in 1928 by warlord troops for the valuables it contained, including an assortment of jade fruit and vegetables. Desecration may have an ideological basis. In 1945 after the Japanese surrendered and the puppet government in Nanjing was swept aside, the grave of its leader, Wang Jingwei 汪精衛, was desecrated, and his remains scattered; he had only been dead for a year, so this must have been quite gruesome.

Great pain came to those who were unable to give their parents a proper funeral. David Chang only heard of his mother's death in 1955 after President Nixon's visit to China in 1972. In the changed political climate he managed to send money to a cousin to have his parents reburied together. Finally, in 1979, he went to his mother's grave. It was a moment of grief and guilt:[11]

My accomplishments, my family, my struggles seemed entirely without significance. I had abandoned my mother, left her to suffer and die without my comfort, her heart broken and crying out for her lost sons, of whom I had been the youngest, dearest, and most culpable for the final tragedy of her life.

The harsh practices of the Mao Era have been reversed in the Reform Era. Elaborate funerals are now the norm: mourners wear white clothing, lamentations are loud. There is a large industry to provide the paper goods that are burnt for the departed.

There is still a strong feeling that burial is preferable to cremation, 'entering the earth for peace' (入土为安 rutu weian). As soon as the madness of the Cultural Revolution was over, graves were restored, and new rites were held for those who had been buried improperly. This is an example of the huge efforts that families may go to to give their dead peace. Chen Huiqin's parents died in the Cultural Revolution. Their bodies were cremated, and the family was only able to perform perfunctory, almost secret, rites for them. In the early 1980s the ashes were reburied, in the family's agricultural plot; they had to be moved soon, when the plot was expropriated for a factory. Later on that site was expropriated too. The parents' ashes were moved to a new cemetery, and reburied, this time

---

Box 12.1 Paper memorial products

To see imagination at full flood look no further than the paper goods provided today for funerals and for the annual commemoration of the dead, all to be burnt at the grave. Money is central, along with share certificates; then come paper cars, air conditioners, cell phones, houses (even apartment buildings), clothing, anything that survivors think the dear departed will need for the coming year. The exuberance and thoughtfulness of the offerings, burnt on the day of commemoration, far surpass the wreaths and bunches of flowers that go on Western graves, only to wither and die.

---

with a proper gravestone. The family paid 5,500 yuan for the plot, only 500 yuan of which came from compensation for the expropriation.[12] Chen found a spirit medium to contact her parents in the afterlife – a profession once banned, now again flourishing. She was relieved to find that they were fine.

Sometimes government has taken the lead in making up for desecration. The tomb of the old warlord Lu Rongting 陸蓉廷 in Wuming 武鳴 (Guangxi) was destroyed by Red Guards. In the 1980s the county government, recognising how much Lu had done for his home place, contacted his children in Hong Kong and worked with them to have the tomb restored. It was rebuilt in a slightly different, more propitious location. In 1995 the ashes of the last emperor of China, Pu Yi, were reburied in the Western Tombs outside Beijing. He had died during the Cultural Revolution, and was given no funeral. Three decades after he died he was reunited with his imperial ancestors.

Chinese funerals were/are less scripted than religious funerals in Western religious traditions, which are conducted by ritual specialists in churches, mosques or synagogues, and follow formal liturgies. There is more room in Chinese practice for demonstrations of mourning, for speaking about the dead and for showing them respect.

Leaders' Remains

Two of China's modern leaders remain unburied, a strange and disturbing coincidence. Mao Zedong's funeral was not followed by burial. His embalmed body lies in a crystal coffin in a mausoleum on Tiananmen Square. I am squeamish; though I have had many opportunities I have never been to see Mao's remains. My squeamishness is reinforced by knowing that this Soviet practice is an abuse of Chinese tradition, which demands that bodies be buried *outside* cities.

Chiang Kai-shek has not broken entirely with tradition. His remains lie in a huge black lacquer coffin, with a white Christian cross on the top. They are in a small pavilion, by a lake outside Taipei, waiting for proper burial in his home place, Fenghua 奉化 (Zhejiang). The Beijing government periodically offers to arrange for his remains to be brought back to Fenghua – a move that would be a sign of reconciliation between the Mainland and Taiwan. His old home in Fenghua has been converted into a tourist site. The future of Mao's remains is uncertain. By custom they should eventually be returned to his birthplace in Hunan.

Wills

In the West the wills of the deceased deal principally with the disposal of property. They are legal documents, written in complex legalese. The will is read by a solicitor, around the time of the funeral. This is a dramatic moment; its contents may be unknown up until that point.

The traditional Chinese concept of wills is quite different. The disposition of property is done by custom, equal portions to sons, with an extra portion for the care of elders and of graves. Wills are a place for advice and exhortation to the younger generations, not for distribution of property. The most famous will is the one that Sun Yat-sen wrote shortly before his death. It was dedicated to the whole Chinese nation:

For forty years I have devoted myself to the cause of the National Revolution with but one end in view, the elevation of China to a position of freedom and equality among the nations. My experiences during these forty years have firmly convinced me that to attain this goal we must bring about a thorough awakening of our own people and ally ourselves in a common struggle with those peoples of the world who treat us on the basis of equality.

The work of the Revolution is not yet done. Let all our comrades follow my Plans for National Reconstruction, Fundamentals of National Reconstruction, Three Principles of the People, and The Manifesto of the First National Convention of the Kuomintang, and strive on for their consummation. Above all, our recent declarations in favor of the convocation of a National Convention and the abolition of unequal treaties should be carried into effect with the least possible delay. This is my heartfelt charge to you.

(Signed) Sun Wen
March 11, 1925

Written on February 20, 1925

His will was learned by heart by all schoolchildren in the decades after his death.

Western common-law wills are transfers of wealth from one generation to the next. There is considerable room for inflicting pleasure or pain. Malice from beyond the grave, ranging from disinheritance to spiteful omissions to unexpected or unwanted bequests, is the stuff of novels. English fiction is full of plots that focus around wills, starting with the greatest novel of all, George Eliot's *Middlemarch*. Its leitmotif is nasty tricks played by elderly men in their last testaments. Crime fiction is solidly based on wills. One of the first questions in murder mysteries is *cui bono*, 'who stands to benefit?'

Wills can be occasions for mischief. My father was hounded in the last decades of his life by his old college, pressing him for mention in his 'testamentary dispositions'. He left an annual barrel of beer to the college's rowing club. The bequest was declined. The will of Charles Millar, a bachelor lawyer in Toronto, was more grandiose. He left his entire estate to the Toronto mother who gave birth to the largest number of children in the decade after his death. In 1936, four mothers, who had each given birth to nine babies, divided $570,000. Madame Elizire Dionne, mother of the Dionne quintuplets, and nine other children, did not qualify because her babies were born in northern Ontario.

In China before the Mao Era property essentially belonged to the family. Sons inherited equally, with the oldest getting an extra share to care for the ancestors. They might choose to divide the family property (*fenjia*), but tradition discouraged them from doing so. Equal inheritance rights meant that migrants, within China or beyond, felt a strong pull to home – they had something to go back for.

For decades inheritance was complicated by the cloudy state of property ownership. This was a fallout of wartime confiscations. Enormous quantities of real estate and movable property had been confiscated between 1937 and the 1980s: by the Japanese occupiers between 1937 and 1945, by the Nationalists (as enemy property) after 1945, by the Communists (as Nationalist property) after 1949. The return of confiscated property to the heirs of people already dead was difficult, complicated by a lack of paperwork; deeds had been destroyed, so that heirs had no proof that their family had once owned a house. Some families retrieved property; others continue to battle (see Box 6.6,Ye Jiaying).

In the Mao Era inheritance rights to land disappeared; land was collectivised, though houses could still be divided. In the Reform Era inheritance rights have been restored, in the Law of Succession (1985). There are changes from the old customary system, chief of which is that women are included; sons and daughters have equal rights to inheritance. Until recently elderly people tended not to write wills, but to rely on the tradition of division of property between sons. Now they write wills that *do* include their daughters. Formal wills can create just as many problems as customary division. The children of the great painter Xu Linlu 徐麟庐 sued their mother when, after his death in 2011, it emerged that his will left all his extremely valuable paintings to her. They lost.[13]

The exception for Chinese wills has been Hong Kong, where inheritance is decided under Common Law. There have been notable, vicious battles within wealthy families over inheritance after the death of a patriarch. These battles are particularly acute in polygamous families. One of the last colonial mansions in Hong Kong, on Pokfulam Road, stood crumbling and empty for decades while the heirs fought with each other over who would benefit from the site's redevelopment.

The Afterlife

The dead in China depend on their living descendants to remember them, to provide for their needs, and to succeed in life to honour them. Their eternity is in their families. Distinguished people live on in wider circles. They are listed in local records. In the past a stele might be erected in their memory, listing their achievements. In Xi'an the Stele Forest 碑林, over a millennium old, houses 3,000 steles. In modern practice a plaque may appear in front of the house a distinguished person lived in, erected by the local cultural bureau. The former home of General Pai Ch'ung-hsi in Guilin has such a plaque. The house is next door to a hotel; the English name is the White House, the Chinese the *Baigong* – the Bai (i.e. Pai) Palace.

Another innovation is naming parks. In Zhong Caojiazhuang 中曹家庄 (Hebei) there is a park named for the village's only famous son, Cao Richang 曹日昌, the pioneer of psychology. There is no memorial anywhere for Cao's wife, Selma Vos, who died in the Cultural Revolution in mysterious and tragic circumstances. Selma was Dutch and Jewish. She survived five years in hiding in Holland under Nazi occupation. She married Cao in Cambridge in 1948 and went to China with him. I worked with her in 1964–1965. The story of her life has been a bestseller in Holland.[14]

Long-range commemoration of the dead rarely arises in the West; ancestors, except in aristocratic families, are remote and unknown, so much so that many people have no idea even of where they come from. Ancestry sites offer to help people find their ancestors, for a fee. A greater concern than ancestors, amongst the religious, is where they will go after death.

As my generation gets closer to the inevitable end, my friends in China and elsewhere have started to think about our legacies and the distribution of wealth and possessions. In China naming buildings has emerged in the Reform Era. At Xiamen University one towering building after another is named for a local Overseas Chinese who did well in the Nanyang 南洋 (the 'Southern Ocean' – South East Asia). Nearby in Jimei 集美 is the Education Village, created by Tan Kha-khee. He founded it as a residential community to educate the children of Overseas Chinese. The beautiful complex of buildings is a lasting memorial to him.

One tradition particular to China is the posthumous rehabilitation (平反 *pingfan*) of a person who died an unjust death. Yue Fei is the most famous example (see Chapter 8). Much more recent examples are those who died in the Cultural Revolution. Families may petition for rectification. If they are successful a ceremony may be held to 'reverse the verdict' and honour the wrongfully attacked person. Marshall Peng Dehuai died in detention in 1974, his death not announced even to his family, so great was Mao's hatred for him. After Mao's death Peng was rehabilitated; his ashes were interred at Babaoshan. A special postage stamp was issued to mark what would have been his ninetieth birthday. In 2015, seventy years after the end of the Resistance War, there was a surge of commemoration of people who perished in the war, but that war still remains one of the least commemorated in modern history, though changes are coming.[15] The latest dead hero is Dr Li Wenliang 李文良, the Wuhan doctor who blew the whistle on COVID, and was punished for his courage. He later died of the disease. He was commemorated informally outside his hospital, with a bank of flowers. The authorities rectified his case soon after his death.

The ancient Chinese traditions around death, commemoration and remembrance have been revived over the past four decades. The dead remain alive so long as they are commemorated and remembered.

13   The Future of the Old

Old age is a time for looking back. The old are observers, retired from serious conflicts, the strongest passions spent.

座山觀虎斗

zuoshan guan hudou

sitting on the mountain watching the tigers fight

This ancient saying, from the *Records of the Grand Historian* (史記 *Shi ji*) (first century BCE), is often used to mean sitting on the fence, refusing to take sides. I use it in a different sense, to apply to old people who no longer have the influence or power to be involved in current disputes. Instead they look back on their lives with a range of emotions: pride in their families, satisfaction in their survival, regret over failures and losses. Women in China may have less to regret than men. Modern China has not been kind to women. Zhang Rong's tribute to her grandmother Yang Yufang encapsulates the hardships that women born a century ago suffered:[1]

She was a great character – vivacious, talented, and immensely capable. Yet she had no outlet for her abilities. The daughter of an ambitious small-town policeman, concubine to a warlord, step-mother to an extended but divided family, and mother and mother-in-law to two Communist officials – in all these circumstances she had little happiness.

Zhang stopped short in her account of her grandmother's life. She did not mention the role that gave her joy, as an old woman, as the dedicated and loving grandmother to five children. She cared for them, stood in for their absent parents and fought for them through the upheavals of the Mao Era (see Chapter 9). Those times of extreme upheaval and pressure, when grandmothers literally had to rescue their grandchildren, have passed. Today's grandmothers have different experiences, different roles, different expectations.

Their future is uncertain. On the positive side they are likely to live longer than earlier generations, and longer than men. Many elderly people are well off; they own their home, bought before housing prices went into the stratosphere. They have a pension and savings. They are part of the 'silver market', a sector of the consumer market less interested in fashion and more in sensible shoes, comfortable clothes and mobility aids. The old have not been demanding; there has been no surge of 'grey power' in China, or for that matter elsewhere. The last time there was an expression of elderly influence was in 1999, when supporters of Falungong staged a sit-in round the central government buildings in Beijing. This sole demonstration triggered repression of Falungong and a cautious recognition that the elderly have to be looked after; serious work on implementing a pension system got under way.

On the negative side there will be more elderly, in proportion to young people. They may be burdens to their children and grandchildren, and to society as a whole. China is not well prepared to deal with the imbalance between retired people and working people. It is described in apocalyptic terms: the 'grey tsunami', the 'ageing time bomb', 'the tidal wave of grey hair'. *The Economist* noted somberly that 'after decades of population control China now stands at the precipice of a population explosion of elderly people'.[2] The threat is intensified by the failure of the birth rate to rebound after the end of the One Child per Family policy. James Liang, entrepreneur and professor at Peking University, claims that 'the collapse of the newborn population is really here', with births in 2020 perhaps almost 10 per cent down from 2019.[3] In something close to desperation the government is now encouraging couples to go beyond the two allowed and have three children.

The intensifying imbalance between old, middle-aged and young looks even grimmer presented in statistical projections. By 2030, according to researchers at Renmin University and Peking University, there will be 365 million people over sixty, as opposed to 222 million in 2016. By 2050, if a straight-line projection is drawn, over 40 per cent of the population will be over the age of sixty. Put in a less scary format, by 2045, 25 per cent of the population will be over sixty-five.[4] Government and university institutes studying ageing, gerontology, dementia and pensions have mushroomed. They produce reports full of foreboding. Their starting point is that the resources to cope with looking after the elderly are not there.

The social safety net has huge holes in it. *The Economist* describes China as having a 'social safety net akin to those of much poorer countries', and the welfare and unemployment systems as 'threadbare'.[5] Full health care does not extend to more than a fraction of the elderly population. The state pension system introduced in the 1990s is inadequate; it covers only a portion of the urban elderly, few of the rural elderly. It is contributory; pensions are only payable to those who have made more than fifteen years of contributions before they start to receive payments. In 2017, 38 per cent of rural elderly (over sixty) received some state support, a subsistence allowance (低保 *dibao*), as did 17 per cent of urban elderly, but the minimal amount of money is not enough to live on.[6] The retirement age, and therefore the pensionable age, will rise;

there are plans to raise it by small increments, so as not to upset people close to retirement. Some elderly people are still able to work, but the proportion of all old people who do so may be small.

The care of the elderly will continue to fall overwhelmingly on their children and grandchildren. This care is enforced by law. In 2018, in a case that attracted national attention, five adult children in Sichuan were convicted of filial neglect, abandoning their father and leaving him to die alone. Their defence that he was abusive and cranky fell on deaf ears. The judgment underlined the principle that care for elders fell on sons rather than on daughters. Zhang Sun'an's only son was sentenced to two years in jail, his four daughters given suspended sentences.[7]

How willing or able will the younger generations be to support their old people? A standard trope is that Chinese honour and care for the aged, whereas Westerners do not. A commonplace assumption in China is that Westerners do not keep their elderly at home, but consign them to old peoples' homes, where they are warehoused, forgotten and miserable. The trope may be exaggerated, though the COVID death rates in long-term care homes in Europe and North America is evidence of serious defects in care for the old.

China has not been without grim views of old age in China, a sad and lonely one. This is Du Fu 杜甫, the Tang poet, writing almost a millennium and a half ago, in a time of great turbulence:[8]

江村獨歸處
寂寞養殘生

Jiangcun dugui qu
Jimo yang cansheng

I go back alone to my village by the river
To eke out the remnants of my life in melancholy.

Du Fu himself lived only to fifty-eight, old age for the times.

How can sad old age be avoided today? Beijing advocates a return to Confucian respect for age as the foundation of elder care; the middle-aged and young have an obligation to care for their seniors. It is a moral and cultural obligation; it speaks to the essence of Chinese civilisation. Confucianism used to be anathema for the Communist Party. Now it has been revived in a utilitarian, instrumental way, as a substitute for social services. There is a huge irony here: the young of the Mao Era, the generation who attacked the old, are now old themselves. Confucius is resurrected to look after them in old age, an old age that coincides with consumerism, and growing numbers of elderly.

As lives get longer, the ranks of elderly in a family swell; the work of the young has to support them all. This is less than attractive to younger generations. They have demands on their incomes – an apartment, a car, school fees, travel. Looking after the elderly may slip down the list of priorities. The old idea that 'having an old person in the family means 'having a golden living treasure' (家有一老黃金活寶 *jia you yi lao huangjin huobao*) may be replaced by the gloomy observation that 'to grow old and not die is to be a thief'.

老而不死是為賊也

Lao er bu si shi wei zei ye

The return to Confucian values does nothing for several categories of old people. One category is those in a family where elders outnumber working members. A working couple may have so many elderly to support that even with the best will and a good income, they cannot care for them all. The worst-case scenario for a working couple, both singletons, is that they have one child, four parents, eight grandparents and a number of great-grandparents, an exacerbation of the 4–2–1 syndrome to 8–4–2–1 (see Chapter 6). Another category contains the elderly who have no son, either because their children were all girls, or because their only son has died. These elderly people, often caring for orphaned grandchildren, face a future of the greatest uncertainty. A third category consists of the childless elderly, without even grandchildren.

The elderly problem is not unique to China. Everywhere people live longer and longer. They are increasingly frail (our mother said 'decrepit'), beset by biomechanical failures – hips, knees, shoulders. They need medical care and institutional care. They may have no pensions, or outlive the ones they do have. They make heavy demands on states with social-service systems. They work their way through their children's inheritance, living on in houses that they bought cheaply, while their children cannot afford an apartment. A three-bedroomed house near my university, which sold for about $30,000 in the 1960s when my generation started working, now costs $3,000,000. Adult children may love their parents, but feelings that range from irritation, to resentment, to rancour are just below the surface. If the elderly complain about how much property taxes have gone up, they will get a salty response. The lifetime jobs that my generation got – in government, academia, banking – are now scarce. In the eyes of the younger the older generation are the lucky ones: now they seem to ask for even more privilege.

Being overburdened with the elderly produces stresses in families. In the worst cases stress boils over into violence. One subject approached with a degree of fear and horror is elder abuse, the maltreatment of the old by their children or by care workers. Abuse has probably always existed. The advent of webcams and other recording devices has brought it into the open, even if only in a limited way. Every now and again a miserable video of an elderly person being abused surfaces. They could just as well be recorded in North America as in China.

The caring capacity of the younger generations is most stressful when they are asked to care for the elderly relatives who have passed into senile decay or dementia. In their second childhood these elderly need constant care, as much as is needed by infants.

返老還童

Fan lao huan tong

The old return to childhood

One way to handle the ageing crisis that has yet to be discussed openly in China: accelerating the end of life, i.e. the solemn debates in the West about 'dying with dignity' or 'medical assistance in dying' (MAID). But they are not impossible in the future, given the cost of medical care and the stress on younger generations. The idea of a timely exit is in fundamental conflict with the longing for longevity.

Longevity 長壽 *changshou*

China's 2010 Census gave impressive evidence of longevity; there were over 48,000 centenarians. The search for longevity, even immortality, has a long tradition in China. Many historical figures lived to extraordinary ages.

Box 13.1 The god of longevity

There are many symbols in the cult of longevity. A favourite portrayal is Shouxing 壽星, the god or star of longevity. He is a thin, bald old man, with a pronounced elongation to his skull. He rides a deer, and holds a peach in one hand, a stick in the other. His image is given out on occasions that celebrate elderly people and their families. The peach carries many happy associations with longevity, the happiest is the Peach Garden outside the World (世外桃源 *shiwai taoyuan*), Paradise or the Garden of Eden with peaches rather than apples.

Box 13.2 Methuselah

Long-lived historical figures have one characteristic in common: no official documentation of their age. Methuselah lived to 969, according to the Book of Genesis. The Yellow Emperor, founding father of the Chinese people, lived to 113, from 2711 to 2598 BCE. Zhao Tuo 趙佗, the king of Nanyue 南越, ruled his kingdom for sixty-seven years, from 203 to 137 BCE. Li Qingyun 李请雲, the great herbalist, lived either 203 or 256 years, from the mid-Qing Dynasty to the Republic. Luo Meizhen 羅美珍, once claimed to be the oldest living person in the world, lived from 1885 to 2013, in Bama. She had no birth certificate; they only appeared in China after 1949.

More than a millennium ago Daoist alchemists searched for the elixir of life, testing combinations of mineral elements, sometimes with unexpected results, such as gunpowder, recorded in Daoist texts as 'not suitable for consumption'. Beyond an elixir, Chinese pharmacology and cuisine have medications and foods that promote long, healthy life.

Longevity is a delicious mystery. It attracts scientists, herbalists and religious groups, and many charlatans. Chinese medicine has many remedies that promote longevity, most of them herbal. Natural products have strong followings. Ginseng (人參 renshen) is a panacea. The most valued roots grow wild in Manchuria, Korea and Canada, and command prices of several hundred dollars a pound. Goji berries (枸杞 gouqi) sound like the next best thing to an elixir, the 'fountain of youth', an 'anti-ageing super-fruit' and an aphrodisiac. Most berries come from Zhongning 中宁 (Gansu), a once impoverished county now basking in the berries' popularity. Some products outdo goji in the number of conditions they claim to cure; they always include longevity. Hawthorn berries (山楂 shancha) promise to promote longevity, and to cure indigestion, anorexia, diarrhoea, dysentery, hepatitis, frostbite and intractable hiccups. That number may sound dubious, until one thinks of quinine, the general prophylactic that once protected Westerners in Asia from almost all infectious diseases. Introduced to Asia from South America by Jesuit priests, quinine allowed Westerners to survive in the tropics. It lives on in gin and tonic.

Chinese cuisine has a special diet to enhance long life for the elderly: nourishing herbal soups, plenty of vegetables and fruit, not too much fat, meat or sugar. It is close to a vegetarian diet.

要想人長壽多吃豆腐小吃肉

Yao xiang ren changshou duo chidoufu shao chirou

If you want to live to an old age eat more bean curd, less meat

This diet may ward off major causes of mortality, heart disease and diabetes; it certainly wards off obesity. The elderly in China look for the freshest possible vegetables, shop for them every day; wilted greens or squashy tomatoes are an offence. Foods have to be easy to eat; lack of a full set of working teeth makes chewing difficult for many elderly. They should be bland, to avoid stomach upsets. Some of the foods are symbolic. Long-life noodles (長壽麵 *changshou mian*), eaten at the New Year, are symbolic of longevity, the longer the noodles the better the chance of a long life. Other foods are eaten every day. The menu of the Congee Noodle House in Vancouver has this to say:

A Sung Dynasty Poet, Lu You, wrote in a poem on congee: 'All mortals crave for long life. They do not understand that the key lies in the present. For me who live in the vale, my philosophy is easy and simple: eating congee brings health and leads to immortality.'

Congee is a pillar of food medicine (食療 *shiliao*) and the ultimate geriatric food; a rice porridge, eaten with vegetables, pork, beef or seafood or on its own, bland, is easily digested, cheap and delicious.

The geriatric diet must include large quantities of garlic and ginger in cooking. 'Eat garlic in summer, ginger in winter and then you will not need doctors or medicines.'

夏吃大蒜冬吃姜, 不用醫生药方

Xia chi dasuan dong chi jiang bu yong yisheng yaofang

Both have protective effects, both help with almost any ailment, and both are cheap. Garlic has one bad effect – halitosis (bad breath), especially common with garlic chewers.

Beyond herbal remedies and a good diet are physical practices that promote serenity and prolong life. Calligraphy is one of the best ways to unite body and mind. The elderly may practise at home, or outdoors, with giant brushes that are dipped in water, not ink. Calligraphy may even be prescribed as a therapy after a heart illness, when tranquility is essential to recovery. Meditation and prayer keep the mind and body calm. Going to a temple or a shrine or even a church allows old people to sit or kneel quietly, without any distractions. The mind is focussed beyond personal problems and issues. Exercise is another way to keep healthy. All over China the elderly gather together to do morning exercises. These were required of all age groups in the Mao Era, now limited to schoolchildren and the elderly.

There are environmental factors attached to longevity. While the northern cities are blanketed in pollution, a particular threat to the elderly, other parts of China have been identified as paradises of longevity. Already in the Song Dynasty, a millennium ago, Hainan Island was identified as a place for longevity, based on its temperate climate: 'In summer it is not extremely hot, in winter not very cold. The villages and towns abound in old men of ninety or a hundred years – all of them still walking around vigorously.'[9]

Bama County 巴馬县 in Guangxi is famous for its large number of centenarians. This poor hill county in a poor province was part of a short-lived soviet (1929) run by the youthful Deng Xiaoping. Longevity there has been associated with the simplicity of life, the cleanness of the air and the water, the lack of meat in the diet – and the daily drinks of wine. These are practical steps to long life, not the magical qualities of the imagined valley of Shangri-la.

Bama has been discovered. It is a major destination for health tourism.[10]

China's affluent elderly are starting to move to parts of China with better climates, as elderly North Americans flock to Florida and Arizona. There is an economic opportunity here, already recognised in Bama. The less affluent elderly may think of leaving cities and going back to their own rural roots,

Box 13.3 Shangri-la

Shangri-la is an imaginary valley in the high mountains, a paradise on earth where time stands still, where two communities, one of ageless, cultivated people, the other of Tibetans, live in harmony and tranquility. The place was imagined by James Hilton, in his 1933 novel *Lost Horizon*. Four assorted Westerners (two diplomats, a lady missionary and a swindler on the run) leave the Northwest Frontier (then India, now Pakistan) by plane. The pilot hijacks the plane and flies it to this earthly paradise. The older diplomat, Conway, has never recovered from the horrors of the First World War. He finds Shangri-La so lovely that he decides to stay, as do the missionary and the fraudster. But first he makes a trip out to help the young diplomat to leave. An old school friend discovers Conway in a hospital in Chengdu and decides to take him back to England. On the ship Conway tells his friend about Shangri-la, and then disappears.

Shangri-la has come to mean a place where mundane cares disappear, and only peace, comfort and civility are left. The name has been appropriated by a chain of hotels, and by a county in western China that claims to be the original Shangri-la. This is improbable; it is too far away from where the plane took off. The most probable model for the imaginary place is the Hunza Valley, in Pakistan, where the sublime 7,788-metre Rakaposhi rises straight out of a rich, fertile valley. Hilton visited Hunza. His Karakal (Blue Moon) is a perfect match for Rakaposhi.

where the cost of living is lower, and help is easy to find. This number may include seniors moving back from abroad; a foreign pension goes much further in China.

One cohort of Chinese seems to have mastered longevity – highly educated intellectuals. The economist Chen Hansheng 陳翰笙 lived to 107, after a life full of creativity, tribulation and adventure. My teacher Jerome Ch'en lived to 100; he died in 2019, his mind acute and lucid to the end. He wrote a memoir of his father and his childhood in Chengdu when he was ninety-eight, written in tiny, perfect characters. The inventor of the Hanyu Pinyin 汉语拼音 romanisation system, Zhou Youguang 周友光, died in early 2017, at the age of 111, having endured Japanese bombing, clinical depression and years in a labour camp during the Cultural Revolution. His mind remained clear; he took advantage of his advanced age to make trenchant criticisms of the current government. Yang Jiang, the playwright and translator, lived to 104, years that included horrible persecution in the Cultural Revolution and the deaths of her only child and her husband Qian Chongshu 錢鍾書. Ma Yinchu 馬寅初, the demographer, lived to 100. Before he died he was rehabilitated and given the tacit recognition that had his advice been taken in the 1950s, China would not have had the population explosion in the 1960s that eventually led to the One Child per Family policy.

We can all make lists of people we would like to see live very long lives. My list would start with David Attenborough. The Queen proves the importance of longevity, given a dubious succession. But admiring longevity in some does not mean that it is desirable for everyone. The world does not have room for all who would like to live long to do so. Being old does not give a person the right to become even older, if getting there puts strain on those who support them. The old have to consider the younger.

Old-Age Behaviour

Elderly people should be careful about how they behave. Being cranky, obstreperous or demanding, in China or elsewhere, may not get them very far. The young are not fond of grumpy old people. The elderly have a responsibility to suppress the cantankerousness that so often comes with old age and infirmity. Positive visions of old age should be emulated, old people who become nicer with age, smiling and nodding gratefully to younger people, especially relatives. There are rewards for behaving well. Being nice in old age makes the elderly feel younger: 'if you smile it takes ten years off your age' (笑一笑十年少 *xiaoyixiao shinian shao*).

Being positive in old age is not easy. Many elderly Chinese have lived through painful pasts that have scarred them and deeply affected their lives in old age. In English the warnings to those young enough to change things is that 'we reap what we sow' or 'as you make your bed so shall you lie in it'. In Chinese the expression is more graphic: 'If you plant melons you will get melons; if you plant beans you will get beans' (種瓜得瓜種豆得豆 *zhonggua degua, zhongdou dedou*). Youthful misbehaviour may return to haunt you. People now in their seventies and eighties have known bitterness and sadness, and endured warfare and political upheaval. Some behaved badly in their youth, as Red Guards, behaviours they prefer to forget (see Chapter 8). They were not always kind to their parents. Many of them have smoked heavily. They have not had good health care or dental care. Dentistry has been a latecomer to China. When I did field research in Shandong in the early 1980s almost all the old people were toothless, or at best nursing one or two front teeth.

Despite or because of what they have been through, the present generation of elderly people are paragons of resilience and adaptability. They have made ideological somersaults, from the traditional, to the revolutionary, to extremism, to 'socialism with Chinese characteristics' and revived Confucianism. Mental gymnastics get tougher with age.

The elderly have obligations to look after themselves, to keep healthy and avoid losing their marbles. They must take responsibility for themselves, even be ready to assert themselves. The Confucius Institute recommends the 'awakening of individualism' amongst the elderly.[11] No example is given of what sounds like a latter-day hippie ideal means in practice.

The sensible elderly everywhere recognise the need to keep improving themselves. They know that they must not give in to resentment and selfishness, must strive to stay open and loving: 'Do not fear growing old, only fear your heart growing old' (不怕人老只怕心老 *bupa ren lao zhi pao xin lao*). One form of improvement is study, taking courses, reading and doing research: 'Live to an old age, study to an old age' (活到老學到老 *huo dao lao xue dao lao*). There are 'old-age universities' (老年大学 *laonian daxue*) that offer courses tailored to the retired, as the retired in North America take courses in university extension programmes or the worldwide University of the Third Age (U3A). There is even a science of geragogy, the study of how to make it easier for the old to learn.

Social media presence is essential, to get the latest news and pictures of grandchildren. It feeds competitive grandmothering; grandmothers put pictures of their precious treasures on social media, thinly veiled efforts to show how superior their darlings are to those of other grandmothers.

What has happened to the idea of the wisdom of age? Confucianism has insisted on the special qualities of old age that make old people repositories of experience and benevolence. Indigenous people stress the knowledge and wisdom of elders – with an important caveat: the title 'elder' is not automatic, but goes only to those old people who are deemed to deserve it. In spite of the promotion of Confucianism by the current government, respect for the wisdom of old age, as elders, to be consulted and listened to, is honoured as much in the absence as in practice. There are no elder statesmen in China. Xi Jinping is not following the example of Deng Xiaoping, exercising remote authority from retirement; instead he holds all the most important positions in China – without term. The Era of Xi Jinping (习近平时代 *Xi Jinping shidai*) has no predetermined ending.

Retreat

For some of the old, life in the 'real world' loses its attraction. They retire from mundane life all together. In China and the West the retreat of the elderly used to be into religious communities, monasteries and nunneries. Old people lived in tranquillity, consuming very little, their lives dedicated to contemplation and prayer. Pope Benedict is living such a life, as portrayed, apparently with Vatican approval, in the 2019 film *The Two Popes*.

The tradition of withdrawal to religious sites continues in Taiwan and Hong Kong.

There is an even more extreme form of withdrawal, a tradition of elderly becoming hermits, living alone in flimsy shelters in the hills, mountains or forests. In the Zhongnan Mountains 终南山 in Shaanxi, and in other hill regions, the tradition continues. Since hermits go out of their way to cut contacts with the outer world, it is impossible to assess their numbers, but there are probably no more than the ageing hippies who live in the forests of British Columbia, living precariously; their income from growing marijuana has disappeared now that the product is legalised.

Search for Peace

People who are dubious about organised religion and even scoff at it observe that it is only the elderly who practise religion. This may be true – but it always has been true. Religion helps people cope with the trials of old age. The only break in religious observance was in the Mao Era. Religious practices of all kinds surged back as soon as the Reform Era started. Hundreds of millions practise Buddhism, Christianity, Daoism and Islam today in China. Many of the practitioners are elderly, looking for calm and acceptance as their lives enter their last stages, looking too for protection and comfort for their descendants.

Tranquility may be as much to do with age itself as with religious practice. The Swedish sociologist Lars Tornstam came up with the awkward neologism gerotranscendence (as awkward as geragogy) to describe the tranquility of old age. His decades of interview research on old people found that they were far more than decayed versions of middle-aged people. Their values had not ossified when they were in middle age; they continued to change. In old age money, status, conformity mattered less than before; solitude, inner peace and enjoyment of small things mattered much more. They were more tolerant, they cared for other people, and they were kinder. The fear of decline and death receded.[12] These observations were based on interviews with elderly Swedes, but it seems to have strong correlations with other, different societies.

The best of the elderly are those who treat younger people well. Kindness and warmth are the most important things that the old have to offer the young. One of the key Confucian virtues is benevolence, *ren* (second tone).

仁

The old have endured; they have learned to be benevolent. They have also learned forbearance, another *ren* (third tone).

忍

The top of the second character is 刀, the blade of a knife, suggesting pain and suffering; the bottom is 心 *xin*, heart. Endurance comes with heart, with love – and love endures. With 仁 and 忍 together they can occupy positions of love and respect in their families and in the world beyond their tight social nexus.

COVID-19

Into the middle of my speculations about the future of the old came an unexpected and dreadful new factor: COVID-19, a global assault on the old. The virus and the pandemic it has created are especially threatening to the old. They are often frail, and have health problems (heart, brain, lungs) that produce co-morbidity. In most countries that publish detailed data, over 70 per cent of the dead are people over seventy. Among the old, people living in long-term care are at greatest risk. In Canada early COVID deaths were mainly in care homes. Statistics that would indicate the age distribution of COVID deaths have yet to be made available for China. What is clear is that China has fared much better through the pandemic than other major countries; so have Taiwan and South Korea, giving the lie to the claim that authoritarianism is better at controlling disease than a democratic system.

At this writing, Beijing has done a remarkable job in controlling the virus and restoring the economy – a difficult task, to bring back exports and to continue work on the Belt and Road. Beijing has taken an offensive stance, led by the wolf warrior (literally 'fighting wolves' 战狼 *zhanlang*) diplomats, imitation martial arts figures who now speak China's truth to the world – a frank and insulting one. The Chinese ambassador to France claimed in April 2020 that French authorities were allowing old people to die in care homes, showing France's lack of concern for the elderly, as compared to China's.

Elderly Chinese will recognise the language: it is the rhetoric of the Cultural Revolution; the diplomats, born in the early years of the Cultural Revolution, must have heard this kind of vituperation in their childhood. The return to a nightmare period, best consigned to amnesia, is profoundly depressing, probably most of all to the generation above the wolf warrior diplomats – their parents, who lost out, their youth and their chances of education ruined by the ten years of chaos.

National and local governments have shown concern for the elderly, reminding them that their survival is thanks to the leadership of the Party and government in promoting disease prevention. A letter to Aged Friends (老年朋友 *laonian pengyou*) from the Dalian City government lists a series of instructions for the proper behaviour of the old in a time of COVID. Some are positive: keep a window open; exercise at home; keep warm during the change of season,

---

Box 13.4 Lu Shaye 卢沙野

Mr Lu is a member of a new group of attack-dog diplomats; their model is the wolf warriors of a popular teen movie. These men present themselves as middle-aged action heroes to promote Beijing's policies. Their forte is vivid invective against foreign critics. Ambassador Lu's skill at insult has led to his rapid promotion within China's foreign service, at the cost of the more sophisticated cohort of diplomats. After postings in Africa, he was briefly ambassador to Canada before getting one of the most prestigious appointments of all, ambassador to France. In Canada he called the country 'white-supremacist', for arresting a Huawei senior executive, Meng Wanzhou, on an extradition request from the USA. In France, in April 2020, he accused French authorities of leaving old people to die in care homes, and called people who welcomed the re-election of Taiwan's president Tsai Ying-wen 'toads'.

---

a time traditionally regarded as a danger for health. Other instructions are stern. The elderly are reminded that 'drinking and smoking have no benefit in preventing infectious disease', a presumed response to a popular belief that smokers are less likely to get the virus. This presumption is corroborated by the instruction not to believe or transmit rumours or 'false and wrong news'. The letter seems to accept the assumption that the disease was transferred from animals to humans in wet markets. 'Do not touch, buy or eat wild animals; avoid going to markets that sell live birds and wild animals.'[13]

The Dalian old people are not mobile; if they follow instructions they are safe. The situation of migrants is more perilous. For the migrants who were back in their home villages for the New Year in 2020 the initial future was clouded. Did they go back to work? Or did they stay at home? Beijing encouraged migrant workers to stay in their villages. The Ministry of Agriculture and Rural Affairs issued this advice, in March: 'Migrants [peasant workers] who have returned to their villages and stayed there should take part in projects such as irrigation, road work, housing improvement and greening the village, encouraging more of these people to work.'[14] This call to return to the villages, if applied widely, would reduce the number of migrant labourers and put some heart back into villages. What was not said was how these village works would be financed. How much could the stay-at-home migrants earn in their villages? How would their resettlement affect the old people who had been caring for the children? They would no longer benefit from their children's remittances. These questions are still open, after a second COVID New Year in 2021.

The impact on personal relations of staying at home may be a silver lining to the pandemic. A letter written by migrant workers Li Qiang and his wife

Wang Yan told a touching story about their relations with their daughter Huihui:[15]

> Although we cannot go out to work, which has brought great financial pressure to our family, we are more and more aware of the importance of our role in Huihui's childhood. We have spent so much time with her, long enough to see her grow a little and witness her happiness. It makes it all worthwhile.

Their present happiness speaks of their previous inability to enjoy their child, to watch her develop and change. It also implies a stark choice: income or time with a child?

Living in a COVID world has upgraded the technical skills of the elderly. People who may have managed up until 2020 without using computers and smartphones are at risk of being ignorant (不知能 *buzhineng*), unable to do the tasks that the social isolation of the COVID world demands – checking bank accounts, ordering meals, keeping in touch with friends and family. The old acceptance of being digitally challenged, getting younger people to help with technical and digital matters, has disappeared. Old people have embraced technology in their isolation. I have been through this myself; I am light years ahead of where I was in early 2020. I can Zoom and Bluejean, and order food, clothes, furniture and books; COVID forced me to advance.

14   Personal Notes

As I was writing about Chinese grandmothers, I kept thinking about my own family, about my grandparents, my parents, my daughters and my grandchildren. There is no such thing as typical but there are universal experiences and similarities that transcend differences between cultures. These are some notes about the Lainson–Symmes–Lary families.

Precious Treasures (Chapter 1)

I have three treasures. Mabel is Meibao 美寶, Jack is Yingbao 英寶 and Misha is Jiabao 加寶 (Beautiful Treasure, Heroic Treasure and Added Treasure). They were given their Chinese names by the great calligrapher Li Zhongzheng 李中正. Their birth days were the three happiest days of my life.

Mabel came into the world on a beautiful May morning, the day before her mother Anna's birthday. She was born at home, but transferred immediately to the Vancouver Women's Hospital for Anna to have a medical procedure. I rushed into the birth centre at the hospital. A nurse asked me, 'Are you the grandmother?' A little papoose was put into my arms. Mabel and I sat very still, gazing at each other. My heart turned over.

Jack was born while I was in the air flying to Ottawa. As I left Vancouver a blazing sun rose above the mountains to the east, a glorious omen. I was met at the airport by my dear friend Denise, whose wide smile told me that the baby was born. It was too late to go to see Tanya and the baby that day, but early the next morning Denise drove me to the hospital. I was handed a heavily wrapped bundle. (This was Ottawa in winter). Only Jack's eyes peeked out from the shawls. He blinked at me. My heart turned over.

Misha came into the world dramatically, an unplanned home delivery. Tanya discounted mild signs of labour, despite my advice that the baby was coming. By the time the midwife arrived, it was too late to go to the hospital. I sat in the kitchen listening for Jack (asleep upstairs) and Tanya (labouring downstairs). I had a powerful ethnic reaction: all I could do was to make a succession of cups of strong, sweet tea. I heard the newborn's cry and rushed down. I was given my third beautiful bundle. My heart was full.

Finding a Husband

The English had very precise rituals for getting the young married off – not arranged marriages, but very close. In Bury St Edmunds, an English county town, at the turn of the nineteenth century to the twentieth, girls from respectable families in their late teens 'came out'. They put up their hair and were escorted to a series of dances at the Athenaeum, the public hall in the town. Their mothers or chaperones sat at the sides of the hall on little gilt chairs while the girls waited to be asked to dance by local youths from acceptable families. The dances were a prelude to courtship and marriage. For unlucky girls, failure to find a match at the dances meant being doomed to spinsterhood.

Cooking

Grandmothers are often remembered for their cooking and their special recipes. There are enough books about grandmothers' cooking to fill many bookshelves. My sisters Polly and Vicky and I were unlucky in this respect. Neither of our grandmothers was strong in the kitchen. Granny Lainson, our father's mother, only learned to cook late in life, when her cook left in 1939 to join the war effort. Her cooking was limited and slapdash, often 'something out of a tin', but she did make wonderful marmalade and quince jelly, both of which I sometimes make myself. Granny Symmes, our mother's mother, made one dish that has passed down to her granddaughters: 'Mix together tiny new potatoes, spring onions, hard-boiled eggs, tomatoes and shredded lettuce. Add olive oil to make a kind of mayonnaise with the egg yolks.' We did not know that we were deprived on the food front; in our childhood the limited English cuisine was undermined by postwar rationing. We ate anything, with relish.

Archetypes and Images of Grandmothers (Chapter 2)

Our Grandmothers

Our grandmothers were born in the Victorian era. Neither went to school; both learned at home the expected accomplishments of girls of their generation – needlework, etiquette, handwriting. Both married late, after a 'disappointment' in their youth – each let down by a vacuous young man with whom they had had an 'understanding'.

Mabel Symmes (Granny S.) was sweet, gentle, patient and kind. She was born in New York to an English army officer and an Irish mother; they met when he was stationed in the west of Ireland and eloped to America. The marriage failed; her father disappeared. Granny, her mother and her brother went to live with her mother's sister, in Cambridge, in a most beautiful, ancient house, Merton Hall. In her twenties she was sent to South Africa with her 'ill' mother. The illness, never specified, may have been an addiction. She spent the happy years of her marriage to a Canadian engineer in Bloemfontain, where her son and daughter were born. Then came tragedy. Her husband was killed (she always said 'fell') on Easter Monday, 1917, along with 3,600 other Canadians. After his death she crossed the Atlantic with her small children, to visit her husband's family in Canada and America, before settling in England. She was a widow for the rest of her long life.

She was sentimental, prone to tears, especially at the mention of 'the finest man who ever lived'. She had only a modest pension to live on – she never contemplated entering the work world – but she was infinitely generous, always had treats for her three granddaughters. She had a repertoire of proverbs: 'Laugh and the world laughs with you; cry and you cry alone'; 'The devil finds work for idle hands'; 'If you are sorry for yourself no one else will be'. I was to discover later that she shared the Chinese love of proverbs. She never lived in Ireland but her Irish heritage was strongly in evidence. She would not set foot outside the house on a Friday the 13th, she never walked under a ladder, or had an open umbrella inside the house. If she spilt salt, she threw a pinch over her left shoulder. I was deeply imprinted by her fear of breaching these 'superstitions'; I still follow them.

Granny S. was a devout Roman Catholic, and a frightened one. She was in mortal sin, for having married a non-Catholic. She could not escape her predicament; her husband was dead and could not be converted to the true faith. She responded to every request for a donation to a Catholic cause, money

ILLUSTRATION 14.1a Granny Symmes

she could not afford. She had no social standing in England; she was a poor widow, a Catholic in an Anglican world, Irish in a world prejudiced against Irish, a woman who had never been to school in a university town. She lived over the road from us throughout our childhood, a constant and loving part of the lives of her 'trio'. She was quite daffy (Polly's word), neither clear-headed nor sensible. She expected nothing of us, but loved us, cared for us and worried about us constantly. No one was more comforting. When you were upset her arms came round, you sank in to her soft bosom, engulfed in the scent of lavender. As she hugged tighter, you reached hard bedrock – like all other women of her age she was a martyr to a corset.

Margaret Lainson (Granny L.), my father's mother, could not have been more different. She was independent, physically tough and even tougher in her opinions. Her entire life was spent in or near Bury St Edmunds, the ancient English abbey town where the barons met to plan Magna Carta. She moved only once when she married, from a house built in the ruins of an abbey chapel to a large house with a beautiful garden three miles south of Bury, in the village of Horringer. Before the Second World War she had a staff to run the house and garden, after the war only a gardener.

She was always busy, 'on the go', gardening, organising the Women's Institute, bottling fruit, making jam and marmalade, harassing the vicar about the state of the churchyard. She drove herself everywhere, relying heavily on her horn. One of her proudest achievements was to have been the first woman to drive in West Suffolk; she drove her doctor father on his rounds. She had standing in the village, as owner of a large house, but stood well below the marquises of Bristol, who dominated the village from their mansion, Ickworth. The Bristols have been described as 'unconventional', 'scandalous' or 'criminal'; their behaviours – which included two spells in jail for the sixth marquis, and drug addiction for the seventh – did not affect their superior standing. Instead they provided an endless and fascinating stream of gossip for the village; outsiders saw the Bristols as the ultimate decay of the hereditary system.[1]

Granny L. did not like to travel, even the twenty-five miles to Cambridge. She seldom came to us but often demanded the presence of one of her granddaughters. The child was put on the train in care of the guard and met at the dramatic Gothic station in Bury. (I started going on my own when I was five; today consigning a young girl to the care of an elderly man would be criminal.) She never hid her preferences or her dislikes. She loved only a few members of her family (I was one), and hated two of her three sisters and my mother, who had dared to marry her adored Arthur. She was a terrible mother-in-law, constantly critical.

She cared little for the opinions of others. She could be a bully, but respected people who stood up to her. She walked with – and gestured with – a stick. She

ILLUSTRATION 14.1b Granny Lainson

had been hit by an army lorry while crossing the road, and left with a hole in her leg, through which the bone could be seen. On rare occasions I was allowed to look at it. She smoked like a chimney; her last words were 'give me a cigarette'. I was touched when I visited the tomb of the Empress Dowager in the Eastern Tombs, to see that Cixi and Granny L. smoked the same brand, Passing Clouds. Many boxes lay in Cixi's tomb, not to the taste of the tomb robbers.

I spent a lot of time with Granny L. as a child. She treated me as an adult. None of the activities we shared would be considered suitable for small children today. We played canasta, backgammon and bezique. We went to auctions – there was a deluge of postwar house sales – and to graveyards to tidy graves. My favourite grave was in Herringswell. Close to the tomb of Granny's grandfather, a grieving widow had erected a broken pillar over the grave of her young husband. A life-size angel hovered beside the pillar. The broken pillar usually symbolises the collapse of a state; in this tiny churchyard it meant the tragic end of a marriage.

Different as they were, my grandmothers shared some deep-seated convictions. One was that the world was full of dangers for children. Two dangers had to do with underwear. The first was that children might 'catch their death' of cold if they were not wearing wool next the skin; English children of my generation were forced to wear scratchy woollen vests (undershirts) and knickers (underpants) in all weathers. One long-lasting brand is actually called Chilprufe. The second was dirty underwear. If a child was hit by a bus and rushed to hospital the doctors and nurses might be so shocked by dirty underwear that they would refuse treatment. Other dangers lurked. You could also 'catch your death' from sleeping in a damp bed; whenever we stayed with either Granny we had a hot-water bottle, to make the bed warm and dry. Sausages and pork pies, staples of the English diet, were lethal in the summer months and forbidden then. Public lavatories carried nameless, appalling dangers and were never to be used; strict bladder control was essential to survival and was instilled in all children of my generation.

Our grandmothers paled in comparison as grandmothers to our mother, M.M.E. Lainson, simply Granny, because the grandmothers of four of her grandchildren were not around; my children's other grandmother had a Russian name, Abu. Granny's six grandchildren, three boys and three girls, were born at regular two-year intervals. She was full of energy, not yet fifty when her first grandchild, Mark, was born. For most of their childhoods she had plenty of space for her grandchildren at Horringer: when Granny L. died, my parents had moved there. Our mother repaired the dilapidated house, added some heating (though it still only had one bathroom) and made it the home from home for her grandchildren.

She never cooked but kept beside her large supplies of the biscuit–chocolate combinations so beloved of the English – Wagon Wheels, Chocolate Marshmallows, Chocolate Fingers, Yoyos, Jaffa Cakes, Penguins. By my grandchildren's time giving sweets/candy to children had become a crime, threatening to ruin their teeth and make them fat. I have never given my grandchildren sweet treats, though I draw the line at ice cream. For years Mabel and I had a weekly date at Dolce Amore, Vancouver's finest gellateria, well named for a grandmother and a beloved grandchild.

The grandchildren had to work in my parents' house and garden. They made their own meals, they picked fruit and vegetables, they collected wood, they searched for eggs laid by the Silkie hens who roamed free. They learned that nature, however beautiful, can be brutal. The silkies were eaten by foxes. The goldfish in the pond were eaten by herons, all except one monster Koi who lurked in the depths – and may have been the real culprit. The mating patterns of the mallards on the pond were horrific, closer to gang rape than to romance. (The pond, the focus of much of the grandchildren's play, dried up after our family left the house in 2011.)

Our mother loved parties and celebrations, and there were many of them – birthdays, Christmases and weddings. These were all-hands-on-deck occasions for the family – planning, shopping, cooking, clearing up. Everyone had to work, before, during and after. We were hosts; the slogan for food and drink was FHB ('family hold back'). They were usually turbulent – at least one person in tears, another drunk – but memorable, and so much associated with our mother that none of us have felt able to replicate them.

ILLUSTRATION 14.2a Two Mabels

Granny was extravagantly loving to her grandchildren. The loving expanded as she got older, thanks to the fall in long-distance phone rates and the coming of cell phones. Mark and William phoned her on their cells as they walked back and forth from work in London. Harriet phoned from wherever she was in the world. Tanya and Anna, the two Canadian granddaughters, phoned every week. Daniel phoned slightly less often (a source of occasional lamentation), though at least once a fortnight.

Like many Chinese grandmothers, our mother's old age was the best part of her long life. She had had an inadequate education in convents, and though she was very well read, an autodidact, with a deep love for poetry and music, her lack of formal education was a deep regret to her. She came into her own as a grandmother. Her greatest joy was the love she gave and received from her grandchildren and great-grandchildren.

When she died at ninety-four she had seven great-grandchildren, Sam, Daisy, Mabel, Jack, Joe, Misha and Luke. She would have loved more, and two more, Helen and John, were born after she died. She was openly envious of her great friend Mrs Burling, who had nineteen grandchildren and a myriad of great-grandchildren. These two grandmothers were fulfilled, bathed in the love of many descendants, all anxieties and grief past, honoured for their longevity and their loving warmth. They were very like their grandmother-sisters in China.

Baby Seekers/Baby Lovers (Chapter 3)

Nine Months

In my youth the months between the wedding and the arrival of the baby were counted assiduously by relatives and neighbours. Only a nine-month interval was acceptable. An empire-style wedding dress was suspicious. I wore an ivory Thai silk dress. The tailor who made it at Number Nineteen, the shop for foreigners in Beijing, must have thought that foreign women only got married when they were pregnant; he gave me a very high waist. Tanya was born five years later. Before then I was often asked about what had happened to my invisible baby.

Mothers-in-Law

Granny L. kept up a long enmity towards her 'unsuitable' daughter-in-law; our mother was half Irish, half Canadian and all Catholic, any one of which cut her out of English county society. Granny L. did not win and towards the end of her life became quite attached to her daughter-in-law. My situation was simpler – and insoluble. My White Russian mother-in-law, Natasha, blamed the deaths of the Russian royal family on Britain, for its failure to send the navy (during the First World War) to rescue the royal cousins. Being British meant that I could never be anything but unacceptable; our relationship started and stayed frigid. My sister Polly's mother-in-law was equally hostile; her son Joel married a non-Jew.

Newborns

Every culture has its own rituals around the handling of a newborn infant, essential for its survival. I experienced a Russian one. Natasha bathed my first baby in olive oil when she was two weeks old. She seized a moment on her own with the baby to oil her from top to toe. Tanya was so slippery that she was almost impossible to hold for days afterwards; she smelt rancid. I was determined that the same would not happen to my second daughter, but I was outwitted – a trip to the bathroom, and Anna too was oiled.

Infant Care

Baby care in the West has been subject to major cycles of belief and practice, with one element that does not change: new mothers doubt the knowledge and skills of older women, especially of their mothers-in-law. The young mothers follow current dogma, not what the older generation says. Here are the views of four generations of my family on infant feeding.

Granny L., despite the Guinness prescribed by her doctor father, did not feed her son for long. She handed him over to a nanny, who fed him Cow and Gate formula, strengthened with nips of gin. He was a placid baby, until Nanny was found drunk in charge of an overturned perambulator; she was gone the next day. Our mother believed in breastfeeding each of her three babies on a rigid four-hour schedule, not broken in the chaos of war. My first baby, Tanya, was given a supplement in hospital and then bottle-fed with delicious Enfalac, on a relaxed schedule. Three years later breastfeeding was back and Anna had no bottles. My grandchildren were breastfed on demand; bottle feeding was considered close to child abuse, a sign of maternal failure.

There were generational changes in advice on baby care. Granny L. turned to her father, the doctor. My mother followed a government manual. I believed in Dr Spock's *Baby and Child Care*, a reassuring book that sold in numbers second only to the Bible. The pages in my copy on 'crying in the early months' were tattered before Tanya was three months old. The good doctor is now considered the Antichrist, if he is not confused with Spock in *Star Trek*. My daughters got their advice not from books but from specialists on lactation and infant nutrition and the Internet. One thing is constant over the generations: the lack of trust a new mother has in older women's ability to care for an infant. Successful grandmothers know to offer no advice, only support to the child-carer.

The principal child-carer has changed in recent times. In poor families grandmothers once played huge roles. In rich families children lived with a nanny in a nursery in a separate part of the house. In between middle-class mothers were principal carers. In the Second World War child care by grand-mothers was universal; the men were away at war, the women in the workforce 'doing their bit'. Granny S. looked after three little girls through much of the war. Granny L. presided over an expanded household – her daughter and our cousin Van, romantic Polish airmen, and occasionally us – without the prewar help she was used to. In my generation mothers were expected to stay at home. Going out to work, except for financial necessity, was close to maternal dereliction. I *did* work and was often criticised, usually by other mothers. My daughters never doubted that they would work, after maternity leave. Today's small children are often in day care.

Baby Names

Most babies have nicknames and pet names. In English they are not system-atised, but in Russian there are formal variants on a child's name. My daughter Tanya was known as Tatiana Nikitovna (formal), Tanya (familiar), Tanechka, Tanyushka (sentimental), Tanka (naughty) – and by generic baby names – dielouschka, douschka, pussischka (some English influence in the last). Olga

Lang, sinologist and lover of Russian literature, called her Tatiana Larina, after the heroine of *Eugene Onegin*.

Child Care (Chapter 4)

Keeping Children Quiet

A key theory of Victorian child raising was keeping the child quiet, absorbed in a gentle pastime. I still have Granny L.'s favourite toy, Marbles, a round board with sockets and a large number of marbles. It is good for hours of quiet play, the child playing against itself. My father's toys were more complicated and expensive. My sisters and I played with them – there were few new toys after the war – a train set, a lovely rocking horse, farm animals and soldiers, made of lead, now known to be toxic. My children and grandchildren have been the targets of toys designed to speed their development, Creative Playthings, Baby Einstein. Ironically the favourite plaything at my house is Marbles, now 140 years old and endlessly challenging. Only three people have succeeded in getting the last marble into the central hole: the first is a nuclear physicist and mathematician; the second was either lucky or (a strong possibility) cheated; the third was my brilliant grandson Jack, who managed it after days of intense practice.

Close Grannies

My sisters and I grew up with Granny S. across the road, a secure and constant present. We were lucky, my grandchildren less so. Jack and Misha live far away in Ottawa, but I am close to Mabel in Vancouver; I pick her up from school, take her to music lessons, to the hairdresser. I look after her when she is sick, take her her favourite invalid food, seafood congee from the Congee Noodle House. I have the daily joy of being close to a grandchild. I am available, though I pale in comparison to my friend Debbie, once a university vice president, who has found great happiness as an almost full-time grandmother.

These happy experiences belie the images of exciting retirement involving travel, self-discovery, new romance, even new careers. Many grandmothers want to live either with or close to their grandchildren, to be active carers. 'Granny flats' are added to existing houses. In Vancouver laneway houses are popular for three-generation families. This is a solution to spiralling house prices, and to the separation of generations. For children it works beautifully. Instead of one or two adults in their life, they have several, at least one available at all times, to provide snacks for children coming home from school, to listen to the stories of what happened during the day.

Ruling the Roost (Chapter 5)

Storerooms

Granny L. prized her food stores as much as any Chinese household manager. In the country, shopping was not a regular practice. She had a walk-in cupboard lined with shelves of bottled fruit, jam and marmalade. The kitchen garden provided vegetables year-round. There were fruit trees and bushes, an asparagus patch and a rhubarb patch. There were bins for potatoes and flour in the scullery and a bread oven. There was an apple loft above the garage, and a pigsty. In season there were pheasants and rabbits hanging in the ice-cold larder. These poor creatures were shot by a local vicar, an inadequate marksman. They were full of shot; we were told to chew each mouthful carefully because a lead pellet could 'be the death' of us.

The pheasants and rabbits were substitutes for rationed meat. Rations dominated our childhood. In wartime and after the war everything was in short supply or unavailable. Everyone had to 'make do', even in private; baths could be no deeper than five inches, only five sheets of toilet paper could be used per evacuation. Granny L.'s essential cigarettes were not rationed, but tea was. I have a dim memory of her laying used tea leaves out to dry on sheets of newspaper, in the hope that there would still be some taste in them that could be revived. We received Bundles for Britain from generous American relatives, but were not allowed to wear the beautiful clothes they sent. We would have stood out from other children who, like us, wore strange clothes made by our grandmothers from old clothes. We three had skirts made from our dead grandfather's pyjamas. Tony Judt's evocative book *Postwar* re-creates the grim, dingy postwar world, though his mention of spam fritters made my mouth water.[2]

Textiles

Older women in China taught the younger ones handwork – sewing, knitting, embroidering, quilting, darning, patching. Granny L. taught me all those skills, with more or less success. She knitted her own very long stockings, turned scraps of fabric into patchwork, darned socks and jumpers, turned sheets sides-to-middle to prolong their lives. After a long hiatus, when cheaper factory-made textiles replaced homemade ones, some of these textile skills are back in vogue in the West, less from need than from pleasure (knitting, quilting), or from eco-consciousness (darning, patching). I have been asked by younger women to teach them how to darn, not easy because darning requires a wooden mushroom – no longer available.

Festivals

In Europe and North America the parallel to the Chinese New Year is Christmas. Our mother adored Christmas. Her preparations were unusual in that she did not worry about food and cooking – she had three daughters to do that. From early November on she made lists of presents and cards. In December the decorating of the house started, with a tree never less than twelve feet tall, laden with lights, glass balls and tinsel. In the days before Christmas the house filled up, never less than fifteen family members. Christmas Day started early; Grandfather had to be got up for his annual visit to church. The daughters were up even earlier, getting the turkey into the oven and the huge lunch ready. After lunch came the conflict between watching the Queen's message or watching soccer; by then the older adults were too tired to do battle and soccer won. We drowsed until present time, the ceremonial demolition of the pile of presents under the tree. Granny received by far the most; she often re-gifted them to her grandchildren. She once gave Mark a whole Stilton to take home after Christmas. He was miffed: it had been his present to her.

Old Age (Chapter 6)

Widowhood

Both our grandmothers were widows. Granny S. was a widow for almost fifty years. She belonged to the sad cohort of women whom the First World War condemned to grief and poverty, with the bleak comfort of knowing that their husbands had fallen in a noble cause. Granny L. was a widow for almost four decades. Her elderly husband left her well off when he died in the fullness of time.

Our mother was a widow for less than a decade. Our father died shortly before he would have had to have a full-time carer (we had actually hired one). In this sense his death was a relief, and she had a spurt of new life. She missed him, but there were signs of him everywhere – photographs, a tower of jigsaw puzzles, a portrait. The carpets and furniture were covered in cigarette burns. Our mother, who never smoked, was always pleased when someone lit up – a reminder of A.

Grandfathers (Chapter 7)

We had no living grandfathers. Our father's father died before we were born. He lived on only in two references to his love of shooting: an empty gun cabinet (the guns were taken for the Home Guard in 1939 and never returned); and a photograph, a gun broken over his arm, off to have a go at the pheasants. He had a kindly face, so his love of slaughtering birds was hard to understand. Our mother's father, dead in the First World War, had a greater presence. His stern visage was inside an ornate brass frame with folding doors on Granny S.'s mantelpiece. The doors were opened every morning, closed at night. He spoke through our grandmother. Our achievements brought praise: 'Your grandfather would be so proud of you.' Rudeness or bad behaviour brought 'Your grandfather would be so disappointed in you'.

Our father made a lovely old man. He stopped driving, after one 'prang' too many, and was always at home. He sank into a happy old age. After breakfast in bed he was usually down by about noon, sitting in the bay window, glancing through the paper, doing a jigsaw puzzle. He chatted to anyone who came in, usually about his passion, transport, and watched television (the news; *Come Dancing*; and *Let the People Sing*) and went back to bed about nine. He made few demands, except for regular meals, constant cups of coffee and a huge supply of cigarettes, up to four packets a day.

He did nothing to help with the housework, never so much as carried a dirty plate to the kitchen; a lifetime of being looked after by the many women in his life made helping inconceivable. He was warm and affectionate to his granddaughters, less so to his grandsons, who threatened his position as the only male in the family.

My children's other grandfather was a gentle, sweet Texan, a brilliant economist and a thwarted handyman. He was a devoted grandfather; he made toys for his granddaughters, notably a doll's house. He took them seriously, talked to them about adult subjects. As they grew older the talks turned to arguments. He was a devout American, and my daughters were Canadian patriots; he found their views on the iniquities of the USA hard to take.

Naming

Our parents' naming practices were haphazard. Polly was named Mary for our father's maiden aunt, a misstep since his mother did not like her sister. She soon became Polly, after Graham Greene's Aunt Mary, a friend of my mother's, who had been Polly as a child. I got Granny L.'s name, Margaret, preceded by Diana. My parents were not sure where Diana came from; the excitement of America's entry into the war a week after I was born distracted them. Vicky was named Victoria Estelle. She was born on 8 May 1944; her first birthday was VE Day. Some Western names have political references. My great friend Marianne Bastid Bruguière was named for the heroine of France, not long after the German invasion of France; her name was her parents' statement of defiance.

Some naming proves to be embarrassing. Alfonso Took, in our village, was named for King Alfonso of Spain; no one could pronounce the name, so he became Fonny. A couple I knew in the 1960s gave their son the names Vladimir

ILLUSTRATION 14.2b Our parents in old age

Che (for Lenin and Guevara), in an access of left-wing fervour; their daughter, born a few years later, was named Esme Anastasia. Intercultural issues with the sound of a name may arise. My granddaughter Mabel was in grade school with a boy named Asul; the children were too young to snigger, older people were not.

Bigamy

The rare Western man has maintained two wives. This is bigamy, not polygamy, and illegal. Our great-uncle Charles/Carlos Symmes, a Canadian engineer, moved to Chile in the 1890s to work on railway building. Eight decades later his grandson Carlos, an early user of the Internet, started on family research. He found more people than he had expected with Symmes as part of their double surname (the Chilean custom). He contacted several of them; they all had a grandfather who had moved to Chile from Canada. The conclusion was inescapable. Charles/Carlos had maintained a household in Santiago, and another at the northern end of the railway line, with a wife and children in each place, in blissful ignorance of his duplicity. His secret was kept, until technology revealed it.

Transmitters of Culture (Chapter 8)

Children's Books

We grew up in a time when there were no new books for children, given postwar paper rationing. We read old books. Granny L. gave me her own favourite book, *Stumps*, by Stella Austin, a book about a little girl who was constantly getting her clothes dirty. I read our father's boyhood books about daring-do in the First World War – a favourite was *Storming the Mole at Zeebrugge*. Our mother's childhood books, read again by her children, were *Pollyanna* and *Little Women*, about wholesome, energetic girls living in America. Another favourite was *Susannah of the Mounties*, about a girl living in Regina at the Mounties training depot – a book unknown in Canada. None of these books has survived over the generations. One that has is *Struwelpeter* (*Slovenly Peter*). The hideous, malevolent stories are about what happens to naughty children: the cover shows a child's long nails about to be cut off with shears, fingers as well as nails. I hated *Struwelpeter* as a child and hated that it survived. Tanya was given two copies as a child, both of which I threw out.

Wartime Praying

Granny S. prayed ardently during the war. Her prayers were answered. Her son survived his many sorties as a navigator in a Lancaster bomber, the most dangerous single job in the Royal Air Force. She herself was saved from a bomb. She was in bed in Cambridge one night, secure in knowing that Cambridge was twinned with Heidelberg and would not be bombed. When she heard a loud bang she thought it was the geyser exploding. It turned out to be a stray bomb, landing in our back garden. It was a dud; though a piece of shrapnel came through the roof above her bed, it did not come through the ceiling. She put this down to the power of her prayers; she could not explain why several people were killed by another bomb at the corner of Station Road, not five minutes away.

Churchgoing

Our grandmothers were both practising Christians, though in very different forms. Granny L. was a pillar of her Anglican village church – named obscurely for the patron saint of prisoners, St Leonard of Limoges (there has never been a prison in Horringer). Her particular concern was the graveyard. She hounded Archdeacon Norton, who returned from fighting the Germans to encounter an even more implacable foe. Anyone who has watched *Midsomer Murders* will have seen formidable church ladies. Granny S.'s Roman Catholic church needed fewer volunteers; the tasks of maintenance were performed by nuns. She went to Mass regularly, lit candles in times of need, and contributed to Catholic charities. Her favourite was the fund for the beatification and canonisation of the English Martyrs, executed during the Reformation.

Family Stories

Our grandmothers talked constantly about their childhoods and their families. The hero of heroes for Granny S. was our grandfather. Granny L. talked about her wonderful father, Dr Image, who ministered selflessly to the sick of Suffolk, going out night and day in all weathers to visit them. On one dramatic occasion he was held up by a highwayman, on the bleak Cavenham Heath. Granny saw him as a hero and still felt indignation that her grandfather had disparaged him, never 'up to' his soldier brother John George, dead at an early age.

We did not learn sad or bad stories from our grandmothers, on the British principle that some things are 'never mentioned', or that 'we don't talk about it', 'it' being something nasty. One sad story came out only when our mother's brother made enquiries about their grandfather, to discover that he had killed himself 'while the balance of the mind was disturbed'. Until this discovery he had never been mentioned; he might as well not have existed. Granny L. never mentioned her sister Joan. Our beautiful Aunt Rosetta told me that Joan was one of twins, born after three daughters. Her twin brother died at birth. The distraught mother brought Joan up as a boy, until it was impossible to disguise her gender. By then the damage was done. Aunt Joan behaved so strangely that she was almost exiled from her family.

Ancestors

People now search for wealthy or distinguished ancestors. Our families seem to have no one of great distinction. Zechariah Symmes, one of two Zechariahs in an early class at Harvard University, seems to have done little with his education. Several generations later, during the American Revolution, some of his descendants moved north, as loyalists (Canada) or traitors (USA). The timing means that we cannot claim John Cleve Symmes, who in the early nineteenth century propounded the theory that there was a world inside the Earth which could be reached through Symmes Holes. He received major funding, some from Congress, to search for them, without success.

The loyalists settled in the Ottawa Valley; the inn that our grandfather's grandfather built in 1831 on the shores of the Ottawa river in Quebec still stands. L'Auberge Symmes (formerly the Symmes Hotel) is a *monument historique*.

Our other grandfather's grandfather had a brief but stellar career. The brilliant son of a crofter from the far north of Scotland, Alexander Nicol was pushed up through the Scottish education system that selected bright boys. He went to an academy and then Oxford, where he became professor of Hebrew and cataloguer of oriental manuscripts in the Bodleian Library. The prodigy died of overwork in his mid-thirties.

Past Events

Talking about past events for our grandmothers often meant talking about war. Granny L. talked about the appearance of a Zep (Zeppelin) over Horringer in 1915, on its way to Bury. In the 'terror raid' several people were killed by bombs that fell on the Buttermarket. Nothing so momentous had happened in Bury since the barons met there 700 years earlier to plan Magna Carta.

Granny S. believed, without any evidence, that her husband had killed four Germans before he died himself. The story was graphic and triumphalist, far away from the misery of the actual, brutal Battle of Arras fought in snow and mud.

Our mother talked to her grandchildren about the shortages and sacrifices of the Second World War. Any grandchild who complained about discomfort might be in for an earful. Tanya said once how hard it had been flying from Ottawa to London with two small children. Her granny retorted, 'I was on a blacked-out train for two days, with Polly and your mother, no food, no heat, constant fear of being strafed.'

I talk to Mabel about school; she loves her school and wants to be a teacher. I tell her about having my nose chalked green for being late to kindergarten. This was at a bizarre establishment run by Scottish twin sisters; one child was singled out for chalking every day. The memory still makes me shudder. I tell her about the fierceness of later teachers (notably Miss Wood and Mrs Laverty). I talk to Jack and Misha, young gourmets, about the horrors of blood pudding and faggots (postwar staples). I am lucky, like most British, Canadian and American grandparents, that our past is relatively anodyne; there are no stories to be hidden. There are weaknesses and injustices in our histories, but no horrors such as the Holocaust.

Amnesia

Laws on state secrecy produce one type of amnesia. My generation growing up in England heard about the brave deeds of our fathers at war. One of my friends could not brag about her father, who apparently never left home. We learned only decades later that he was doing top-secret work at Bletchley Park, probably making a greater contribution to the war effort than all the other fathers put together.

National shame is another reason. When I spent a term in Frankfurt in 1957 the war was taboo; too much suffering, too much war guilt. In our weekly class at the Herderschule on *Entnazifizierung* (denazification) Herr Hess tried manfully to get the girls to accept what was in the textbook, but few did. In England we were taught at school to refuse to recognise the present. The decline of Britain was ignored. We learned geography from prewar atlases that showed much of the world a deep pink. We did no history on North America after 'the French Intervention', when foolish people threw 'perfectly good tea' into Boston harbour. In our Girl Guide anthem we sang of ourselves as 'loyal daughters of the empire'; no one told us the empire was gone.

Absent Parents (Chapter 9)

Boarding School

British who can afford it send their children away from home, to a boarding school. The system started to provide choristers for cathedrals (Winchester, Eton, Westminster), later to educate boys whose parents were abroad (Rugby), but morphed in the late nineteenth century to places for the education of sons of wealthy parents. Going away to school was traumatic. Our father, in his eighties, once (and only once) said when I asked him something about the house, 'I was sent away from this house when I was eight and three-quarters.' He spoke with something between sadness and bitterness. He left a house of comfort for a bleak prep school on the cliffs above the Wash (a grim stretch of mud and sea), followed by a public school in north London. He was certainly beaten, perhaps abused in other ways. He was hungry. His mother sent him a box of extra food every week. She missed him terribly, worried about him constantly but never thought of bringing him home except for holidays.

The Pleasures of Old Age (Chapter 11)

Gardens and Competitions

Flower traditions for older women differ. Japanese women arrange flowers in intricate, minimalist patterns. English women love to grow flowers, especially herbaceous borders, a riot of flowering plants, which, if carefully cultivated, provide a 'show' for months on end. On a fine day my mother would be out in the garden for all the hours of daylight, encouraging plants, watering them, engaged in a ceaseless fight against bugs and weeds. All her battles were with natural enemies, not with humans.

In English villages the garden had a gender division. Women grew flowers, men vegetables; their aim was to grow as large specimens as possible – a two-foot-long marrow, eighteen-inch carrots, foot-long beans. The competition was ferocious; the judges at the annual fete had to watch their backs.

The only fiercer competition I have come across was for the most beautiful baby, at the Canadian National Exhibition. The competition had to be abandoned after the judges received threats – from grandmothers. I am sure the year was 1973. My plump, rosy, smiley baby Anna would have been ineligible; she was not yet three months old when the competition should have been held. I felt a twinge of *Schadenfreude* when the competition that my baby would have won if she had been a month older was cancelled.

Television

Television arrived in China in 1964, just in time to announce China's first nuclear test. In Britain it arrived just in time for the coronation of Queen Elizabeth II in 1953. The day-long ceremonies were televised, in black and white. Forty or so of us were packed into Mrs Mason's tiny sitting room; she was the first person in our street to get a set. We were not allowed to move for the duration of the ceremonies (good bladder control again).

Our grandmothers became television addicts. Granny S. loved her set most because it brought her granddaughters over to her house every day – we did not have a television. Granny L. claimed not to watch, but she did. Her world expanded beyond the narrow confines of West Suffolk.

Marriage Age

Our generation knew the fear of missing the marriage boat. We had spinster great-aunts who had not married and war widows who had not remarried as dread examples. We experienced the anxiety at a much earlier age than Chinese girls do now. We expected to be married in our very early twenties, just after leaving university. (Girls who did not go to university married earlier.) The thought of not being at least engaged by twenty-one was so awful that we did not let it happen. Those days seem far away. Young marriage is considered risky, as it was – the success rate of our marriages was low; two of the few still married are our sister Polly and our cousin Van, both married for more than sixty years.

Travels

My travels with my grandchildren were three of the best journeys of my life. Mabel and I went to Hong Kong and Guilin in 2016 and sailed down the Li river with our friends Chi-yuet and David. She saw the nearest possible thing to a slice of old China. Jack, my sister Vicky and I went to the centenary of the Battle of Vimy Ridge in France (2017). He heard his great-great-grandfather's name read out on the roster of the Canadian men who fell. Misha and I had a week in Rome in 2019, with my lovely school friend Clare. He hung out with real Italians, ate real Italian food; he was allowed a small glass of wine at every meal.

Leaving This Life (Chapter 12)

Graves

Five people are buried in our family's grave in Horringer: grandfather, his first wife, grandmother, father and mother. The custom in rural England is to reopen graves for a new burial, provided a decent time has elapsed between deaths. If not reused, graves fall into disrepair, tombstones topple over, the inscriptions fill with moss. Eventually the stones are moved and stacked against the wall of the churchyard. Granny S. was buried in the same grave as her brother in the part of the Cambridge Cemetery reserved for Roman Catholics; they are surrounded by Irish and Polish neighbours. Our mother had the startling inscription placed on their tombstone: 'Same womb, same tomb.'

Funerals

Church funerals are scripted occasions, with an established liturgy. This makes things easier for the family. We had only to choose the hymns and the music. Our father had asked for 'Oh Hear us when we pray to thee for those in peril on the sea'. We nixed the lugubrious hymn, not realising that it was the Royal Navy's official hymn. He left the church to Elgar's *Dream of Gerontius*. Our mother left to Handel's 'Hallelujah chorus'.

Secular Western funerals or memorials are demanding of the mourners, since so little is preordained. They can be awkward affairs, put together by people in grief, who have to come up with an appropriate memorial ceremony for someone they loved, without benefit of the ritual specialists – priests, rabbis or imams.

Afterlife

Anglicans tend to assume that they will go to Heaven, a happy place. They will meet those who have 'gone on before'. After our father died my cousin Van and

I pictured Granny L. and her beloved Arthur reunited on a cloud, puffing away at their Passing Clouds.

Roman Catholics used to worry about where they would go after death: directly to the fires of Hell, or to a prolonged stay in Purgatory with a distant promise of Heaven. Granny S. lived in chronic anxiety that her mortal sin (marrying a non-Catholic) was bound to send her at least to Purgatory. Our mother beat the system. She left the Roman Catholic Church in her late teens but she had already had the last rites, when she was dangerously ill as a child, i.e. before the age of sin. She was guaranteed a safe ride to Heaven, to become a cherub. She lived for almost nine decades after she nearly died, but the rites could only be performed once.

The Future of the Old (Chapter 13)

Keeping Young

Granny S. had a nostrum about keeping the lines of age at bay. She warned us against making faces; if the wind changed while we were scowling we would be stuck with that expression for life. The best thing was to smile as much as possible, since we never knew when the wind would change. With or without the wind, scowling or frowning sets nasty lines into a face; laugh lines are much better. As my friends and I have aged, I have learned what good advice this was.

Afterword

Writing this book has been a great pleasure. My admiration for the hardworking, devoted and loving grandmothers of China has grown and grown. Beyond this praise for their contributions, hard and fast conclusions are dangerous. I have been looking at a constantly changing scene. A recent example is the government's proposal to raise the retirement age. The proposal has been met with open opposition, not from those about to retire but from the young who fear their mothers will be too old when they retire to care for their grandchildren.

Some things have not changed. The sadness of being separated from their children is shared by tens of millions of parents. They miss the precious early years of their children, the most attractive stage of life, and their children are put at risk. Credit or recognition for grandmothers in China's economic boom is still missing. The Confucian respect for age is official dogma, but in question; the demands of modern life leave little space for elder care.

I hope I have shown how valuable Chinese grandmothers are and always have been to their families, and have shown that being a grandmother and caring for grandchildren can be rewarding and joyful, a huge compensation for growing old.

Notes

Introduction

1. Pearl Buck, *The Good Earth*, Kindle edition, p. 315 (originally published New York: John Day, 1931).
2. Li Jie, *Shanghai Homes* (New York: Columbia University Press, 2015), p. xi.
3. Yu I-li, Fei Hsiao-t'ung and Chang Tse-i, *Three Types of Rural Economy in Yunnan* (New York: Institute of Pacific Relations, 1943), pp. 17–18.
4. Chiang Yee, *A Chinese Childhood* (London: Methuen, 1940), p. 104.
5. The title of China's greatest novel can be translated as *Dream of the Red Chamber* or *Dream of Red Mansions*. Another title is *The Story of the Stone*. There are many translations of *The Dream*. I use Tsao Hsueh-ch'in (Cao Xueqin), *A Dream of Red Mansions*, translated by Yang Hsien-yi and Gladys Yang (Beijing: Foreign Languages Press, 1978).
6. Sheng Cheng, *A Son of China* (New York: Norton, 1930); Tan Shih-hua, *Testament of Youth* (London: Gollancz, 1934); and Ling Su Hua, *Ancient Melodies* (London: Hogarth, 1953).
7. Ida Pruitt, *Daughter of Han: The Autobiography of a Chinese Working Woman* (New Haven: Yale University Press, 1945).
8. Gail Hershatter, *The Gender of Memory: Rural Women in China's Collective Past* (Berkeley: University of California Press, 2011).
9. Ba Jin, *The Family* (Shanghai: Kaiming shudian, 1933); Francois Cheng, *Le dit de Tianyi* (Paris: Éditions Albin Michel, 1998); English translation *The River Below* (New York: Welcome Rain, 2002). The novel won France's most prestigious literary prize, the Prix Femina.
10. Sally Taylor Liebermann, *The Mother and Narrative Politics in Modern China* (Charlottesville: University Press of Virginia, 1998), p. 1. Cheng was the first ethnic Chinese to be elected to the Academie française.
11. Hershatter, *The Gender of Memory*, p. 269.

Chapter 1

1. Fei Hsiao-tung, *Peasant Life in China: A Field Study of Country Life in the Yangtse Valley* (New York: Dutton, 1939), pp. 40–45.
2. Nie Zeng Jifen, *Testimony of a Confucian Woman: The Autobiography of Mrs Nie Zheng Jifen, 1852–1942* (Athens: University of Georgia Press, 1993). Translated and annotated by Thomas Kennnedy and Micki Kennedy.

3. Ida Pruitt, *Daughter of Han* (New Haven: Yale University Press, 1945), pp. 42, 50.
4. Peng Hui, 'A brief autobiography', in Jing Wang, ed., *Jumping through Hoops* (Hong Kong: Hong Kong University Press, 2003), p. 143.
5. Tong Te-kong and Li Tsung-jen, *The Memoirs of Li Tsung-jen* (Boulder: Westview, 1979), p. 10.
6. *Reading the Story of the Stone*, with Pai Hsien-yung and Susan Chan Egan, UCLA webinar, 26 February 2021.
7. Cited in Penelope Farmer, *The Virago Book of Grandmothers* (London: Virago, 2000), p. 2.
8. Amy Chua, *Battle Hymn of the Tiger Mother* (New York: Penguin, 2011), pp. 3–4.
9. Chua, *Battle Hymn of the Tiger Mother*, pp. 87, 170.
10. Margery Wolf, *Women and Family in Rural Taiwan* (Stanford: Stanford University Press, 1972), p. 221.
11. Jian Ping, *Mulberry Child* (New York: Morrison, 2008), p. 82.
12. Leslie Li, *Daughter of Heaven: A Memoir with Earthly Recipes* (New York: Arcade, 2006), p. 2.
13. Liang Hsing. *Liu Hu-lan: The Story of a Girl Revolutionary* (Beijing: Foreign Languages Press.1953), pp. 2–3.
14. Zhu Xiaodi, *Thirty Years in a Red House* (Amherst: University of Massachusetts Press, 1998), p. 19.
15. Wu Zhihong 武志红, *Juyingguo* 巨婴国 (Nation of Giant Infants) (Hangzhou: Zhejiang renmin chubanshe, 2016). The book was banned in China shortly after publication.
16. Chen Ran, *A Private Life* (New York: Columbia University Press, 2004), p. 90. Translated by John Gibbon.
17. Peng Xiaoling 彭晓玲, *Kong Chao* 空巢 (Empty Nest) (Beijing: Zuojia chubanshe, 2016), pp. 176–180.
18. Tsai Chin, *Daughter of Shanghai* (New York: St Martin's, 1998), p. 75.

Chapter 2

1. Tsao Hsueh-ch'in (Cao Xueqin), *A Dream of Red Mansions* (Beijing: Foreign Languages Press, 1978), Volume I, p. 26. Translated by Yang Hsien-yi and Gladys Yang.
2. Ibid., Volume I, pp. 481–2.
3. Ibid., Volume III, pp. 556–7.
4. Delia Davin, *Women-Work* (Oxford: Clarendon, 1976), p. 75.
5. Margery Wolf, *Women and Family in Rural Taiwan* (Stanford: Stanford University Press, 1972), p. 233.
6. Nie Zeng Jifen, *Testimony of a Confucian Woman: The Autobiography of Mrs Nie Zheng Jifen, 1852–1942* (Athens: University of Georgia Press, 1993), p. ix. Translated and annotated by Thomas Kennedy and Micki Kennedy.
7. *China Daily*, 2 September 2019.
8. Zeng Baosun, *Confucian Feminist* (Philadelphia: American Philosophical Society, 2002), p. 5. Translated by Thomas Kennedy.

9. Vivienne Poy, *Profit, Victory and Sharpness: The Lees of Hong Kong* (Toronto: York University, 2006), pp. 59–63.
10. Martin Yang, *A Chinese Village: Taitou, Shandong Province* (London: Paul, Trench, Trübner, 1948), p. 57.
11. Ellen Judd, *Gender and Power in Rural North China* (Stanford: Stanford University Press, 1994), p. 196.
12. Zhu Yisheng, *Chronique d'une illustre famille à Shanghai* (Chronicle of an Illustrious Family in Shanghai) (Paris: Éditions Rive Droite, 2002), pp. 83–6.

Chapter 3

1. Susan Mann, *Gender and Society in Modern Chinese History* (New York: Cambridge University Press, 2011), pp. 4–5.
2. Tsao Hsueh-ch'in (Cao Xueqin), *A Dream of Red Mansions* (Beijing: Foreign Languages Press,1978), Volume II, p. 99.
3. Fei Xiaotong, *Chinese Village Close-Up* (Beijing: New World Press, 1983), p. 40.
4. Lu Xun, 'What happens after Nora leaves home', in *Silent China* (Oxford: Oxford University Press, 1973), p. 151. Translated by Gladys Yang.
5. Pearl Buck, *East Wind West Wind* (New York: John Day, 1932).
6. Sheng Cheng, *A Son of China* (New York: Norton, 1930), p. 70.
7. T.C. Lai, *Ch'i Pai Shih [Qi Baishi]* (Hong Kong: Swindon, 1973), p. 3.
8. Ye Zhongyin, 'My autobiography', in Jing Wang, ed., *Jumping through Hoops* (Hong Kong: Hong Kong University Press, 2003), p. 168.
9. Yu Chun-fang, *Kuan-yin* (New York; Columbia University Press, 2000), p. x.
10. Zhou Weihui, *Marrying Buddha* (London: Robinson, 2005).
11. Yang Chao Buwei, *Autobiography of a Chinese Woman* (New York: John Day, 1947), pp. 9–13.
12. Isaac Headland, *Home Life in China* (London: Methuen, 1914), pp. 110–111.
13. Chin Annping, *Four Daughters of Hofei* (New York: Scribner, 2003), p. 68.
14. Gao Yaojie 高耀潔, *Gaojie de linghun* 高耀潔的靈魂 (The Soul of Gao Yaojie) (Hong Kong: Mingbao, 2008), p. 7.
15. For a detailed description of a birth around the Xinhai Revolution, see H.Y. Lowe, *The Adventures of Wu* (Princeton: Princeton University Press, 1983), pp. 7–10. The book is based on articles published in Beijing in 1940, loving tributes to the city's old culture, which was disappearing under Japanese occupation.
16. Heng Ou et al., *The First Forty Days: The Essential Art of Nourishing the New Mother* (Los Angeles: Motherbees, 2016).
17. Père Doré, *Manuel des superstitions chinoises* (Manual of Chinese Superstitions) (Shanghai: Mission Catholiques, 1926).
18. Gail Hershatter, *The Gender of Memory: Rural Women in China's Collective Past* (Berkeley: University of California Press, 2011), pp. 154 ff.
19. Pearl Buck, *Dragon Seed* (New York: John Day, 1942), p. 56.
20. Erich Maria Remarque, *Three Comrades* (New York: Ballantyne, 1964), p. 69 (first German edition 1936).
21. Pearl Buck, *My Several Worlds* (New York: John Day,1954), p. 14.
22. Isabella Beeton, *Book of Household Management* (London: Ward, Locke, 1880). Online edition, Section 2471.

23. Olga Lang, *Chinese Family and Society* (New Haven: Yale University Press, 1946), p. 23.
24. Martin Yang, *A Chinese Village: Taitou, Shantung Province* (London: Paul, Trench, Trübner, 1948), p. 239.
25. Yang, *A Chinese Village*, pp. 116–117.
26. Ye Weili with Ma Xiaodong, *Growing up in the People's Republic of China* (New York: Garland, 2005), pp. 18–9.
27. Shih Kuo-heng and T'ien Ju-k'ang, *Labor and Labor Relations in the New Industries of Southwest China* (New York: Institute of Pacific Relations, 1943), p. 37.
28. C.K. Yang, *The Chinese Family in the Communist Revolution* (Cambridge: Technology Press, 1959), pp. 205–206.
29. Xia was the mother of Jung Chang, *Wild Swans* (New York: Anchor, 1991), p. 155.
30. *Lan Fengzheng* 蓝风筝 (The Blue Kite), 1993, director Tian Zhuangzhuang 田壮壮.
31. Chen Huiqin, *Daughter of Good Fortune* (Seattle: University of Washington Press, 2015), pp. 131–133.
32. Cong Zhang et al., 'Rise of maternal grandmother child care in urban Chinese families', *Journal of Marriage and the Family*, October 2019, pp. 1174–1191.
33. Janet Salaff, *Working Daughters of Hong Kong* (New York: Cambridge University Press, 1981), p. 198.
34. Li Xia 李霞, *Niangjia yu pojia* 娘家与婆家 (Natal Family and Marital Family) (Beijing: Shehui kexue chubanshe, 2009), pp. 1–3.
35. Hershatter, *The Gender of Memory*, p. 277.

Chapter 4

1. Michael Meyer, *In Manchuria* (London: Bloomsbury, 2015), p. 33.
2. Nancy Mitford, *The Pursuit of Love* (London: Hamish Hamilton, 1945), pp. 197–198.
3. Ye Zhongying, 'My autobiography', in Jing Wang, ed., *Jumping through Hoops* (Hong Kong: Hong Kong University Press, 2002), p. 170.
4. Hsieh Ping-ying (Xie Bingying), *Autobiography of a Chinese Girl* (London: George Allen and Unwin, 1943).
5. Chen Hansheng 陳翰笙, *Sige shidai zhi wo* 四个时代之我 (Myself through Four Periods) (Beijing: Zhongguo wenshi chubanshe, 1988), p. 3.
6. Aisin-Gioro Pu Yi, translated by W.J.F. Jenner, *From Emperor to Citizen* (Beijing: Foreign Languages Press, 1964), p. 26.
7. Martin Yang, *A Chinese Village: Taitou, Shantung Province* (London: Paul, Trench, Trübner, 1948), p. 66.
8. Chin Annping, *Four Sisters of Hofei* (New York: Scribner, 2002), pp. 38–59.
9. Gao Yaojie 高耀潔, *Gao Yaojie de linghun* 高耀潔的靈魂 (The Soul of Gao Yaojie) (Hong Kong: Mingbao, 2008), p. 19.
10. Jade Snow Wong, *Fifth Chinese Daughter* (London: Hurst and Blackett, 1952), p. 18.
11. Jun Chang, *Wild Swans* (New York: HarperCollins, 1991), pp. 208, 249.

12. Jian Ping, *Mulberry Child* (Glasgow: Morrison McNae, 2008), pp. 81–82.
13. *Root*, Spring 2019, p. 23; *Macleans*, 18 December 2017; and *Hello!*, 7 September 2018.
14. Tan Shih-hua, *Chinese Testament* (London: Gollancz, 1934.), p. 26.
15. Dorothy Ko, *Every Step a Lotus* (Berkeley: University of California Press, 2001), p. 54.
16. Melissa Brown et al., 'Marriage mobility and foot-binding in pre-1949 rural China', *Journal of Asian Studies*, 12 November 2012, pp. 1035–1067.
17. Gao Yaojie, *Gao Yaojie de linghun*, pp. 19–21.
18. Emily Honig, *Sisters and Strangers* (Stanford: Stanford University Press, 1996), p. 183.
19. Chen Da 陈达, *Woguo KangRi zhanzheng shiqi shizhen gongren shenghuo* 我国抗日战争时期市镇工人生活 (The Life of Urban Workers in China during the Resistance War) (Beijing: Xinhua shudian, 1992) p. 527.
20. Ah Jung, 'Problems of an ideal couple', in Li Yuning, ed., *Chinese Women through Chinese Eyes* (New York: M.E. Sharpe, 1992), p. 125.
21. Zhongguo renmin gongheguo quanguo funu lianhehui 中華人民共和國全國婦女聯和會, *Zhongguo jiefangqu de ertong* 中國解放區的兒童 (Children in the Liberated Areas of China) (Beijing, 1949), p. 3.
22. Felix Wemheuer, *A Social History of Maoist China* (Cambridge: Cambridge University Press, 2019), pp. 32–33.
23. Cong Zhang et al., 'The rise of maternal grandmother child care in urban Chinese families', *Journal of Marriage and the Family*, October 2019, pp. 1174–1191.
24. Delia Davin, *Women-Work* (Oxford: Clarendon Press, 1976), p. 138.
25. Gail Hershatter, *The Gender of Memory: Rural Women in China's Collective Past* (Berkeley: University of California Press, 2011), p. 196.
26. *Women in the Peoples Communes* (Beijing: Foreign Languages Press, 1960), n.p.
27. Davin, *Women-Work*, p. 125.
28. Li Huaiyin, *Village China under Socialism and Reform* (Stanford: Stanford University Press, 2009).
29. C.K. Yang, *The Chinese Family in the Communist Revolution* (Cambridge, MA: Harvard University Press, 1959), p. 153.
30. *Women in the People's Communes*, n.p.
31. Li, *Village China under Socialism and Reform*, p. 95.
32. Zhou Xun, *Forgotten Voices of Mao's Great Famine* (New Haven: Yale University Press, 2013); Frank Dikötter, *Mao's Great Famine* (New York: Walker, 2010); and Yang Jicheng, *Tombstone* (New York: Farrar and Strauss, 2008).
33. Wu Yulin 吴玉林, *Zhongguo renkou Shandong fence* 中国人口山东分册 (China's Population: Shandong) (Beijing: Zhongguo caifeng jingji chubanshe, 1989), pp. 293–294.
34. Kelly Yang, 'In China it's the grandparents who lean in', *Atlantic Monthly*, 30 September 2013; *China Daily*, 26 July 2018.
35. Gao Yuhua, 'Family relations: the generation gap at the table', in Jun Jing, ed., *Feeding China's Little Emperors* (Stanford: Stanford University Press, 2000), pp. 94–113.
36. Yan Hairong, *New Masters, New Servants* (Durham, NC: Duke University Press, 2008), pp. 88–98.

37. Chen Huiqin, *Daughter of Good Fortune* (Seattle: University of Washington Press, 2015), p. 250.
38. Ni Dandan, *Sixth Tone* (online), May 2019; and State Council Document on Child Care, May 2019.

Chapter 5

1. Lee Yan Phou, *When I Was a Boy in China* (Boston: Lothrop, 1887), p. 26.
2. Ibid., p. 33.
3. For accounts of the labour involved in raising silkworms see Mao Dun's story 'Spring silkworms', in *Spring Silkworms and Other Stories* (Beijing: Foreign Languages Press, 1956), n.p; and Pere Dore, *Manuel des superstitions chinoises* (Shanghai: Mission Catholique, 1926), pp. 115–117.
4. Lin Yueh-hwa (Lin Yaohua) 林耀华, *The Golden Wing* (New York: Oxford University Press, 1947), p. 16.
5. Li Jie, *Shanghai Homes: Palimpsests of Private Life* (New York: Columbia University Press, 2015), pp. 157–158.
6. Margery Wolf, *Women and Family in Rural Taiwan* (Stanford: Stanford University Press, 1972), pp. 223–224.
7. H.D. Fong, *Rural Industries in China* (Shanghai: Institute of Pacific Relations, 1933), has a detailed discussion of cottage industries.
8. James Flath, *The God of Happiness* (Vancouver: UBC Press, 2006).
9. L.K. Tao (Tao Menghe) 陶孟和, *The Standard of Living among Chinese Workers* (Shanghai: Institute of Pacific Relations, 1931), p. 1.
10. Francis Hsu, *Under the Ancestors' Shadow* (Stanford: Stanford University Press, 1971), p. 219.
11. Chin Annping, *Four Daughters of Hofei* (New York: Scribner, 2003), pp. 4–5.
12. Mao Dun, 'The shop of the Lin family', in Mao Dun, *Spring Silkworms and Other Stories*, p. 131. Translated by Sidney Shapiro.
13. Zhao Ma, *Runaway Wives, Urban Crimes, and Survival Tactics in Wartime Beijing, 1937–1949* (Cambridge, MA: Harvard East Asian Center, 2015).
14. Chang Kia-ngau, *The Inflationary Spiral: The Experience of China, 1939–1950* (Cambridge, MA: Massachusetts Institute of Technology, 1958), p. 79.
15. *Children of China* (Beijing: Zhongguo renmin baowei ertong quanguo weiyuanhui, 1956), pp. 5–6.

Chapter 6

1. John Lossing Buck, *Land Utilization in China* (Chicago: The University of Chicago Press, 1938), cited in Frank Price, *The Rural Church in China* (New York: Agricultural Missions, 1948), p. 50.
2. Janet Salaff, *Working Daughters of Hong Kong* (Cambridge: Cambridge University Press, 1981), p. 11,
3. Sheila Kitzinger, *Becoming a Grandmother: A Life Transition* (New York: Scribner. 1996), p. 75.

4. Margery Wolf, *Women and the Family in Rural Taiwan* (Stanford: Stanford University Press, 1972), p. 41.
5. Tsao Hsueh-chin (Cao Xueqin), *A Dream of Red Mansions* (Beijing: Foreign Languages Press, 1978), Volume II, pp. 520–524.
6. H.Y. Lowe, *The Adventures of Wu* (Princeton: Princeton University Press, 1983), pp. 214–220 .
7. Lin Yueh-hwa (Lin Yaohua) 林耀華, *The Golden Wing* (New York: Oxford University Press, 1947), pp. 67–68.
8. Susan Mann, *Gender and Sexuality in Modern Chinese Histroy* (New York: Cambridge University Press, 2011), p. 75.
9. Thomas Gottschang and Diana Lary, *Swallows and Settlers* (Ann Arbor: University of Michigan Press, 2000), p. 77.
10. Lin Yutang, *My Country and My People* (New York: John Day, 1935), p. 52.
11. Pearl Buck, *My Several Lives* (New York: John Day, 1954), p. 336.
12. George Kates, *The Years That Were Fat* (New York: Harper, 1952), p. 96.
13. Su Hua (Ling Shuhua) *Ancient Melodies* (London: Hogarth Press, 1953), pp. 176–191.
14. L.K. Tao, 'Social changes', in Sophia Zen, ed., *Symposium on Chinese Culture* (Shanghai: China Institute of Pacific Relations, 1931), p. 252.
15. Ibid., p. 254.
16. L.K. Tao, *A Study of the Standard of Living of Working Families in Shanghai* (Shanghai: Institute of Pacific Relations, 1931), pp. 22–24.
17. Diana Lary, 'The waters covered the earth: China's war-induced natural disasters', in Mark Selden and Alvin So, eds, *War and State Terrorism* (Lanham: Rowman and Littlefield, 2004), pp. 143–170; Micah Muscolino, *The Ecology of War in China* (New York: Cambridge University Press, 2015).
18. Yun Xia, *Down with Traitors: Justice and Nationalism in Wartime China* (Seattle: University of Washington Press, 2017).
19. Lao She, *Yellow Storm*, abridged version of *Four Generations under One Roof* (New York: Harper, Brace, 1951), p. 37. Translated by Ida Pruitt.
20. Marion Levy, *The Family Revolution in Modern China* (New York: Octagon, 1971), pp. 205–206. Originally published 1949.
21. Francis Hsu, 'China's new social spirit', *Asia*, September 1942, p. 508.
22. Chu Fu-sung, 'China's career girls: women enjoy new status', *China Newsweek*, 114 (23 November 1944), p. 8.
23. Hsu Meng-hsiung, 'The free women of Free China', *Asia*, March 1941, p. 123.
24. Pai Hsien-yung 白先勇, *Fuqin yu Minguo* 父親與民國 (Father and the Republic) (Taipei: Shibao, 2012), pp. 206 ff; Cheng Siyuan 程思远, *Bai Chongxi zhuan* 白崇禧傳 (Biography of Pai Ch'ung-hsi) (Beijing: Huayi chubanshe, 1991), pp. 222–224; Diana Lary 戴安娜拉里, 流離歲月 (translation of *Chinese People at War*) (Taipei: Shibao, 2015), p. 204.
25. T.C. Lai, *Ch'i Pai Shih* [Qi Baishi], (Kowloon: Swindon, 1973), p, 109,
26. Li Jie, *Shanghai Homes: Palimpsests of Private Life* (New York: Columbia University Press, 2015), p. 74.
27. *Women in the People's Communes* (Beijing: Foreign Languages Press, 1960), n.p.
28. *Chinese Women in the Great Leap Forward* (Beijing: Foreign Languages Press, 1960), pp. 91–97.

29. Mu Aiping, *Vermillion Gate* (London: Little, Brown, 2000), p. 180.
30. Hugh Baker, *Chinese Family and Kinship* (London: Macmillan, 1997), p. 200–201,
31. Zhou Xun, *Forgotten Voices of Mao's Great Famine, 1958–1962: An Oral History* (New Haven: Yale University Press, 2014), p. 169.
32. *Women of China*, December 2001.
33. Chen Sheying, *Social Policy of the Economic State* (Aldershot: Avebury, 1996), pp. 304–306.
34. Nathan Vanderklippe, *Globe and Mail*, 13 January 2017; *South China Morning Post*, 22 June 2015. 'China's elderly offer rich pickings for private developers'.
35. *South China Morning Post*, 30 December 2017.
36. *Sixth Tone*, 9 February 2021.
37. Cai Fang, John Giles, Philip O'Keefe and Wang Dewen, *The Elderly and Old-Age Support in Rural China* (Washington, DC: World Bank, 1992), pp. 3, 48.
38. Zhang Hong, 'Living alone and the rural elderly: strategy and agency in post-Mao rural China', in Charlotte Ikels, ed., *Filial Piety* (Stanford: Stanford University Press, 2008), p. 71.
39. Charlotte Ikels, *The Return of the God of Wealth* (Stanford: Stanford University Press, 1996), p. 107.

Chapter 7

1. *Qi Baishi nianpu* 齊白石年譜 (Qi Baishi Chronology) (Shanghai: Suda, 1949), p. 38.
2. H.Y. Lowe, *The Adventures of Wu* (Princeton: Princeton University Press, 1983), pp. 63–64.
3. Lin Yueh-hwa (Lin Yaohua), *The Golden Wing* (New York: Oxford University Press, 1947), p. 2.
4. Lao She, *Yellow Storm*, abridged version of *Four Generations under One Roof* (New York: Harper, Brace, 1951), p. 4. Translated by Ida Pruitt.
5. Zheng Da, *Chiang Yee: The Silent Traveller from the East* (New Brunswick: Rutgers University Press, 2010), p. 3.
6. Lowe, *The Adventures of Wu*, p. 155.
7. Wang Fan-sen, *Fu Ssu-nien: A Life in Chinese History and Politics* (Cambridge: Cambridge University Press, 2000), pp. 15–16,
8. *The Chin Family Tree* (Vancouver, private publication, 1980).
9. Yang Jiang 楊絳我們仨 *Women sa* (We Three) (Hong Kong: Oxford University Press, 2003), pp. 130, 148.
10. Chen Shehong, *Chen Huiying: Daughter of Good Fortune* (Seattle: University of Washington Press, 2015),
11. Adeline Yen Mah, *Falling Leaves* (London: Penguin, 1997), p. 96.
12. Wu Erqin 乌尔沁, 老人 *Laoren* (Old People) (Beijing: Xiyuan chubanshe,2000), pp. 61–65.
13. Anna Chao Pai, *From Manchurian Princess to the American Dream* (private publication, 2019).
14. C.F. Yong, *Tan Kha-kee: The Making of an Overseas Chinese Legend* (Singapore: Oxford University Press, 1987), pp. 35–39.
15. Su Hua [Ling Shuhua], *Ancient Melodies* (London: Hogarth, 1953).

16. Ibid., p. 92.
17. Gu Hongming, *The Spirit of the Chinese People* (Peking: Peking Daily News, 1915), p. 83.
18. Ye Weili with Ma Xiaodong, *Growing Up in the People's Republic of China* (New York: Garland, 2005), pp. 11–12.
19. Lady Hosie, *Brave New China* (London: Hodder and Stoughton, 1938), p. 12.
20. Tan Shih-hua, *Chinese Testament* (London: Gollanz, 1934), p. 268.
21. Chen Ta, *Emigrant Communities in South China* (New York: Institute of Pacific Relations, 1940), p. 109.
22. Ibid., pp. 119–123.
23. Chen Jieru 陈洁如, 我做了七年的蒋介石妇人 *Wo zuole qinian de Jiang Jieshe furen* (I Was Chiang Kai-shek's Wife for Seven Years) (Beijing: Tuanjie chubanshe, 2002).
24. Neil Diamant, *Revolutionizing the Family* (Berkeley: University of California Press, 2000), p. 106.
25. James Gao, *The Communist Takeover of Hangzhou* (Honolulu: University of Hawaii Press, 2004), p. 198.

Chapter 8

1. An excellent collection of stories is Moss Roberts, *Chinese Fairy Tales and Fantasies* (New York: Pantheon, 1979).
2. Ni Ping, 'My grandmother and I', *Women of China*, December 1998, at womenofchina.cn.
3. This film was directed by Zhang Yimou. It was approved for distribution by the Beijing film authorities. Zhang's most recent film, *One Second*, was not, possibly because it is set in the Cultural Revolution.
4. Very Reverend Peter Elliott, sermon at Christ Church Cathedral, Vancouver, 24 February 2019.
5. Kang Xiaofei, *The Cult of the Fox* (New York: Columbia University Press, 2005), p. 124.
6. Francis Hsu, *Under the Ancestors' Shadow* (Stanford: Stanford University Press, 1971), pp. 204–205.
7. Pearl Buck, *East Wind West Wind* (London: Methuen, 1931), p. 210.
8. Francis Hsu, p. 131.
9. Yu Chun-fang, *Kuan-yin* (New York: Columbia University Press, 2000), p.x.
10. Jiang Weixin 蒋纬新, 壮战二十七君 *Zhuangzhan ershi qi jun* (Twenty-Seven Brave Warriors) (Chongwu: s.n., 2010).
11. Fan Lizhu, 'The cult of the Silkworm Mother', in Daniel Overmyer, ed., *Religion in China Today* (New York: Cambridge University Press, 2003), pp. 53–66.
12. Rae Yang, *Spider Eaters* (Berkeley: University of California Press, 1997), pp. 21–22.
13. Peng Xiaoling 彭晓玲, 空巢 *Kongchao* (Empty Nests) (Beijing: Zuojiachubanshe, 2016), pp. 12–15.
14. Kong Zhaoqi 孔昭琪 and Kong Jian 孔见, 方言与普通话语音对照 *Fangyan yu Putonghua yuyin duizhao* (Sonic Comparison between Dialect and Putonghua) (Jinan: Shandong renmin chubanshe, 2016), is a meticulous study of a 'dialect' spoken by tens of millions of people.

Chapter 9

1. Zheng Da, *Chiang Yee: The Silent Traveller from the East* (New Brunswick: Rutgers University Press, 2010), p. 3.
2. Xiao Jun 蕭軍, 我的童年 *Wode tongnian* (My Childhood) (Harbin: Heilongjiang Renmin Chubanshe, 1981), pp. 3–12.
3. Peng Dehuai, *Memoirs of a Chinese Marshall* (Honolulu: University of the Pacific Press, 2005), p. 21.
4. Lin Beili, 'My motive for writing', in Jing Wang, ed., *Jumping through Hoops* (Hong Kong: Hong Kong University Press, 2003), p. 167.
5. Chi Pang-yuan, *The Great Flowing River* (New York: Columbia University Press, 2018), pp. 39–40. Translated by John Balcom.
6. Shu Ji (Lao She's daughter), 'My father's four generations', *Chinese Literature*, Autumn 1986, pp. 209–216.
7. Sun Benwen 孫本文, 現代中國社會問體 *Xiandai Zhongguo shehui wenti* (Contemporary China's Social Problems) (Shanghai: Commercial, 1943), p. 202.
8. Chiang Yee, *A Chinese Childhood* (London: Methuen, 1940), pp. 303–304.
9. Ye Weili with Ma Xiaodong, *Growing Up in the People's Republic* (New York: Palgrave, 2005), p. 20.
10. Mu Anping, *Vermillion Gate* (London: Time Warner, 2000), p. 179.
11. Dominic Meng-Hsuan Yang, *The Great Exodus from China* (Cambridge: Cambridge University Press, 2020).
12. Lo Jiu-jung 羅久蓉 et al., 烽火歲月下的中國婦女 *Fenghuo suiyue xia de Zhongguo funü* (Chinese Women in the Fires of War) (Taipei: Zhongyang yanjiuyuan Jindaishi suo, 2004), pp. 370–4, 396.
13. Amy Tan, *The Joy Luck Club* (New York: Putnams, 1989).
14. Tsai Chin, *Daughter of Shanghai* (New York: St Martin's, 1994).
15. François Cheng, *The River Below* (translation of *Le dit de Tianyi*) (New York: Welcome Rain, 2000).
16. For detailed description of the processes see William Hinton, *Fanshen* (New York: Monthly Review, 1997).
17. Wang Ning, *Banished to the Great Northern Wilderness* (Vancouver: UBC Press, 2017), p. 58.
18. Rae Yang, *Spider Eaters* (Berkeley: University of California Press, 1997), pp. 47–48.
19. Guo Xiaolu, *Nine Continents: A Memoir in and out of China* (New York: Grove Press, 2017), pp. 73–75. Her novel *Village of Stone* is in part a fictionalized account of her childhood.
20. Jian Ping, *Mulberry Child*, pp. 119ff; and Jung Chang (Zhang Rong), *Wild Swans* (New York: HarperCollins, 1991), pp. 273ff.
21. Rae Yang, *Spider Eaters*, p. 11.
22. Wen Chihua, *The Red Mirror: Children of the Cultural Revolution* (Boulder: Westview, 1995), p. 71.
23. Jiang Wen 姜文, director, 阳光灿烂的日子 *Yangguang canlan de rizi* (In the Heat of the Sun) (Beijing, 1994).
24. Zhang Zhimei, *Les traces d'un papillon* (The Traces of a Butterfly) (Montreal: VLB, 1995), p. 158.
25. Ye Weili, *Growing Up in the People's Republic*, p. 87.

26. Zhu Xiaodi, *Thirty Years in a Red House* (Amherst: University of Massachusetts Press, 1998), p. 121.
27. Lu Min-zhan, *Shanghai Quartet* (Pittsburgh: Duquesne University Press, 2001), p. 67.
28. Denise Chong, *The Concubine's Children* (Toronto: Penguin, 1994).
29. Donald Longmead, *Maya Lin* (Santa Barbara: Greenwood, 2011), p. 24.
30. William Kessen, *Childhood in China* (New Haven: Yale University Press, 1975), pp. 36–37.
31. Li Jie, *Shanghai Homes* (New York: Columbia University Press, 2015), p. 86.
32. Liu Haiming, *Transnational History of a Chinese Family* (New Brunswick: Rutgers University Press, 2005), p. xi.
33. *All China Women's Federation*, 24 September 2013.

Chapter 10

1. Peng Xiaoling 彭晓玲, 空巢 *Kong Chao* (Empty Nest) (Beijing: Zuojia chubanshe, 2016), pp. 65–70.
2. Fan Lixin, interview, October 2009.
3. The American economist Hal B. Lary predicted inherent problems in the growth of LIMs in international trade in *The Import of Manufactures from Less Developed Countries* (New York: National Bureau of Economic Research, 1968). His concern was the impact of imports on the US economy.
4. *The Economist*, 23 June 2018, pp. 41-2.
5. 国家统计局 Guojia tongji ju, 2019 年农民工监测调查报告 *2019 Nian nongmingong jiance diaocha baogao* (Observation and Survey Report on Peasant Workers in 2019), www.stats.gov.cn/tjsj/zxfb/202004/t20200430_1742724.html.
6. *All China Women's Federation*, 19 September 2013.
7. *The Economist*, 10 April 2021.
8. Liu Dan 刘旦 et al., 留守中国 *Liushou Zhongguo* (Left-Behind China) (Guangzhou: Guangdong renmin chubanshe, 2013), p. 68.
9. UNICEF China, 中国儿童发展指标图集 *Zhongguo ertong fazhan jibiaotuji* (Tables of Normative Development of Chinese Children) (Beijing: 2018). 'Floating' suggests separation for shorter periods from parents, rather than the full year of 'left-behind'.
10. Leslie Chang, *Factory Girls: From Village to City in a Changing China* (New York: Spiegel and Grau, 2008), p. 105.
11. Michael Mu, *Building Resilience of Floating Children and Left-Behind Children in China* (London: Routledge, 2018).
12. Dexter Roberts, *The Myth of Chinese Capitalism* (London: St Martin's 2020), p. 160.
13. Scott Rozelle and Natalie Hell, *Invisible China* (Chicago: The University of Chicago Press, 2020). Reviewed in *The Economist*, 23 January 2021.
14. *6th Tone*, 16 January 2021.
15. Cai Fang et al., *The Elderly and Old-Age Support in Rural China* (Washington, DC: World Bank, 1992), p. 46.
16. Peter Hessler, *Driving China: A Journey through China from Farm to Factory* (New York: HarperCollins, 2010), p. 92.

17. Chang, *Factory Girls*, pp. 283–4.
18. Ibid., p. 272.
19. Goncalo Santos, 'Multiple mothering and labour migration in rural South China', in Goncalo Santos and Stefan Harrell, eds., *Transforming Patriarchy* (Seattle: University of Washingto Press, 2017), p. 98.
20. Peng Xiaoling, *Kong Chao*, pp. 56–61.
21. Ibid., pp. 189–195.
22. Liu Dan et al., *Liushou Zhongguo*, pp. 30–32.
23. Nathan Vanderklippe, *Globe and Mail*, 20 August 2016, p. A11.
24. Peng Xiaoling, *Kong Chao*, pp. 251–259.
25. Ibid., pp. 286–290.
26. Ibid., pp. 280–286.
27. Ibid., pp. 50–56.
28. Ye Jingzhong 叶敬忠, 别养童年:中国农村留守儿童 *Bieyang tongnian: Zhonguo nongcun liushou ertong* (Differentiated Childhoods: Children Left Behind in Rural China) (Beijing: Shehui kexue wenxian chubanshe, 2008), pp. 119–121, 139–140, 177–178, 219.
29. Ibid., p. 219.
30. Yang Wu, 'Changing faces in the Chinese Communist Revolutionary Party members in two Jiaodong counties', Ph.D. thesis, University of British Columbia, 2013.
31. Liu Dan et al., *Liushou Zhongguo*, pp. 33–37.
32. Ibid., pp. 28–32.
33. Jun Jing, 'Food, nutrition and cultural authority in a Gansu village', in Jun Jing, ed., *Feeding China's Little Emperors* (Stanford: Stanford University Press, 2010), pp. 139–140.
34. Peng Xiaoling, *Kong Chao*.
35. Li Minghuan, *Seeing Transnationally: How Chinese Migrants Make Their Dreams Come True* (Hangzhou: Zhejiang University Press, 2013), p. 88. Li is the leading expert on migration in Fujian.
36. Emily Feng, 'China's globetrotting labourers face danger and debt', *Financial Times*, 15 January 2019.
37. Peng Xiaoling, *Kong Chao*, p. 22.
38. Anne Cornelison's study of the left-behind wives and grandmothers in Calabria, *Women of the Shadows* (New York: Vintage, 1976), was a pioneering work.
39. Fei Xiaotong 費孝通, 郷土重建與郷镇發展 *Xiangtu chongjian yu xiangzhen fazhan* (Rural Reconstruction and the Development of Villages and Towns) (Hong Kong: Oxford University Press, 1994); Kate Merkel-Hess, *The Rural Modern: Reconstructing the Self and State in Republican China* (Chicago: The University of Chicago Press, 2016).
40. Ellen Judd, *Gender and Power in Rural North China* (Stanford: Stanford University Press, 1994), p. 45. See also pp. 10–13, 99, 195.
41. Yan Lianke, *Lenin's Kisses* (New York: Grove, 2004).
42. *South China Morning Post*, 16 February 2018; YouTube, www.youtube.com/watch?v=7IQH2HIVspg.

Chapter 11

1. Amy Tan, *The Valley of Amazement* (New York: HarperCollins, 2013); and Ming Mei Yip, *Peach Blossom Pavillion*, Kindle edn (2008).
2. Lady Hosie, *Brave New China* (London: Hodder and Stoughton, 1938), p. 64,
3. Michael Meyer, *The Last Days of Old Beijing* (New York: Walker, 2008), p. 42.
4. *NBC News*, 24 March 2015.
5. *All China Women's Federation*, 6 January 2016, 4 June 2011.
6. *China Daily*, 25 April 2017.
7. Huang Fali et al., *Love, Money and Old Age* (Washington, DC: World Bank, 2015).
8. A positive view of 'left-over women' is found in Roseann Lake, *Leftover in China: The Women Shaping the World's Next Superpower* (New York: Norton, 2018).
9. *All China Women's Federation*, 13 August 2013.
10. *South China Morning Post*, 18 December 2020.

Chapter 12

1. *The Farewell*, dir. Lulu Wang, 2019.
2. H.Y. Lowe, *The Adventures of Wu*, reprint (Princeton: Princeton University Press, 1983), pp. 232–233.
3. Michal Meyer, *In Manchuria* (New York: Bloomsbury, 2015), p. 145.
4. Francis Hsu, *Under the Ancestors' Shadow* (Stanford: Stanford University Press, 1971), p. 60.
5. Chin Annping, *Four Daughters of Hofei* (New York: Scribner, 2003), p. 69.
6. Ida Pruitt, *Old Madam Yin* (Stanford: Stanford University Press, 1979), p. 108.
7. For exquisite details of the rituals surrounding a funeral, see Mrs J.G. Cormack, *Chinese Birthday, Wedding, Funeral and Other Customs* (Beijing: Commercial Press, 1923).
8. Lowe, *The Adventures of Wu*, p. 111.
9. C.F. Young, *Tan Kha Kee* (Singapore: Oxford University Press, 1967), p. 24.
10. Wang Xiaoxuan, 'The state and religion in the PRC', in Jeremy Brown and Mathew Johnson, eds., *Maoism at the Grassroots* (Cambridge, MA: Harvard University Press, 2015), pp. 269–270.
11. David Chang and A.R. Carter, *The Scholar and the Tiger* (Lanham: Rowman and Littlefield, 2009), p. 162.
12. Chen Huiqin, *Daughter of Good Fortune* (Seattle: University of Washington Press, 2015), pp. 274–277.
13. *China Daily*, 6 November 2014.
14. Carloijn Visser, *Selma: aan Hitler ontsnapt, gevangene van Mao* (Selma: Escaped Hitler, Caught by Mao) (Antwerp: Augustus, 2016).
15. Diana Lary, 'Memory times, memory places: memories and commemoration of war in China', in Mark Frost, Daniel Schumacher and Edward Vickers, eds., *Remembering Asia's World War Two* (Routledge: London, 2019), pp. 56–71. Rana Mitter, *China's Good War* (Cambridge, MA: Harvard University Press, 2020).

Chapter 13

1. Jung Chang (Zhang Rong), *Wild Swans* (New York: HarperCollins, 1991), p. 400.
2. 'Paying for the grey', *The Economist*, 5 April 2014.
3. *South China Morning Post*, 9 February 2021.
4. Nathan Vanderklippe, *Globe and Mail*, 31 March 2016; *BBC*, 12 December 2015; *The Economist*, 2 November 2019, p. 64.
5. *The Economist*, 9 May 2020, p. 30.
6. UNICEF, 中国儿童发展指标图集 *Zhongguo ertong fazhan zhibiao tuji* (Indices of Chinese Children's Development) (Beijing: UNICEF, 2018), p. 37.
7. *Sixth Tone*, 18 September 2018.
8. Du Fu, *Four Poems to see off Duke Yan.*
9. Edward Schafer, *Shore of Pearls* (Berkeley: University of California Press, 1970), p. 32.
10. *The Guardian*, 30 December 2013.
11. Readers Club, Confucius Institute, September 2010.
12. Rev. Alistair Smith, Christ Church Cathedral, Vancouver, 18 March 2018. For Tornstam's book, see *Gerotranscendence: A Theory of Positive Aging* (Uppsala: Uppsala University Press, 2005). Torstam himself did not live to old age; he died in his early seventies.
13. Dalian City Committee for the Old-Aged, '给老年朋友的一封信' 'Gei laonian pengyou de yifeng xin' (A letter to aged friends), 30 January 2020.
14. 农业农村部办公厅 Nongye nongcun bangongting (Office of Agriculture and Villages), 30 March 2020.
15. *One Sky*, 8 June 2020.

Chapter 14

1. For the sins of the Bristols, see Marcus Scriven, *Splendour and Squalor* (London: Atlantic Books, 2011).
2. Tony Judt, *Postwar* (London: Penguin, 2004). Spam was a hideous meat-type product, made of normally inedible parts of the pig. It is very popular in Hawaii and was immortalised by the Pythons.

Bibliography

Ba Jin 巴金. *The Family* 家. Shanghai: Kaiming shudian,1933.

Brigitte Baptandier. *The Lady of Linshui*. Stanford: Stamford University Press, 1988.

Isabella Beeton. *Book of Household Management*. London: Ward Locke, 1880.

Juliet Bredon, *Peking*. Shanghai: Kelly and Walsh, 1920.

Melissa Brown et al. 'Marriage mobility and foot binding in pre-1949 rural China', *Journal of Asian Studies*, 12 November 2012.

Mary Bryson. *Child Life in Chinese Homes*. London: Religious Tract Society, 1885.

Pearl Buck. *East Wind West Wind*. New York: John Day, 1932.
  The Good Earth. New York: John Day, 1931.
  My Several Lives. New York: John Day, 1954.

Cai Fang, John Giles, Philip O'Keefe and Wang Dewen, *The Elderly and Old-Age Support in Rural China*. Washington, DC: World Bank, 1992.

David We-wei Chang and A.R. Carter. *The Tiger and the Scholar*. Lanham: Rowman and Littlefield, 2009.

Jung Chang. *Wild Swans*. New York: Anchor, 1991.

Chang Kia-ngau. *The Inflationary Spiral: The Experience of China, 1939–1950*. Cambridge, MA: Massachusetts Institute of Technology, 1958.

Leslie Chang. *Factory Girls: From Village to City in a Changing China*. New York: Spiegel and Grau, 2008.

Chen Hansheng 陳翰笙. *Sige shidai zhi wo* 四个时代之我 (Myself through Four Decades). Beijing: Zhongguo wenshi chubanshe, 1988.

Chen Huiqin. *Daughter of Good Fortune*. Seattle: University of Washington, 2015.

Chen Jieru 陳洁如. *Wo zuole qinian de Jiang Jieshi furen* 我做了七年的蒋介石夫人 (I was Chiang Kai-shek's Wife for Seven Years). Beijing: Tuanjie chubanshe, 2002.

Ran Chen. *A Private Life*. New York: Columbia University Press, 2004. Translated by John Gibbon.

Sophia Chen 陳衡哲. *The Chinese Woman*. Beiping: Private publication, 1934.

François Cheng. *The River Below* (translation of *Le dit de Tianyi*). New York: Welcome Rain, 2000.

Ch'i Chao-t'ing. *War-Time Economic Conditions in China*. New York: Institute of Pacific Relations, 1939.

Chi Pang-yuan. *The Great Flowing River*. New York: Columbia University Press, 2018. Translated by John Balcom.

Chiang Yee. *A Chinese Childhood*. London: Methuen, 1940.

Chin Annping. *Four Daughters of Hofei*. New York: Scribner, 2003.

Chinese Women in the Great Leap Forward. Peking: Foreign Languages Press, 1960.
Denise Chong. *The Concubine's Children.* Toronto: Viking, 1994.
Nelson Chow and Alex Kwan. *Elderly: A Study of the Changing Life-Style of the Elderly in Low Income Families in Hong Kong.* Hong Kong: Writers and Publishers Cooperative, 1986.
Amy Chua. *Battle Hymn of the Tiger Mother.* New York; Penguin, 2011.
Mrs J.G. Cormack, *Chinese Birthday, Wedding, Funeral and Other Customs.* Peking: Commercial Press. 1923.
Deborah Davies Freedman, *Long Lives: Chinese Elderly and the Communist Revolution.* Cambridge, MA: Harvard University Press, 1983.
Delia Davin. *Women-Work.* Oxford: Clarendon Press, 1976.
Neil Diamant. *Revolutionizing the Family.* Berkeley: University of California Press, 2000.
Frank Dikötter. *Mao's Great Famine.* New York: Walker, 2010.
Père Doré. *Manuel des superstitions chinoises* (Manual of Chinese Superstitions). Shanghai: Missions Catholiques, 1926.
Fan Lizhu. 'The cult of the Silkworm Mother', in Daniel Overmyer, *Religion in China Today.* New York: Cambridge University Press, 2003.
Penelope Farmer, *The Virago Book of Grandmothers.* London: Virago, 2000.
Fei Xiaotong, *Chinese Village Close-Up.* Beijing: New World Press, 1983.
   Peasant Life in China: A Field Study of Country Life in the Yangtse Valley. New York: Dutton, 1939.
James Flath. *The God of Happiness.* Vancouver: University of British Columbia Press, 2005.
H.D. Fong (Fang Xianting). *Rural Industries in China.* Shanghai: Institute of Pacific Relations, 1933.
Mark Frazier. *Social Insecurity.* Ithaca: Cornell University Press, 2010.
James Gao. *The Communist Takeover of Hangzhou.* Honolulu: University of Hawaii Press, 2004.
Gao Yuhua. 'Family relations: the generation gap at the table', in Jun Jing, ed., *Feeding China's Little Emperors.* Stanford: Stanford University Press, 2000.
Ge Jianxiong 葛剑雄 *Zhongguo renkou shi* 中国人口史 (A History of China's Population). Shanghai: Fudan, 2002.
Esther Goh. *China's One-Child Policy and Multiple Care-Giving.* New York: Routledge, 2011.
Thomas Gottschang and Diana Lary. *Swallows and Settlers.* Ann Arbor: University of Michigan, 2000.
Barbara Graham. *Eye of My Heart.* New York: Harper, 2009.
Gu Hongming (Ku Hung-ming). *The Spirit of the Chinese People.* Peking: Peking Daily News, 1915.
Guangxi funü ertong tongji ziliao 广西妇女儿童统计资料 (Materials on Guangxi's Women and Children). Nanning: Guangxi nianjian chubanshe, 1993.
Guo Xiaolu. *Nine Continents: A Memoir in and out of China.* New York: Grove Press, 2017.
   Village of Stone. London: Chatto and Windus, 2005.
Stevan Harrell and Giancalo Santos. *Transforming Patriarchy: Chinese Families in the Twenty-First Century.* Seattle: University of Washington, 2017.

Kristen Hawkes, 'Human longevity: the grandmother effect', *Nature* 428, March 2014
Isaac Taylor Headland. *Home Life in China*. London: Methuen, 1914.
Gail Hershatter. *The Gender of Memory: Rural Women in China's Collective Past.* Berkeley: University of California Press, 2011.
    Women in China's Long Twentieth Century. Berkeley: University of California, 2002.
Emily Honig. *Sisters and Strangers.* Stanford: Stanford University Press, 1986.
Lady Hosie. *Brave New China.* London, Hodder and Stoughton, 1938.
Hsieh Bao-hua. *Concubinage and Servitude in Late Imperial China.* London: Lexington, 2014.
Hsieh Ping-ying. *Autobiography of a Chinese Girl.* London: George Allen and Unwin, 1941.
Hsiung Ping-chen. *A Tender Voyage: Children and Childhood in Late Imperial China.* Stanford: Stanford University Press, 2005.
Francis Hsu. *Under the Ancestors' Shadow.* Stanford: Stanford University Press, 1971.
Huang Fali et al. *Love, Money and Old Age.* Washington, DC: World Bank, 2015.
Charlotte Ikels. 'Grandparents in cross-cultural perspective', in Maximiliane Szinovacz, ed., *Handbook on Grandparenthood.* Westport: Greenwood Press, 1998.
    The Return of the God of Wealth. Stanford: Stanford University Press, 1996.
Tamara Jacka, *Rural Women in Urban China.* Armonk: M.E. Sharpe, 2005.
Jian Ping. *Mulberry Child.* New York: Morrison, 2008.
Jiang Weixin 蒋纬新. *Zhuangzhan ershiqi jun* 壮战二十七君 (Twenty-Seven Brave Warriors). Chongwu, 2010.
Jun Jing. *Feeding China's Little Emperors.* Stanford: Stanford University Press, 2000.
Kay Johnson. *Women, the Family and Peasant Revolution in China.* Chicago: The University of Chicago Press, 1983.
Ellen Judd. *Gender and Power in Rural North China.* Stanford: Stanford University Press, 1994.
Tony Judt, *Postwar.* London: Penguin, 2004.
Kang Xiaofei. *The Cult of the Fox Fairy.* New York: Columbia University Press, 2005.
George Kates. *The Years That Were Fat.* New York: Harper, 1952,
William Kessen, ed. *Childhood in China.* New Haven: Yale University Press, 1975.
Sheila Kitzinger. *Becoming a Grandmother: A Life Transition.* New York; Scribner, 1996.
Dorothy Ko. *Every Step a Lotus.* Berkeley: University of California Press, 2001.
Kong Zhaoqi 孔昭琪 and Kong Jian 孔见. *Fangyan yu putonghua yuyan duizhao* 方言与普通话语言对照 (Sonic Comparison between Dialect and Putonghua). Jinan: Renminchubanshe, 2016.
Daniel Kulp. *Country Life in South China.* New York: Columbia, 1925.
T.C. Lai. *Ch'i Pai Shih.* Hong Kong: Swindon, 1973.
Roseann Lake. *Leftover in China: The Women Shaping the World's Next Superpower.* New York: Norton, 2018.
Hua Lan and Vanessa Fong. *Women in Republican China.* Armonk: M.E. Sharpe, 1989.
Olga Lang. *Chinese Family and Society.* New Haven, Yale University Press, 1946.
Diana Lary. *China's Civil War.* Cambridge: Cambridge University Press, 2015.
    Chinese Migration from Antiquity to the Present. Lanham: Rowman and Littlefield, 2012.

The Chinese People at War. Cambridge: Cambridge University Press, 2010.
Liuli suiyue 流離歲月 (translation of *The Chinese People at War*), with preface by Pai Hsien-yung. Taipei: Shibao, 2015.
'The waters covered the earth', in Mark Selden and Alvin So, eds., *War and State Terrorism*. Lanham: Rowman and Littlefield, 2004.
Lao She (Lau Shaw, S.Y. Shu). *The Yellow Storm.* New York: Harcourt Brace, 1951. Translated by Ida Pruitt.
Lee Yan Phou (Li Yanfu). *When I Was a Boy in China.* Boston: Lowthrop, 1887.
Y.K. Leong and L.K. Tao. *Village and Town Life in China.* London: George Allen and Unwin, 1915.
Marion Levy. *The Family Revolution in Modern China.* New York: Octagon, 1971. First published 1949.
Li Haimin. *Transnational History of a Chinese Family.* New Brunswick: Rutgers University Press, 2005.
Li Huaiyin. *Village China under Socialism and Reform.* Stanford: Stanford University Press, 2009.
Li Jie. *Shanghai Homes: Palimpsests of Private Life.* New York: Columbia University Press, 2015.
Leslie Li. *Daughter of Heaven: A Memoir with Earthly Recipes.* New York: Arcade, 2006.
Li Xia 李霞. *Niangjia yu pojia* 娘及与婆家 (Mother's Home and Mother-in-Law's Home). Beijing: Shehui kexue chubanshe, 2009.
Li Yongji 李泳集. *Xingbie yu wenhua: kejia funü yanjiu* 性別与文化: 客家妇女研究. (Gender and Culture: Research on Hakka Women). Guangzhou: Guangdong renmin chubanshe, 1996.
Li Yu-i, Fei Hisao-tung and Chang Tse-i. *Three Types of Rural Economy in Yunnan.* New York: Institute of Pacific Relations, 1943.
Liang Hsing. *Liu Hu-lan: Story of a Girl Revolutionary.* Peking: Foreign Languages Press, 1953.
Lin Yueh-hua. *The Golden Wing.* New York: Oxford University Press, 1947.
Lin Yutang. *My Country and My People.* New York: John Day, 1935.
Ling Shuhua. *Ancient Melodies.* London: Hogarth, 1953.
Liu Dan 刘旦 et al. *Liushou Zhongguo: Zhongguo nongcun liushou ertong funü laoren diaocha* 留守中国: 中国农村留守儿童妇女老人调查 (Left-Behind China: Investigation on Children, Women and Old People Left Behind in China's Countryside) Guangzhou: Guangdong renmin chubanshe, 2013.
Sally Taylor Lieberman. *The Mother and Narrative Politics in Modern China.* Charlottesville: University Press of Virginia, 1998.
Lo Jiu-jung 羅久蓉 et al. *Fenghuo suiyue xia de Zhongguo funü* 烽火歲月下的中國婦女 (Chinese Women in the Fires of War). Taipei: Zhongyang yanjiuyuan Jindaishi suo, 2004.
H.Y. Lowe. *The Adventures of Wu.* Princeton: Princeton University Press, 1983.
Lu Min-zhan. *Shanghai Quartet.* Pittsburgh: Duquesne University Press, 2001.
Lu Xun. 'What happens after Nora leaves home', in Gladys Yang, *Silent China.* Oxford: Oxford University Press, 1973. Translated by Gladys Yang.
Zhao Ma. *Runaway Wives, Urban Crimes, and Survival Tactics in Wartime Beijing, 1937–1949.* Cambridge, MA: Harvard East Asia Center, 2015.

Adeline Yen Mah. *Falling Leaves*. London: Penguin, 1997.
Susan Mann, *Gender and Society in Modern Chinese History*. New York: Cambridge University Press, 2011.
Mao Dun. *Spring Silkworms and Other Stories*. Beijing: Foreign Languages Press, 1979. Translated by Sidney Shapiro.
Michael Meyer. *In Manchuria: A Village Called Wasteland and the Transformation of Rural China*. New York: Bloomsbury, 2015.
  The Last Days of Old Beijing. New York: Walker, 2008.
Robert Mitchell. *Family Life in Urban Hong Kong*. Taipei: Oriental Cultural Service, 1972,
Nancy Mitford. *The Pursuit of Love*. London: Hamish Hamilton, 1945.
Rana Mitter. *China's Good War*. Cambridge, MA: Harvard University Press, 2020.
Micah Muscolino. *The Ecology of War in China*. Cambridge: Cambridge University Press, 2015.
Mo Yan. *Red Sorghum*. Beijing: Zuojia chubanshe, 1987. English translation by Howard Goldblatt, New York: Viking, 1993.
Mu Anping. *Vermillion Gate*. London: Abacus, 2000.
Nie Zeng Jifen. *Testimony of a Confucian Woman: The Autobiography of Mrs Nie Zheng Jifen, 1852–1942*. Athens: University of Georgia Press, 1993. Translated and annotated by Thomas Kennnedy and Micki Kennedy.
Henry Ou et al. *The First Forty Days*. Los Angeles: Motherbees, 2016.
Daniel Overmyer. *Local Religion in North China*. Leiden: Brill, 2009.
Anna Chao Pai. *From Manchurian Princess to the American Dream*. Private publication, 2019.
Pai Hsien-yung 白先勇. *Fuqin yu Minguo* 父親與民國 (My Father and the Republic). Taibei: Shibao, 2012.
Peng Dehuai. *Memoirs of a Chinese Marshall: The Autobiographical Notes of Peng Dehuai*. Honolulu: University Press of the Pacific, 1994.
Peng Hui. 'A brief autobiography', in Jing Wang, ed., *Jumping through Hoops* (Hong Kong: Hong Kong University Press, 2003.
Peng Xiaoling 彭晓玲, *Kong Chao* 空巢 (Empty Nest). Beijing: Zuojia chubanshe, 2016.
Vivienne Poy. *Profit, Victory and Sharpness*. Toronto: York University, 2006.
Frank Price. *The Rural Church in China*. New York: Agricultural Missions, 1948.
Ida Pruitt. *Daughter of Han*. New Haven: Yale University Press, 1945.
  Old Madam Yin. Stanford: Stanford University Press, 1979.
Erich Maria Remarque. *Three Comrades*. New York: Ballantyne, 1964. First German edition 1936.
Mark Rosenzweig. *Co-residence, Life-Cycle Saving and Inter-generational Savings Support in Urban China*. New York: National Bureau of Economic Research, 2014.
Janet Salaff. *Working Daughters of Hong Kong*. Cambridge: Cambridge University Press, 1981.
Edward Schaffer. *Shore of Pearls*. Berkeley: University of California Press, 1970.
A.C. Scott. *Mei Lan-fang: The Life and Times of a Peking Actor*. Hong Kong: Hong Kong University Press, 1971.
Shen Chonglin 沈崇麟, *Dangdai Zhongguo chengshi jia ting* 当代中国城市家庭 (Contemporary Urban Families in China). Beijing: Shehui kexue yuan, 1995.

Sheng Cheng. *A Son of China*. New York: Norton, 1930.

Shih Kuo-heng and T'ien Ju-kang. *Labor and Labor Relations in the New Industries of Southwest China*. New York: Institute of Pacific Relations, 1943.

Kristin Stapleton. *Fact in Fiction*. Stanford: Stanford University Press, 2016.

Amy Tan. *The Joy Luck Club*. New York: Putnams, 1989.

Where the Past Begins. New York: Harper Collins, 2017.

Tan Shih-hua. *Chinese Testament*. London: Gollancz, 1934.

L.K. Tao. 'Social changes', in Sophia Zen ed., *Symposium on Chinese Culture*. Shanghai: China Institute of Pacific Relations, 1931.

The Study of the Standard of Living among Working Families in Shanghai. Shanghai: Institute of Pacific Relations, 1931.

Lars Tornstam, *Gerotranscendence: A Theory of Positive Aging*. Uppsala: Uppsala University Press, 2005.

Tsai Chin. *Daughter of Shanghai*. New York: St Martin's, 1998.

Tsao Hsueh-chin. *A Dream of Red Mansions*. Beijing: Foreign Languages Press, 1978. Translated by Yang Hsien-yi and Gladys Yang.

Carolijn Visser. *Selma: aan Hitler ontsnapt, gevangene van Mao* (Selma: Escaped Hitler, Captured by Mao). Antwerp: Augustus, 2016.

David Wakefield. *Fenjia: Household Division and Inheritance in Late Qing and Republican China*. Honolulu: University of Hawaii, 1998.

Ban Wang. *Illuminations from the Past: Trauma, Memory and History in Modern China*. Stanford, Stanford University Press, 2004.

David Der-wei Wang. *The Monster That Is History: History, Violence and Fictional Writing in Twentieth-Century China*. Berkeley: University of California Press, 2004.

Wang Fan-sen. *Fu Ssu-nien*. Cambridge: Cambridge University Press 2000.

Jing Wang, ed. *Jumping through Hoops*. Hong Kong: Hong Kong University Press, 2003.

Felix Wemheuer. *A Social History of Modern China*. Cambridge: Cambridge University Press, 2019.

Wen Chihua. *The Red Mirror: Children of China's Cultural Revolution*. Boulder: Westview, 1999.

Endymion Wilkinson. *Chinese History: A New Manual*, 3rd edition. Cambridge, MA: Harvard University Asia Center, 2013.

Margery Wolf. 'Child training and the Chinese family', in Arthur Wolf, ed., *Studies in Chinese Society*. Stanford: Stanford University Press, 1978.

The House of Lim. New York: Appleton, 1968.

Women and Family in Rural Taiwan. Stanford: Stanford University Press, 1972.

Women in New China. Peking: Foreign Languages Press, 1949.

Women in the People's Communes. Beijing: Foreign Languages Press, 1960.

Jade Snow Wong. *Fifth Chinese Daughter*. London: Hurst and Blackett, 1952.

Wu Erqin 乌尔沁. *Laoren* 老人 (Old People). Beijing: Xiyuan chubanshe, 2000.

Wu Yulin 吴玉林. *Zhongguo renkou Shandong fenci* 中国人口山东分册 (China's Population: Shandong). Beijing: Zhongguo caifeng jingji chubanshe. 1989.

Wu Zhihong 吴志红. *Zhuying guo* 巨婴国 (Nation of Giant Infants). Hangzhou: Zhejiang renmin chubanshe, 2016.

Xia Yun. *Down with Traitors*. Seattle: University of Washington Press, 2017.

Xiao Jun 蕭军. *Wode tongnian* 我的童年 (My Childhood). Harbin: Heilongjiang Renmin Chubanshe, 1981

Yan Hairong. *New Masters, New Servants*. Durham, NC: Duke University, 2008.

Yan Lianke. *Lenin's Kisses*. Beijing: Chunfeng, 2004. English edition New York: Grove, 2004.

Yan Yunxiang. *Private Life under Socialism*. Stanford: Stanford University, 2003.

Yang Buwei. *Autobiography of a Chinese Woman*. New York: John Day, 1947.

C.K. Yang. *The Chinese Family in the Communist Revolution*. Cambridge, MA: Harvard University Press, 1959.

Dominic Yang. *The Great Exodus from China*. Cambridge: Cambridge University Press, 2020.

Yang Jicheng. *Tombstone*. New York: Farrar and Strauss, 2008.

Yang Jiang 楊絳. *Women Sa* 我們仨 (We Three). Hong Kong: Oxford University Press, 2003.

Martin Yang. *A Chinese Village: Taitou, Shantung Province*. London: Paul, Trench, Trübner, 1948.

Rae Yang. *Spider Eaters*. Berkeley: University of California Press, 1997.

Ye Jingzhong 叶敬忠. *Bieyang tongnian: Zhongguo nongcun liushou ertong* 别养童年: 中国农村留守儿童 (Differentiated Childhoods: Children Left Behind in the Rural Areas). Beijing: Shehui kexue wenxian, 2008.

Ye Weili and Ma Xiaodong. *Growing Up in the People's Republic of China*. New York: Garland, 2005.

Ye Zhongyin. 'My autobiography', in Jing Wang, ed., *Jumping through Hoops*. Hong Kong: Hong Kong University Press, 2003.

C.F. Yong, *Tan Kha-kee: The Making of an Overseas Chinese Legend*. Singapore: Oxford University Press, 1987

Yu Ch'un-fang. *Kuan-yin*. New York: Columbia University Press, 2000.

Yu I-li, Fei Hsiao-t'ung and Chang Tse-i. *Three Types of Rural Economy in Yunnan*. New York: Institute of Pacific Relations, 1943.

Zeng Baosun. *Confucian Feminist*. Philadelphia: American Philosophical Society, 2002. Translated by Thomas Kennedy.

Cong Zhang et al. 'The rise of maternal grandmother child care in urban Chinese families', *Journal of Marriage and the Family*, October 2019.

Zhang Hong. 'Living alone and the rural elderly: strategy and agency in post-Mao rural China', in Charlotte Ikels, ed., *Filial Piety*. Stanford: Stanford University Press, 2008.

'Recalibrating filial piety', in Stevan Harrell and Giancarlo Santos, eds., *Transforming Patriarchy*. Seattle: University of Washington Press, 2017.

Zhang Zhimei. *Les traces d'un papillon* (Traces of a Butterfly). Montreal: VLB, 2019.

Zheng Da. *Chiang Yee: The Silent Traveller*. New Brunswick: Rutgers University Press, 2010.

Zhongguo funü 中国妇女 (Chinese Women). Beijing: All China Women's Federation, n.d.

Zhongguo renmin gongheguo quanguo funü lianhehui 中華人民共和國全國婦聯和會. *Zhongguo jiefangqu de ertong* 中國解放區的兒童 (Children in the Liberated Areas of China). Beijing: Xinhua, 1949.

Zhou Weihui. *Marrying Buddha*. London: Robinson, 2003.

Zhou Xun. *Forgotten Voices of Mao's Great Famine*. New Haven: Yale University Press, 2013.

Zhu Xiaodi. *Thirty Years in a Red House*. Amherst: University of Massachusetts Press, 1998.

Zhu Yisheng, *Chronique d'une illustre famille à Shanghai* (Chronicle of an Illustrious Family in Shanghai). Paris: Éditions Rive Droite, 2002.

Index

Lightning Source UK Ltd.
Milton Keynes UK
UKHW020909050722
405332UK00021B/595

9 781009 073622